SEEING THE
BIG
PICTURE

SEEING THE
BIG
PICTURE

Exploring
American Cultures
on Film

**Ellen Summerfield
and Sandra Lee**

INTERCULTURAL PRESS, INC.

First published by Intercultural Press. For information contact:

Intercultural Press, Inc.
PO Box 700
Yarmouth, Maine 04096 USA
001-207-846-5168
Fax: 001-207-846-5181
www.interculturalpress.com

Nicholas Brealey Publishing
36 John Street
London, WC1N 2AT, UK
44-207-430-0224
Fax 44-207-404-8311
www.nbrealey-books.com

Printed in Canada

05   04   03   02   01   1   2   3   4   5

Library of Congress Cataloging-in-Publication Data
Summerfield, Ellen, 1949–
    Seeing the big picture: exploring American cultures on film/Ellen
Summerfield and Sandra Lee.
        p. cm.
    Includes bibliographical references.
    Contents: Native American Culture: Dances With Wolves,
Thunderheart—African American culture: The long walk home—Chinese
American culture: Joy Luck Club—Japanese American culture: Come see
the Paradise—Mexican American culture: Lone Star—Mainstream white
culture—Gay culture: Wedding banquet—Deaf culture: Children of a lesser
god.
    ISBN 1-877864-84-6
    1. Minorities in motion pictures.   2. Motion pictures—United States—
History. I. Lee, Sandra.   II. Title.

  PN1995.9.M56 S86 2001
  791.43'6520693—dc21   2001   024425

To Phil and Mom

To Kate and Daniel

Permissions

Contents

Acknowledgments

The authors wish to express gratitude to many groups and individuals who have lent support and assistance during the making of this book. At Linfield College we have often relied on the expertise of our wonderful library staff. In past years the student group Fusion has made regular visits to our classes, helping us and our students understand issues affecting gays, lesbians, and bisexuals. We owe enormous thanks to our Linfield work-study students, especially Hildi Nicksic and Stephanie Sayles. For his splendid work on the maps and drawings, we are grateful to Steven Shoffner.

We have enjoyed and appreciated the contributions of the many American and international students at Linfield College who have thoughtfully worked with revisions of the evolving manuscript. We also wish to thank Linfield College for supporting our requests for sabbatical and leave time to devote to the book.

The Oregon School for the Deaf has welcomed us and our students to its campus many times, and we have greatly appreciated the expert advice of Fred Farrior, Patti Togioka, and Alan Yankus. We are indebted to Dr. Hyung-a Kim (Australian National University) for her suggestions on the Chinese American chapter and to Dr. Toni Humber (California State Polytechnic University, Pomona) for her assistance with the section on Black English.

We consider ourselves most fortunate to work with the staff of Intercultural Press, who have helped shape the manuscript in important ways. Both of us extend heartfelt thanks to Toby Frank for her wisdom and encouragement; to Judy Carl-Hendrick for her consummate editing skills and tactful, helpful criticism; and to Patty Topel for her creativity in layout and design.

Finally, Sandra Lee thanks her children, Kate and Daniel, who have watched *Dances with Wolves* far too often; and Ellen Summerfield acknowledges with special affection her husband, Phil, a talented editor who has also watched more than his share of cross-cultural films.

To the Students

Sneak Preview

You are about to embark on an exciting journey through America's*
diverse cultures as presented in contemporary feature films. This
journey will be more meaningful to you if you have a rough idea of the
itinerary. The following two sections will give you essential background information on the two areas we consider: cultures and film.

Why American Cultures?

Did the title of this book surprise you? Shouldn't we speak of American culture rather than American cultures? Is there, after all, more
than one American culture? Is the United States to be thought of in
the singular or the plural?

   These questions are at the heart of the current identity crisis in the
United States. Put bluntly, America no longer knows who she is. This
crisis is all the more astonishing in view of the fact that, not too many
decades ago, she knew exactly what she represented to herself and to

---

* For reasons of economy and convenience, we have elected to use
America and Americans to refer to the United States and citizens
thereof, though we realize that the word actually belongs to the entire continent and that Latin Americans, for example, generally refer
to us as *norteamericanos,* or North Americans.

the world. Having emerged victorious from World War II, she considered herself to be "number one," the greatest nation on earth. Her belief in her own superiority—that she represented the ideal political, social, and economic system—was borne out by unequaled military and financial success. Many Americans assumed without question that their values and way of life were a model for the entire world.

This way of life was distinctly Anglo in nature. Because of the country's grounding in the language, government, religion, and system of laws of England, the core identity of the country was white, Anglo-Saxon, and Protestant (WASP). Admittedly, as a nation of immigrants, the United States was populated by millions of people who did not fit the Anglo mold, but they were expected to leave behind their old lives, languages, and selves and to assimilate. The *melting pot theory*, popularized at the turn of the century, expressed this ideal: differences, however vast, will be melted away, and newcomers will be reborn as "Americans."

The problem is that for many people the differences have never really melted away. Even ardent supporters of the melting pot idea admit, for example, that African Americans were "unmeltable." They and many other "minority" people and groups were excluded from the system, ignored, left out. They were never part of the "American Dream."

Unable or unwilling to "melt," and no longer content to be deprived of full and equal participation in American life, African Americans and many other groups began to demand change during the civil rights movement of the 1960s. In this book you will learn about the momentous struggles of the civil rights era, and you will see that this is where the rethinking of America began. In those tumultuous years African Americans, Latinos, Native Americans, Asian Americans, women, people with disabilities, gays and lesbians, and other marginalized groups began to claim their right to help define what this country is and what it represents. Why, they asked then (and continue to ask now), should they always be the ones to conform and adapt to the mainstream society? Could not the larger society also adapt to, and learn from, them?

Forty years later, as we begin a new millennium, the idea of the so-called *multicultural* or *pluralistic* society has widely replaced the idea of assimilation. In a multicultural society, cultural pluralists argue, many different ways of life can coexist, all contributing to the whole but not necessarily becoming identical. Rather than a melting pot, a more appropriate metaphor is a tossed salad, a mosaic, or a patchwork quilt. In contemporary America, so the theory goes, we can actually value and celebrate diversity rather than ignoring or devaluing it.

Of course not everyone applauds or believes in the multicultural ideal. Especially those whose faces match the old American portrait and who have benefited from the old system can feel uncertain and threatened. They may be reluctant to welcome others to the table if they fear that the other person's gain may be their loss. And they may find it hard to share what in the past has been exclusively theirs.

Should this seem a bit too abstract, try to imagine some of the things that are now to be shared. If you are white, think about sharing coveted spaces in prestigious universities or professional employment opportunities with people of color. Other examples include sharing space on store shelves (with African American hair products and Mexican foods), on the airwaves (with Cuban American music), and in history books (with heretofore neglected stories of women and minorities). Depending on who you are and what you have come to expect as privileges, life may be getting a bit crowded with all the new competitors.

These competitors are undeniably engaged in a power struggle with the dominant, or mainstream, society. As you study the films presented in this book, always remember to keep in mind the issues of power and control. The multicultural society does not take shape quietly; it is generating fierce debate and opposition. Ongoing battles in the so-called "culture wars" are being fought in government, the courts, the schools and universities, the media, and in many other contexts of our everyday lives. One of the most divisive disputes has to do with curricula in schools and universities. Whose history, for example, should be taught? That of conquerors, presidents, and military leaders—or perhaps of women, children, workers, and slaves? In this book you will learn about compelling histories that have long been neglected in America's schools.

Some claim that the multicultural struggles are tearing the country apart and threatening its very existence. These traditionalists fear that the nation's most cherished values of freedom, democracy, equality, hard work, honesty, and self-reliance are being shattered, to be replaced with many competing sets of values. Opponents of multiculturalism use terms such as *fraying* or *disuniting* to suggest that in a multicultural society there will no longer be a common American ground, no glue to hold all the parts together. They fear that there will no longer be anything that is distinctly "American" and that we will disintegrate into dozens of separate, squabbling, disunited groups.

In this book you will become familiar with many Americas. Do you think that all these different cultures can live together peacefully? What will America look like—and represent to the rest of the world—once the old portraits are abandoned? What can hold together such a diverse collection of peoples, ideas, histories, religions, and ways of life?

If you are from a country other than the United States, think as well of multicultural issues and struggles in your own country. While the issues and controversies presented in this book are identified with American society, there is virtually no corner of the earth untouched by multiculturalism. Other societies and nations are facing their own multicultural issues, and many are becoming acutely aware of the need for new approaches and creative ideas.

If you look through the Table of Contents, you will notice that in addition to white mainstream culture the book contains five ethnic cultures as well as two other types of *subcultures* (also called *cocultures*). Admittedly, many ethnic and other subcultures are missing. We included Mexican Americans, for example, but not Puerto Ricans, and we included a discussion of Deaf culture but not of people with other disabilities. Nor do we have a chapter on Jewish culture or Arab American culture or the culture of the elderly. Clearly, in a single book, we had to make choices. The choices are based on our attempt to give you a representative sample. We also had to base our decisions on the feature films that are available and of sufficiently high quality. We hope that this introduction to cultures on film will entice you to fill in the gaps on your own.

Finally, we need to explain that while each chapter heading focuses on one single culture, in reality neither film nor life presents single cultures in isolation. Cultures are always multiple and interrelated. In any group, for example, you have people not only of different ethnic backgrounds but also of different religions, geographical origins, ages, genders, and so on. In each chapter we will try to bring out this inter-relatedness of cultures. For example, in the chapter on *Lone Star*, the main focus is on issues related to Mexican Americans, but we can also look at African Americans and Texans. As we go along, try always to keep in mind the complexity of cultural interactions.

Viewing Films in New Ways

This is a book about cultures, and it is also a book about film. We will not, however, study the history of film or learn more than just a smatter-ing about the technical aspects of filmmaking. What we will do is ask you to look at films in new ways. Most of you have undoubtedly grown up with film, television, and video. You already possess a rich store of experiences with film. But you are probably used to viewing feature films primarily as entertainment. This is not to say that we are deny-ing the value of entertainment. We are great fans of all the films dis-cussed in this book, and we hope you will enjoy them as much as we do. But we also want you to develop a new set of eyes. Your "film eyes" need to be alert, skeptical, and always questioning.

What the eight films discussed in this book present are different interpretations of the cultures of this country, as developed by directors, producers, writers, camera operators, and actors. Your job is to decide whether—or to what extent—you trust and respect their interpretations. You will be asked to give your own evaluations of the films in terms of their validity, integrity, and reliability in depicting cultures.

But on what basis can you make your evaluation? How will you know if a film portrays a culture in ways that are superficial, distorted, or erroneous? How can you recognize whether a film is the product of in-depth familiarity with a culture and whether it is respectful of that culture's complexities? When you see *Thunderheart*, for example, how can you determine if life on the South Dakota reservation has been depicted truthfully and knowledgeably? When you see *The Long Walk Home*, how can you tell if the mood of the 1955 Montgomery bus boycott has been reliably captured?

Furthermore, can we justifiably hold a feature film to particular criteria of truthfulness and accuracy? Don't filmmakers have the right to fictionalize even historical events? This question of truth and fiction is fascinating and far-reaching, and it will come up again and again. As you think about it, remember that even though plot and characterization may be fictionalized, feature films, like literary fiction, can reveal profound truths about people and cultures, or they can misconstrue and misrepresent.

We will help you deal with these complicated issues. Throughout the book you will be exposed to essential tools and skills that will further your ability to view films critically. One of these tools, for example, is simply to view a film twice. In any first viewing it is hard to be critical, since you are caught up in the plot and simply enjoying the film. The second viewing is quite different; you can step back and look at the inner workings of the film, at the *how* and *why* rather than the *what* of the presentation. Another tool is to read reviews, and yet another is to explore the director's background.

When you have developed your new film eyes, you will find that they will enable you to look at other forms of media differently as well. You will begin to see how everything we read, watch, and hear in our media-filled world is presented from a particular point of view. Even relatively "objective" media forms such as documentaries and *New York Times* articles are still to be understood as interpretations; the filmmakers and journalists inevitably have their own unique slant, their personal "take" on the material. One documentary filmmaker may, for example, tell a story about the successes Deaf students experience at Gallaudet University, while another may present a story on the failures. While both stories may be "true," they leave us with entirely different impressions.

The more you understand the notion of "point of view," the less vulnerable you will be to manipulation by the media. Where, you will always ask, is this particular author or journalist or filmmaker coming from? How is the medium at hand being used to convince me to agree with what is presented? Are the tactics legitimate?

Of course filmmakers are not simply manipulators but are also artists who use their medium to the best possible advantage. As the various films are considered in the book, you'll be introduced to some of the basic techniques and vocabulary of filmmaking. For example, to give you an idea of how a familiarity with film techniques can illuminate viewing, look at the following quotation (from Michael Hilger's *The American Indian in Film*), which explains how film techniques in traditional westerns are used to bias viewers against Indians.

> *The long shot, which emphasizes the setting, often stresses the landscape of the West, with either hostile Indians hiding or threatening to attack or conquered Indians vanishing into the horizon in long processions. High angle shots, in which the audience looks down on the subject, may suggest the vulnerability of the whites about to be ambushed by Indians. Low angle shots…can emphasize the threat of the Indian lurking above his victims or the power of the hero. (1986, 4)*

Hilger further explains how editing, especially cross-cutting between pursuers and pursued (rapidly alternating shots of the two groups), heightens fear of the threatening Indians. Composition, which is how the picture is organized within the camera frame, places white heroes in higher or more central positions, reinforcing the idea that Indians are inferior. Music and sound, such as hostile-sounding drums and rescuing bugle calls, and acting roles that reduce the Indians to wooden masks that barely speak or to fierce, war-whooping warriors also send clear messages to the audience about who the enemies and the heroes are.

- In the section entitled Why American Cultures? you will find a number of provocative questions. Choose two of the questions that interest you most and respond to them in the film notebook that you will keep throughout this course.
- Think about the cultures to which you belong, and write a short entry in your film notebook describing who you are, culturally.
- Which cultures other than your own would you like to know more about, and why?
- Review the film techniques described in Viewing Films in New Ways (page 4). Were any of them familiar to you? In your notebook write briefly about a film you have seen in which you recall one of these techniques being used. What do you think was the

filmmaker's intention? Was the use of this technique effective for that purpose? (A more comprehensive list of film terms is provided in the next section.)

Your film notebook will be a personal record of all of your writing, from rough notes to more polished formal entries. Use your notebook not only for exercises in the text but also as a place to jot down your thoughts as you watch the films and listen to class discussions. Include in it your reactions to class field trips and any information you gather from fieldwork, surveys, interviews, or other assignments from the section entitled Hands-on Activities.

Your film notebook will also become a valuable repository of ideas you may wish to use in oral reports and research papers.

Always bring your notebook to class, since your instructor may wish to collect it or may ask you to read a specific entry to the class. We suggest you use a three-ring binder and that you date your entries.

One form of writing that you will be asked to do in your film notebook—and that may be new to you—is called freewriting. Freewriting means simply to put your pen to paper and let your ideas flow over the page. When you are freewriting, you are "thinking aloud on paper" and recording what comes to mind without worrying about organization, sentence structure, grammar, or spelling. You may find it useful to freewrite often as an initial way of getting thoughts and reactions on paper before attempting to write or speak in a more organized fashion.

Whenever the icon depicted above appears in the text, you'll be asked to freewrite, write, or draw in your film notebook and to be prepared for class discussion.

The clapboard icon indicates that an activity or a discussion will take place, often accompanied as well by some form of writing in your film notebook.

Script

To deepen your understanding of cultures and films and to express your own ideas more clearly and powerfully, you will need to acquire new vocabulary. The following two sections will help you get started. Familiarize yourself with the terms now, but don't try to learn them all at this point. Instead, refer back to the lists as you work through each chapter and try to use the terms in class discussions. Also, as the course proceeds, add terms of your own to the lists. The definitions below are necessarily brief, so check your dictionary and other references for additional clarification. Philip Herbst's *The Color of Words* is an excellent resource.

Read the definitions on the following pages with pen in hand, and jot down in your film notebook at least five terms that are new to you or about which you have questions or comments.

Essential Vocabulary on Cultures

There are many definitions of *culture*, but an easy one to remember is that it is the entire way of life of a group of people. It is usually, but not always, passed from one generation to the next. It may be acquired either by birth or by choice. It includes things that are observable, such as food, clothing, dress, housing, and behavior, and things that are not observable, such as beliefs, knowledge, values, and attitudes. The cultures you belong to, or with which you identify, play a major role in determining who you are, how you think, and how you behave.

Terms having to do with cultural distinctions and groupings

assimilation   Process of being absorbed into a new culture; usually refers to minority or immigrant groups becoming part of the mainstream society.

bicultural   People who were born into, or who have acquired, two different cultural identities and who can successfully switch back and forth between them, both mentally and behaviorally.

class   Group within society that shares a common socioeconomic background and thus tends to share common tastes, values, behaviors, and aspirations.

diversity   Range of different cultural backgrounds present in a given group or society.

ethnic group   Group with a shared heritage, usually possessing common language, religion, and appearance, e.g., African American, Greek American, Italian American.

mainstream culture, dominant culture   Cultural group possessing sufficient economic and political power to determine the nature and direction of a given society. Usually the dominant culture is the one in the numerical majority, e.g., white European Americans in the United States.

minority   Word that has fallen out of favor when used to refer to a subculture or coculture. Many people of color feel that minority connotes "lesser" or "subordinate." A minority group is usually in the numerical minority, but the term more often refers to power than to numbers; thus women, for example, are often seen as a minority group.

multiculturalism or **cultural pluralism**   Ideal in which diverse groups in a society coexist amicably.

race   Term used to classify people into broad groups according to inherited physical characteristics, e.g., Mongoloid, Caucasian, and Negroid races. The term is widely used and has sociological and historical usefulness, but anthropologists and scientists generally agree that the term has no scientific validity and that there are no clear-cut distinctions among races.

subculture, coculture   Culture within a larger culture. Examples of subcultures existing within U.S. society include Native Americans, the elderly, Southerners, and the homeless.

values   Set of enduring views on what is considered right, good, useful, and true that members of a particular culture tend to hold in common. Values provide a basis for choices and guide the behavior of individuals within a given culture.

Terms having to do with prejudice

discrimination   Prejudice in action, such as refusing to give a person a job because of the person's ethnicity rather than because of individual qualifications.

ethnocentrism   Assumption that one's own cultural group is superior to all others and that it is appropriate to judge others by one's own standards.

institutionalized racism, sexism, homophobia, etc.   Form of discrimination built into the structure of an entire society such that certain groups are advantaged over others; also referred to by terms such as **white, male,** or **heterosexual privilege.**

internalized oppression   Phenomenon that occurs when individuals in subjugated groups begin to believe that they are inferior and thus participate in their own subjugation.

prejudice, bias, bigotry   Preconceived, negative attitudes about a group of people or about individuals based on their membership in a specific group.

racism, sexism, ageism, classism, ableism, anti-Semitism   Different types of prejudice based on notions of the inherent inferiority of the indicated group.

stereotype   Oversimplified, exaggerated, usually negative notion of what all people in a group are like, e.g., "Americans don't take marriage very seriously." Often based on a kernel of truth that is distorted and rigidly applied.

Terms having to do with intercultural communication

empathy   Ability to put oneself in another's position, to relate to another's feelings and point of view; recognized as a basic element of effective intercultural communication.

intercultural communication   Communication among people of different cultural backgrounds by both verbal and nonverbal means. Barriers to effective intercultural communication can be formidable. Not only do spoken languages differ significantly from culture to culture, but patterns of nonverbal communication do as well.

kinesics   Commonly called "body language"; communication that takes place through movement, such as gestures, posture, facial expressions, and eye contact.

nonverbal communication   Communication by means other than words (estimated by experts to be 60–90 percent of what we communicate). For example, we send each other messages by the way we dress, by how we touch one another, and by our use of time. Other common means of nonverbal communication include:

paralanguage   Not *what* we say, but *how* we say it; includes voice qualities (such as pitch, tone, volume, rate), silences, and sounds accompanying speech (groans, exclamations, sighs, yells).

proxemics   Communication through the use of space, e.g., physical distance between people, seating arrangements.

verbal communication   Communication that takes place through the spoken word.

Essential Film Vocabulary

As you study the films presented in this book, you will frequently encounter the terms and techniques defined on pages 12 and 13. Make a habit of looking out for them as you watch the movies. Jot down examples. Be sure to note where they occur in the film in minutes/seconds. Your notes will be a useful reference for oral or written presentations.

Before we provide definitions, you need to know that films are made up of many different *shots*. A shot is simply the flow of visual images photographed by one camera from the time the camera is turned on to the time it is stopped. One shot might last just an instant, another several minutes or longer. The *editor* is the person who cuts the shots to the desired length, arranges them, and splices them together to make *scenes* or *sequences*. For example, if you wanted to film your grandmother telling a story to her grandchildren, you could combine different shots: first the empty chair, then your grandmother sitting down, then a shot just of her face, then of the children listening, then of her hand gestures, and finally of her getting up to get some lemonade. Or you could film one long shot, perhaps by holding the camera still and focusing on the entire scene or just on her face, or possibly by moving the camera from her profile in the chair, to her face, to the children, to her hands, and back to her face.

The editor also links different scenes. For example, the scene of your grandmother telling the story might be followed by a scene in which the children run outside and act out the story Grandma has just told them. The *transition* occurs when the film moves from one scene to another. The way the director arranges characters, props, and setting in a *frame* (the area encompassed by the borders of a shot) is called *composition* or *mise-en-scène*.

Filmmakers

cinematographer Directs the photography. Supervises the camera operators and works with the director to film the specific shots. Responsible for the lighting and quality of the camera work.

director Shapes the film by determining how it should be shot. The director usually supervises the entire cast, selects the location(s), and has ultimate responsibility for artistic decisions. The director's vision is essential to the effectiveness of a film.

editor Assembles, cuts, organizes, and joins the available shots to create the film sequences.

producer Is responsible for obtaining financing and establishing and managing the budget. The producer's responsibilities may go beyond financial matters to other aspects of making the film, such as hiring the director and lead actors, working with the director on artistic matters, and solving problems and disputes.

screenwriter Writes the script for the film, often adapting it from a novel or other source.

Types of Shots

close-up Focuses on a subject in great detail to emphasize its significance or meaning. Whereas a long shot might show the entire forest and a medium shot might show several branches, a close-up would show only one leaf.

long shot Gives an overview of the action, often introducing a scene. Commonly used in epics or historical movies to show the setting or locale from a great distance, with humans appearing as tiny specks.

medium shot Is often used in introducing characters and for dialogue where characters are shown from the knee or waist up.

Types of Lenses

telephoto Functions like a telescope, magnifying objects from a distance.

wide angle Allows the camera to photograph an area wider than normal.

zoom Allows the camera to move a distant subject closer or to make a close subject more distant, moving the viewer rapidly into or out of a scene.

Moving Camera Shots

boom shot Can move in any direction; camera is mounted on a long pole or support.

pan or **panning shot** Moves horizontally; short for panorama.

tilt shot Moves vertically in either direction.

tracking/trucking or **dolly shot** Moves with the subject; camera is placed on a moving vehicle.

Types of Camera Angles

bird's-eye view   Views a scene from high overhead, often creating an illusion of power or omniscience.

eye level or **flat angle shot**   Views the subject at eye level.

high angle shot   Is not as high and imposing as a bird's-eye view, but gives an overview of the scene in which the characters seem less important than the setting.

low angle shot   Shoots upward to make characters and objects appear taller and bigger. This shot can be used to make the subject seem powerful, fearful, or important.

oblique angle shot   Views subject at an angle and is achieved by tilting the camera. Characters and objects appear to be falling over. This angle is disorienting and is often used to create anxiety.

over the shoulder shot   Usually focuses on two characters in dialogue. The viewer sees the back of the head and shoulder of the person speaking, often causing that person to dominate the scene.

point of view shot   Views the world from the "eyes" of a character. To obtain a little girl's point of view, for example, the camera would be placed at her eye level and thus view things as she would.

Other Techniques

cross-cutting   Alternates rapidly from one film shot to another occurring in a different setting to indicate that both are taking place simultaneously.

dissolve   Occurs when a scene slowly fades out and a new scene fades in. At one point the images usually seem to be blended together.

fade-in   Occurs when a scene gradually becomes brighter and clearer from black to normal light, usually indicating that a new sequence is beginning.

fade-out   Occurs when the brightness of the scene gradually decreases and becomes black, usually indicating the end of a sequence.

fast motion   Speeds up the action.

flashback   Interrupts actions and events in the present time to take the viewer back to a previous time.

flashforward   Interrupts actions and events in the present time to take the viewer forward in time.

slow motion   Occurs when the action seems to be occurring at a pace slower than reality; may give the scene a dreamlike quality or prolong the emotional impact.

voice-over   Conveys the thoughts or memories of a character who is not speaking on camera; the spoken commentary is recorded separately from the filmed sequence.

Stage Directions: Guidelines for Discussion

 In this course you will learn a great deal about American cultures and cocultures, not only by watching the films and reading the texts but also by listening to your classmates' points of view. Your peers will bring to the discussions cultural backgrounds and experiences different from your own, and at times you may find yourself reacting to what they say with surprise, disbelief, or even shock. Whatever your reaction, try to realize that your differences are valuable resources for learning. It is precisely these differences that will lead to more interesting, enlightening discussions and to a clearer understanding of the films you have viewed together.

To help make your discussions as productive, satisfying, and worthwhile as possible, we wish to suggest some guidelines. These will allow you to express yourself more freely, confident that your peers will treat your comments with respect and interest, regardless of their own perspectives. Please read the suggestions below and add to the list any others you wish.

1. Listen considerately and respectfully to each other.
2. Take risks by discussing topics about which you may have previously been reluctant to air your views.
3. Develop trust by supporting your peers whenever they have difficulty expressing their ideas or when they express views that may be unpopular.
4. Respond frankly but sensitively so as not to hurt others' feelings.
5. Avoid sarcasm and cynicism at all costs.
6. Maintain a sense of humor without trivializing the discussion.
7. Do not judge what a classmate says quickly; instead, ask questions that will help you better understand the point being made.
8. Try not to be afraid of emotions; the topics you will discuss can be sensitive and upsetting, and emotions will surface. Regard them as a source of learning.

Depending on the topic or exercise, you may be asked to work with a partner, in groups, or with the entire class. If you find it difficult to speak in front of groups, you might try one or more of the specific discussion roles outlined below, especially during the early stages of the course. Many of these roles allow you to contribute to a discussion without having to feel pressured to make a brilliant remark, have special oral skills, or be an expert on the topic at hand. Gradually, as you grow more accustomed to group discussions, you can begin to drop the roles. Also remember that in any discussion you may adopt multiple roles.

The roles are also useful for those who may already be confident and experienced in group discussions but who tend to play the same roles all the time. You can improve your discussion skills as well as your ability to function constructively in groups by becoming more aware of the different roles you can assume.

1. **Initiator** You help to get the discussion started or recharged whenever it begins to lag.
2. **Information Provider** You give the group information about a topic when you think it will enhance the discussion.
3. **Feedback Provider** You listen and respond to the Initiator and/or Information Provider verbally or nonverbally. For example, you might explain why you agree with what was just said or simply nod your head in affirmation.
4. **Idea Clarifier** If you think an idea or piece of information is not sufficiently clear, you can ask for clarification. Remember, if you don't understand something, chances are that others don't either. Or you can restate the idea in your own words to confirm whether you and others understand. You can also provide a personal experience as an example of the point being made in order to clarify an idea further and to get confirmation from the Information Provider.
5. **Encouragement Provider** If you become aware that a group member is being left out, you can verbally or nonverbally encourage that person to join in. You might express your interest in hearing the person's point of view or simply make an encouraging gesture.
6. **Group Tension Reliever** If you are discussing a particularly sensitive and controversial topic, the discussion may become quite heated. Without trivializing the topic, you may be able to inject a lighter note or make the group laugh.
7. **Misinformation Tracker** This is a difficult role, because it involves confronting and/or disagreeing with information that has been given. If you hear something you believe is incorrect, you can step in politely and correct it in a nonthreatening way. For example, you can say something like "I'm not sure that date is correct—I'd be glad to check it" or "I wonder if we have correctly understood the difference between ASL and Signed English. Let's check in the text." Remember, you are confronting the information, not the person.

8. **Idea Challenger**   You have the most sensitive role because you are challenging another person's ideas or opinions. Always proceed carefully and respectfully. Usually it's a good idea to acknowledge something you liked or agreed with before bringing up the point of contention. You might say, for example, "Yes, I do think it is very important for Latino children to learn English, but I really believe that their Spanish language skills and culture should be maintained."

9. **Discussion Tracker**   As a discussion progresses, it may go off on a tangent or become confusing. Your role is to keep an eye on the discussion and bring it back on track if it strays too far. A comment such as "I think we are getting away from the main point here—can we return to the discussion of the Issei and Nisei?" is entirely appropriate.

10. **Questioner**   You ask questions to gain information, to provoke thought, and to stimulate further discussion.

11. **Timekeeper**   If you become aware that one group member is dominating the discussion or that your group is running out of time, you help to keep the discussion moving or bring it to a close. You can politely interrupt and remind people how much time is available to finish certain tasks by saying, for example, "I think that's a good thought, but we've only got a couple of minutes left, so can we quickly review our main points?"

12. **Summarizer**   Your role is to jot down the main points your group has made. You may be called upon in the last few minutes of a discussion to summarize the group's ideas in preparation for a class discussion or to take notes for a group presentation, such as for the Spotlight section in each chapter of this book.

In your film notebook, identify two roles: one you feel you can play easily and another that you feel less confident in assuming or that you have never tried. Give reasons for your choices, perhaps with examples from previous discussion experiences.

Sequel: Further Suggested Resources

Herbst, Philip H. 1997. *The Color of Words: An Encyclopædic Dictionary of Ethnic Bias in the United States.* Yarmouth, ME: Intercultural Press.

Hilger, Michael. 1986. *The American Indian in Film.* Metuchen, NJ: Scarecrow Press.

2

Native American Culture: *Dances with Wolves* and *Thunderheart*

Dances with Wolves
Setting the Scene: Freewriting and Discussion

> *Like most children of the fifties, my first impressions of Native American people were not very positive. Indians were widely portrayed as devils, whose destruction was purely a matter of necessity in the process of taming the West. Every publication or film I saw as a child was slanted in this way.*
>
> *But from the first, I sensed somehow that the story was incomplete.* (Costner, Blake, and Wilson 1990, xv)

These words by Michael Blake, author of the *Dances with Wolves* screenplay, reveal that his early ideas about Native Americans* were formed by stereotypes. First review the concept of stereotyping from the Essential Vocabulary on Cultures (page 10), and then jot down in your film notebook some stereotypes of Indians that are prevalent in American culture. Freewrite about the extent to which you are personally affected by these stereotypes. Discuss and compare your thoughts in small groups.

---

*For alternative terms and definitions, see Related Terms, page 23.

Wide-Angle Lens: Historical and
Geographical Perspectives

History of Westward Expansion

The nineteenth century, during which the film is set, was a time of great westward expansion beyond the Mississippi River and of accompanying major conflicts throughout the West between Native Americans and white citizens (see Map 3, page 26). In popular language this is the era of the "Wild West," the "frontier," the "cowboys and Indians." It has given rise to enduring and cherished national myths about the heroism of white settlers who conquered the frontier.

Actually, when the nineteenth century began, the United States of America had only been in existence a short time. Having emerged victorious in 1783 from the War of Independence against England, this new nation was soon to become the sole possessor of immense territories once claimed by the major colonial rivals England, Spain, and France (see Map 2, page 25). The purchase of the huge Louisiana Territory from France in 1803, coupled with several major annexations at midcentury (explained below), meant that America stretched from coast to coast. But, in truth, the claims to this vast land by the new settlers ignored the rightful ownership of its original inhabitants—the American Indians.

Let's recall that at the time of Columbus' landing in the New World in 1492, hundreds of Indian groups occupied a vast stretch of territory equivalent to one-fourth of the earth's habitable land, extending from northern Alaska to Cape Horn. The population at the time of Columbus is uncertain, but estimates for those Indians living in North America (north of present-day Mexico) suggest that there were at least two million native inhabitants.

As the colonial powers waged their campaigns for land and riches in the new continent during the three centuries subsequent to Columbus' landing, the Indians were forced to deal with the invaders, many of whom were originally received with hospitality. Despite periods of relative peace, uneasy truces, and accommodation, the first three hundred years of contact with Europeans overwhelmingly demonstrated to the Indians that the white man's presence ultimately meant betrayal, destruction, and death. Indian groups repeatedly tried to resist the white man's attempts to convert, deceive, subjugate, enslave, and dispossess them, fighting numerous battles as well as major wars—ranging from the Pueblo Revolt (1680) to Little Turtle's War (1790–1795)—but their struggles were fruitless. By the nineteenth century, European-borne disease and the depredations of continuous warfare had decimated or in some cases completely wiped out entire Indian populations. As Indians struggled to survive, the young nation was flexing its muscle.

In 1830 a new era of oppression was launched by the U.S. government under President Andrew Jackson in the form of the Indian Removal Act. Though greatly reduced in land and numbers, most eastern Indian tribes still occupied portions of their original homelands—until Jackson forcibly relocated them west of the Mississippi. Some groups, such as the Florida Seminoles and the Georgia Cherokees, resisted removal, but the decade between 1830 and 1840 saw more than fifty tribes (80,000 Indians) driven from their homelands. The removal had tragic consequences. Not only did many Indians perish on the trek west, but subsequent clashes occurred between the displaced peoples and those Indians already occupying the western territories. In return for uprooting the tribes, Jackson's government set apart an "ample district west of the Mississippi…to be guaranteed to the Indian tribes as long as they shall occupy it" (Richardson 1896, 458).

This promise of security was soon broken. From 1845 to 1853 the sudden acquisition of enormous additional western lands (Texas, California, Oregon Territory, and parts of the Southwest) stretched the country from ocean to ocean. Still, the western lands might have remained remote, inhospitable, and uninteresting to white settlers had not gold been discovered in California in 1848. That event decided the fate of western Indians forever. While trappers, traders, and missionaries had roamed the territories and some wagon trains of settlers had been rolling westward on the Oregon Trail across Indian lands since the early 1840s, suddenly tens of thousands of fortune hunters surged westward through Indian territory. This relentless migration and the accompanying growth of railroad and communications lines severely disrupted Indian hunting and fishing practices, destroyed food-gathering grounds, depleted natural resources, and spread hitherto unknown diseases.

The whites called this encroachment on Indian lands *Manifest Destiny*, a doctrine proclaiming that they, as superior, civilized, white Europeans, had both a right and an obligation to expand the nation westward to its furthermost borders and rule over it. To protect settlers and secure control of the newly claimed land, the government established an increasing number of military forts along lines of travel and communication. Such forts play a role in *Dances with Wolves*. Lieutenant Dunbar receives his orders at Fort Hays in present-day Kansas and is stationed at the frontier Fort Sedgewick, located somewhere in the Dakotas in the territory of the Great Plains Indians.

In the 1860s white migration westward slowed somewhat because of the Civil War (*Dances with Wolves* opens with a scene on a battlefield in Tennessee). At that time the population of Indians living in the United States, mostly west of the Mississippi, had dwindled to three hundred thousand. Whites numbered approximately thirty million.

The powerful Sioux stand out among those Indians who resisted westward expansion. The fifteen-year period referred to in American history as the Sioux Wars included clashes such as the Minnesota Uprising (1862), the War for the Bozeman Trail (1866–1868), and the Battle of the Little Bighorn (1876), where George Armstrong Custer died. The Sioux way of life has given us many of the cultural features now associated (often mistakenly) with all Indians: tipis, warbonnets and eagle feathers, buffalo hunting, and superior horsemanship. The great Sioux leaders—Little Crow, Red Cloud, Sitting Bull, Black Elk, Crazy Horse, and Spotted Tail—have achieved legendary status in American history.

Sioux are classified as Great Plains Indians, one of ten labels commonly used to classify North American Indians according to geography, language, and culture (see Map 1, page 24). Within each of these ten large groupings are numerous subdivisions. The Great Plains Indians, for example, include Caddoan and Athapaskan as well as Sioux. The Pawnee, whom we will also meet in *Dances with Wolves*, are a Caddoan tribe. The Sioux themselves traditionally comprised three major groups—the Santees, Yankton, and Lakota—each of whom spoke distinct Sioux dialects. *Dances with Wolves* deals with the Lakota, the westernmost Sioux group living on the plains of North and South Dakota and Nebraska. Note that the Lakota were further divided into seven tribes. *Dances with Wolves*, however, does not specify which Lakota tribe we are encountering.

Related Terms

Aleuts, Inuits (Eskimos)   Indigenous peoples of Alaska and other regions. *Eskimo* is falling into disfavor among most groups.

American Indian, Indian   Terms widely used to refer to the many different indigenous peoples who inhabited this country before the European conquest. The word *Indian* originated with Christopher Columbus who, falsely believing he had landed in India, used the Spanish word *indios* to refer to the people he encountered.

First Americans   Term sometimes used to refer to American Indians.

Hawaiian Natives, Native Hawaiians   Terms used to refer to indigenous peoples of Hawaii.

indigenous people   Term often used by anthropologists and others to refer to groups native to a region. It avoids the word *native*, which sometimes has pejorative associations with the idea of primitiveness.

Native American   Term that came into widespread usage in the 1980s as a respectful way of referring to American Indians. The term, however, is used more by non-Indians than by Indians, who often dislike being lumped together and prefer to be called by the name of their tribe or nation.

redskin, red man   Terms referring to the skin color of Native Americans, which is not really red; generally considered dated and offensive. "Red Power" was a slogan used by Indian activists during the civil rights movement.

squaw, injun   Derogatory terms for Indians.

tribe   In common usage, a group of American Indians sharing a common heritage. Indians themselves also use the term *nation,* which suggests political independence, though in a legal sense not all tribes are actually nations.

Map Exercise: Working with a partner, study and discuss the three maps on the following pages. What do they tell you that you did not already know? How do they help you understand the Indian history you have just read? After discussing, write your answers to these questions in your film notebook.

Map 1. Ten Indian Culture Areas in North America

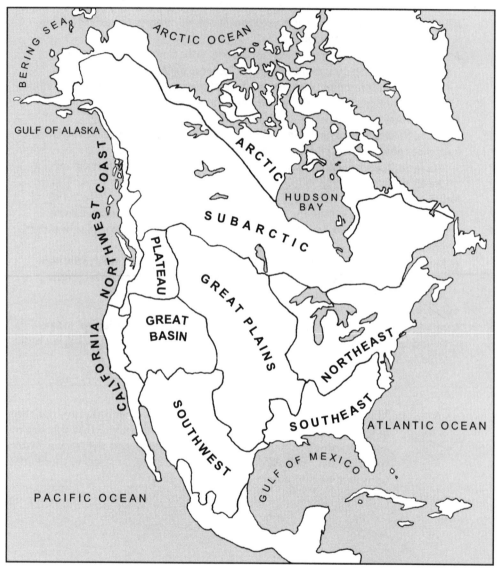

map by Steven Shoffner

Map 2. Growth of the United States by Region and Appropriation of Indian Lands (1776–1867)

OREGON
TERRITORY
FROM
BRITAIN
(1846)

LOUISIANA PURCHASE
FROM FRANCE
(1803)

UNITED STATES
AFTER
AMERICAN
REVOLUTION
(1783)

MEXICAN CESSION
AFTER
MEXICAN WAR
(1848)

ORIGINAL THIRTEEN COLONIES
(17th –18th Centuries)

TEXAS
ANNEXATION
FROM
MEXICO
(1845)

ALASKA
PURCHASE
FROM RUSSIA
(1867)

GADSDEN
PURCHASE
FROM MEXICO
(1853)

FLORIDA ACQUISITION
FROM SPAIN
(1819)

map by Steven Shoffner

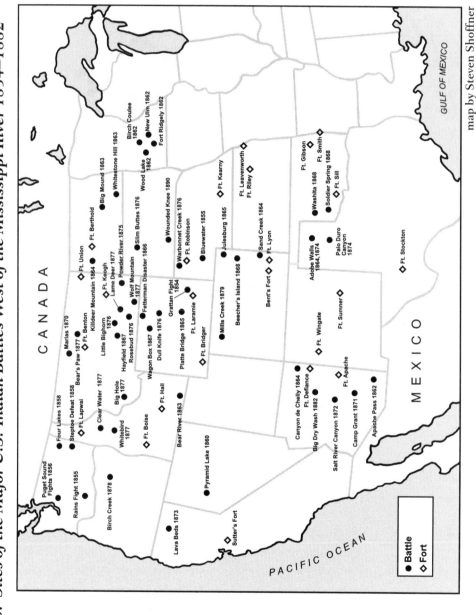

Map 3. Sites of the Major U.S.-Indian Battles West of the Mississippi River 1854–1882

CANADA

Marias 1870
Bear's Paw 1877
Ft. Benton
Ft. Union
Ft. Berthold
Big Mound 1863
Whitestone Hill 1863
Birch Coulee 1862
New Ulm 1862
Fort Ridgely 1862
Wood Lake 1862
Killdeer Mountain 1864
Ft. Keogh
Lame Deer 1877
Powder River 1875
Slim Buttes 1876
Wounded Knee 1890
Little Bighorn 1876
Wolf Mountain 1877
Warbonnet Creek 1876
Ft. Robinson
Hayfield 1867
Rosebud 1876
Fetterman Disaster 1866
Bluewater 1855
Ft. Kearny
Four Lakes 1858
Steptoe Defeat 1858
Ft. Lapwai
Clear Water 1877
Big Hole 1877
Wagon Box 1867
Dull Knife 1876
Grattan Fight 1854
Platte Bridge 1865
Ft. Laramie
Julesburg 1865
Ft. Leavenworth
Ft. Riley
Washita 1868
Ft. Gibson
Ft. Smith
Soldier Spring 1868
Ft. Sill
Whitebird 1877
Ft. Boise
Ft. Hall
Bear River 1863
Ft. Bridger
Mills Creek 1879
Beecher's Island 1868
Sand Creek 1864
Ft. Lyon
Bent's Fort
Adobe Walls 1864, 1874
Palo Duro Canyon 1874
Puget Sound Fights 1856
Rains Fight 1855
Birch Creek 1878
Pyramid Lake 1860
Canyon de Chelly 1864
Ft. Defiance
Big Dry Wash 1882
Salt River Canyon 1872
Camp Grant 1871
Ft. Wingate
Ft. Apache
Ft. Sumner
Apache Pass 1862
Ft. Stockton
Lava Beds 1873
Sutter's Fort

PACIFIC OCEAN

MEXICO

GULF OF MEXICO

Battle
Fort

map by Steven Shoffner

Lights Out: Viewing the Film

Dances with Wolves (1990) was a phenomenal success, grossing over four hundred million dollars at box offices around the world and winning dozens of awards, including seven Academy Awards, three Golden Globe Awards, and four awards at the American Indian Film Festival. The lead actors—Kevin Costner, Graham Greene, Rodney Grant, Floyd Crow Westerman, and Mary McDonnell—director Kevin Costner, cinematographer Dean Semler, costume designer Elsa Zamparelli, and screenplay author Michael Blake have all been recognized for their work.

Why is this film important? At first glance it might seem only to retell a familiar story—the struggle between whites and Indians over the American West—already captured countless times in books, on television, and in films. In particular Hollywood's tradition of westerns has shaped the way many Americans have viewed Indians throughout the twentieth century. If you have seen even a few of the hundreds of westerns filmed, you know that Indians are routinely depicted in stereotypical fashion, either as "bloodthirsty savages" or "noble savages"—but almost always as savages. They are rarely given names or personalities, do not speak English or any other language (but do emit fierce sounds or grunts), and relish killing and scalping whites.

Throughout this chapter you will observe how *Dances with Wolves* breaks with tradition to create a different type of western. Actually, Costner was not the first to deviate from the old pattern: well-known films such as *Broken Arrow* (1950), *Soldier Blue* (1970), and *Little Big Man* (1970) are also considered innovative. Costner's film, however, was the first to reach such a wide national and international audience, and he achieves significant breakthroughs, such as his decision to film major portions of the movie in the Lakota Sioux language, his commitment to use Native American actors in all of the Indian roles, and his painstaking attention to historical detail in the creation of tipis, costumes, and sets.

As you view the film, write down any questions you have concerning content in your film notebook (e.g., Why did Stands With A Fist cut herself?[†]).

[†] Women in mourning for a deceased husband made small incisions on their bodies as part of the grieving process. It seems that Stands With A Fist accidentally cut herself too deeply, or perhaps she was carried away by sorrow.

To bring to life the world of the nineteenth century Sioux, costume designer Elsa Zamparelli undertook extensive research, which was shared by technical advisor Cathy Smith, who grew up in the Black Hills and specializes in Plains Indians. They searched the country for the hundreds of deerskins and buffalo skins needed to make the numerous period costumes. In addition, scarce items such as authentic feathers, beads, and jewelry were used to achieve the distinct designs and patterns of the Sioux and Pawnee clothing.

In the costume production, Smith used traditional Lakota techniques such as intricate beading, quilling (accenting with porcupine quills), and brain tanning (rubbing buffalo brains on skins to soften them). She explains that the Plains tribes "probably had the most flamboyant, highly decorated dress of any Indians." Significantly, "all this clothing was made to be worn on horseback, moving through the wind. Not only did the fringe look wonderful, it helped shed water off the buckskin."

Another advisor, Larry Belitz, was responsible for recreating the Sioux village of the 1860s with its tipis, cooking utensils, and weapons. To achieve authenticity he used buffalo hair for robes and pillows, buffalo stomachs for cooking pots, and buffalo bladders for canteens. He made a total of about four hundred pieces worth approximately $60,000.‡

Major Characters and Locations in the Film

Lieutenant John Dunbar Wounded officer posted to Fort Sedgewick

Major Fambrough Commander at Fort Hays

Timmons Teamster who drives Dunbar to Fort Sedgewick

Kicking Bird Sioux medicine man

Ten Bears Sioux chief

Wind In His Hair Sioux warrior

Stone Calf Sioux elder

Stands With A Fist White woman adopted as a child by Sioux

Otter, Worm, Smiles A Lot Sioux children

Pretty Shield Ten Bears' wife

Black Shawl Kicking Bird's wife

Cisco Dunbar's horse

Two Socks Dunbar's wolf companion

Fort Hays Dakota plains fort where Dunbar receives orders

Fort Sedgewick Furthermost outpost where Dunbar is posted

---

‡ We have used Costner, Blake, and Wilson's *Dances with Wolves: The Illustrated Story of the Epic Film* and Diana Landau's "How Dances Got Real" (*Entertainment Weekly,* 8 March 1991) as sources for this information.

Spotlight on Culture and Communication

This spotlight will focus on nonverbal communication.

Review this concept from the Essential Vocabulary on Cultures (page 10), including the terms *kinesics*, *proxemics*, and *paralanguage*. Then, working in small groups, choose a short film clip from *Dances with Wolves* that seems to you to be rich in nonverbal communication, and analyze it, trying to pick up even the smallest details. Also think about how various film techniques reinforce or enhance the nonverbal cues you observe.

Time permitting, one or more of the groups can show their clip to the entire class, identifying the nonverbal cues they found most interesting and valuable.

Point of View: What the Critics Have to Say

The following pages provide a sample of how *Dances with Wolves* has been received by reviewers, both Indian and non-Indian.[§] A good review should open your film eyes wider and help you reevaluate what you have seen. It may lead you to appreciate the film more, or on the other hand, to see its faults more clearly. In any case, the reviewer should capture and hold your attention while stimulating thought and provoking questions.

In your film notebooks, evaluate the extent to which each review helped you to gain a new perspective on the film. Did any of the reviewers' points surprise or disturb you? Which of the four did you find most thought-provoking?

[§] Of the reviewers presented here, Shoots the Ghost is Native American, as was Michael Dorris.

Yet, *Dances with Wolves* dances around real issue

by Coretta Scott King   © 1990

THE OREGONIAN, WEDNESDAY, DECEMBER 5, 1990: Kevin Costner's epic film *Dances with Wolves* has critics across the country raving, but among American Indian leaders the reviews are mixed. While many Indian leaders have applauded *Dances with Wolves,* hoping that it heralds a new era in filmmaking about Indians, others have expressed concern about the overall effect of the film.

They do not disparage its cinematic depiction of Indians, which is said to be positive, rather they question its relevance to their current concerns, specifically the deplorable social and economic conditions being forced on the nation's more than 1.4 million Indians.

"The film perpetuates a romanticized image of a culture that would take attention away from the needs of native peoples today," explains Aaron Two Elk, Southeast regional coordinator of the International Indian Treaty Council.

Perhaps it's a little harsh to fault a filmmaker for his choice of time frame, but there is an undeniable need for films that are relevant to the current experience of American Indians. Film can be a powerful medium for promoting awareness about the need for social reforms.

Unemployment approaches 70 percent in many of the nation's 260 Indian reservations, where about half of the Native American population lives. It is estimated that at least one-third of the families on reservations live in poverty. Alcoholism, suicide and infant mortality rates are all three to four times the national average. Tales of how the U.S. government and industry created these conditions need to be told.

American Indians possess a unique vantage point, and they have much to teach the rest of the country about their concerns: land and fishing rights, the desecration of their sacred burial grounds and religious sites, the plundering of their religious freedom and, most importantly, protection of their tribal self-determination rights.

Two Elk, who was quoted in a recent Atlanta Constitution article on Indians' perspective on the film, is also concerned that the success of *Dances with Wolves* will prompt Hollywood producers to exploit the Native American heritage. "It's a subtle attempt to prostitute the culture for monetary gain," Two Elk said.

Our nation has such a rich, multicultural heritage, it's a shame that there are so few minority producers, directors and screenwriters. It will be a great day for American culture when some socially responsible investor funds the production of a major feature film about Indians, which is also produced, directed, written and acted by Indians.

The old excuses about not being able to find "qualified" minorities, so often used to justify the lack of support for minority filmmakers, were never credible. Every ethnic group has first-rate writers and artists. What so many of them lack are authentic films about their people's experience.

As Martin Luther King Jr. said in 1963,

Our nation was born in genocide when it embraced the doctrine that the original American, the Indian, was an inferior race… . We are perhaps the only nation that has tried as a matter of policy to wipe out its indigenous population… . Indeed, even today we have not permitted ourselves to reject or feel remorse for this shameful episode. Our literature, our films, our drama, our folklore all exalt it. ■

Dances with Wolves

by Dan Georgakas   © 1991

Utterly unforgivable in what touts itself as a pro-Native American film is the portrayal of the Pawnees. These heavy-duty villains are assigned every negative characteristic ever attributed to "the red man." To call the depictions two-dimensional would be a compliment. The Pawnee make their first appearance by sadistically waylaying a lone mule skinner, reach full stride with a raid on women and children, and end by hounding their Lakota enemies as scout/spies of the U.S. Army. Pawnee society, in reality, was a Plains culture quite similar to that of the Lakota....

The film begins to show some vitality when Dunbar makes his first contacts with the Lakota. These initial meetings are among the most successful in the film. They offer strong portraits of the Lakota as a people with a rich culture, and they establish Dunbar's desperate need to be perceived as friendly. Unfortunately, the filmmakers are not up to the challenge of exploring cultural and political diversities. The language problem gets a convenient jump start when Stands With A Fist is able to recall her English. Although much of the dialog is spoken in Lakota with English subtitles, the real problems of transcultural communication have been aborted.

Dunbar can only express his admiration of the Lakota by writing in his logbook that they are "just like us," that they are clean and are devoted to their families. The historical Lakota were indeed devoted to families and were clean, but they were not at all like Europeans. Their views of marriage, religion, nature, property, parenting, war, medicine, and animals, among other things, were profoundly different. Two distinctive cultures were coming into conflict, and the one with superior weapons technology would slaughter its rival. There is no hint in *Dances with Wolves* of the tragic nature of the clash between two equally complex cultures, each with its own merits and liabilities. The cultural issues become thoroughly cheapened when Dunbar renounces his evil white ways to become an adopted Indian. This cultural abdication is unconvincing and will prove fruitless.

Director Costner scores best when presenting the physical aspects of Lakota life. The splendid costumes, ornaments, hairstyles, and artifacts are all accurate and are lovingly rendered. The symbiotic relationship of the Lakota camps to specific physical settings is captured in beautifully filmed sequences, the winter camp being most notable. There is also a good sense of the council process in which the traditional chief, the war chief, and the religious chief each plays a distinctive role in what is a consensus judgment. Equally successful are scenes which indicate how Lakota women had significant, if indirect, input into day-to-day decision making in a decidedly patriarchal society....

Given that the filmmakers have made their casting a point of pride, it must be noted that of the three major Lakota roles, only one is played by a Lakota. Perhaps the filmmakers believe that, unlike Europeans, all Native Americans look alike. In any case, the real problem facing actors of Native American descent is not being overlooked for parts in the few westerns being made but in not getting a fair share of nonethnic roles....■

Good Indians Live, Bad Indians Die: A Critique of *Dances with Wolves*

by Shoots the Ghost © 1993

Indians In Aspic: Costner Falls Back on Myths

by Michael Dorris © 1991

Shoots the Ghost is Oglala Lakota, born on the Pine Ridge Indian Reservation. His birth name is Marlon Sherman; Shoots the Ghost was his grandfather's grandfather's name. As an undergraduate at the University of California, Santa Cruz, Shoots the Ghost wrote this essay in 1991 for American Studies 101.

…While it [*Dances with Wolves*] does portray the Lakota more fairly than any movie in recent past, it is still a white man's movie about white male choices….

Dunbar is always in control, always the hero. When he comes upon a grieving Indian woman, catching her unaware, he subdues her and takes her back to her village, managing to ride right past the sentries and enter the village unnoticed from above. Later, it is Dunbar who finds the buffalo herd, and who saves a young hunter from certain death during the hunt. During the attack by the Pawnees, it is Dunbar who saves the village by unearthing his cache of firearms. Near the end of the movie Dunbar displays great knowledge of White ways and wisdom when he advises the tribe to move further into the wilderness. These incidents show that our hero is extremely competent in all situations, and we have to wonder how the Indians got as far as they did without him….

Historically, the movie is often incorrect. There are no real badlands between Kansas and South Dakota, where the Pawnee and Sioux territories would overlap. Also, the Pawnee were never such a threat to the Lakota. They were a more sedentary people who lived in earth lodges and only followed the buffalo herd briefly each year. If anything, the Lakota terrorized them, pushing them ever southward….

This is a movie Americans can feel good about. The good Indians live, the bad Indians die, the white hero marries a white woman and the wolf is howling on the cliff, still wild, still beautiful. ∎

…With such tremendous popularity, the film is sure to generate a bubble of sympathy for the Sioux, but hard questions remain: Will this sentiment be practical, translating into public support for native American religious freedom cases before the Supreme Court, for restoration of Lakota sacred lands (the Black Hills) or water rights, for tribal sovereignty, for providing the money desperately needed by reservation health clinics? Pine Ridge is the most economically impoverished corner of America today, the Census Bureau says, but will its modern Indian advocates in business suits, men and women with laptop computers and perfect English, be the recipients of a tidal wave of good will?

Or will it turn out, once again, that the only good Indians—the only Indians whose causes and needs we can embrace—are lodged safely in the past, wrapped neatly in the blanket of history, magnets for our sympathy because they require nothing of us but tears in a dark theater? ∎

Indian Languages

The Lakota language, heard in *Dances with Wolves,* is one of the few Indian languages that may have a secure future. At the time of Columbus' landing an estimated five hundred native languages were spoken in the territory that is now the United States and Canada. Miraculously, as many as two hundred of these have survived to the present day, but most of them are now threatened with extinction.

Traditionally, Indian languages were unwritten, transmitted orally from one generation to the next. In the seventeenth and eighteenth centuries missionaries attempted to capture various languages in writing, primarily in order to translate the Bible for use in converting the Indians to Christianity. In the early 1800s a Cherokee from Tennessee named Sequoyah, fascinated by what he called the "talking leaves" of the English, worked for twelve years to create a written language for his tribe. His brilliant, innovative writing system gained rapid acceptance among the Cherokee. Today the giant redwood trees in California bear his name.

The fate of Indian languages is of course inseparable from the fate of the people themselves. During the colonial period and the age of westward expansion, as entire Indian populations and tribes succumbed to war and disease, their languages, too, disappeared. In more recent history when the last Indian wars were fought and surviving Indians were driven onto reservations, government policy focused on forcing Indians to give up their "Indianness" and to adopt white ways. Over several generations, from the 1880s to the mid-twentieth century, Indian children were removed from their parents and taken to boarding schools, where only English was allowed. If caught speaking their native languages, the children were often beaten. This deliberate, sustained attempt to wipe out Indian culture and language achieved considerable success, as another 150 languages were lost.

An intriguing exception to the universal disrespect shown for Indian languages was their use by the U.S. government as codes during the two world wars. The first language to be used was Choctaw; fourteen Indian speakers are credited with helping to win critical battles against the Germans in France during World War I. Choctaw was used again in World War II, as were Comanche and Navajo. The Navajo Code Talkers in particular—eventually a group of approximately four hundred men—achieved heroic status for their ingenuity in constructing the code and their accuracy in delivering it. They were especially active in the Pacific, where their greatest achievement was the delivery of hundreds of messages to communicate the plan to capture Iwo Jima. The Indian Code Talkers rendered invaluable service in codes that were never deciphered or broken.

Reversing its long-standing policy of suppression, the federal government in 1990 passed the Native American Languages Act. This legislation protects the right of Native Americans to use and develop their languages in the recognition that "languages are critical to the survival of the cultural and political integrity of any people." The 1990 act is an important step, but the federal government's support in the form of funding to save Indian languages (currently some two million dollars a year) to many minds reflects only a tepid commitment.

For most of the languages, it may be too late; Michael E. Krauss, professor of linguistics at the University of Alaska, estimates that a mere twenty languages are still being taught to children by their parents. The others are spoken almost entirely by the older generations, in many cases by fewer than ten elderly tribal members. The urgency of the situation has prompted many Indian groups to action: elders are teaching children in summer language camps; radio stations are offering native language broadcasts; tribal colleges are offering language courses; and tribal members are capturing the language of elders on tape.

This sense of the value of indigenous languages is growing worldwide. As more and more languages vanish—approximately half of the world's six thousand languages have no children speakers—so does a wealth of knowledge and human experience. People from many different countries and cultures now realize that indigenous languages are not only vital to the cultural preservation of the peoples directly affected, but they also serve all of us as a link to the human past. They are repositories of historical events and political institutions, of religious and literary thought, and of ecological and medical wisdom. Once a language is gone, this knowledge cannot be recaptured.

Approximately two thousand Indian words and hundreds of place-names have been incorporated into the English language. As Arlene Hirschfelder and Martha Kreipe de Montaño explain, Americans "use native words when they speak about food (squash), the weather (hurricane), transportation (canoe), animals (coyote), and shoes (moccasin)" (1993, 88).

Names of places reveal the Indians' profound relationship to the land and natural world. Many cities, towns, and states as well as rivers, lakes, mountains, and other geographical features today bear names of Indian origin. See box on the next page for some examples.

Use of Lakota in the Film

The Lakota language, once nearly lost, is now being used and taught on Sioux reservations in South Dakota. In order to bring the language into the film, producer Jim Wilson contacted Doris Leader Charge, an instructor of Lakota language and culture at Sinte Gleska College on the Rosebud Reservation (see map on page 43). In her capacity as technical advisor, Leader Charge translated the script into Lakota and trained the actors.

Not only were Kevin Costner and Mary McDonnell tutored by Leader Charge, but the Indian actors (including Graham Greene, an Oneida Iroquois from Ontario, Canada, and Rodney Grant, an Omaha from Nebraska) were as well. Even the three boys who played Smiles A Lot, Otter, and Worm, themselves Sioux from Leader Charge's reservation, had to be taught their language. Leader Charge explains that Lakota "was forbidden by the Bureau of Indian Affairs for many generations, until the Freedom of Religion Act was passed in the 1970s. They figured if they outlawed our language and ceremonies, we'd become assimilated, but it never really happened" (Costner, Blake, and Wilson 1990, 53). The only native Lakota speakers in the film are Floyd Crow Westerman as Ten Bears and Leader Charge herself, who plays Ten Bears' wife, Pretty Shield.

Geographical Names of Indian Origin

Kansas   From Kansas Sioux tribe word for "south wind people" or "wind people"

Massachusetts   From Algonquian, meaning "great-hill-small-place"

Ohio   From Iroquois word for "beautiful river"

Oklahoma   From Choctaw word for "red people"

- Listen again to any sections of the film in which Lakota is spoken. Write down adjectives that come to mind as you hear the melody of the language. Using this list as a starting point, write a poem or short essay about the language, describing its sounds and tones as well as the feelings it evokes in you.
- Imagine that you are an elder in your Indian nation and the last speaker of your language. Write a letter to your grandchildren describing your thoughts and emotions as you face the loss of your language.

Zoom Lens: Choosing Your Own Topic of Interest

Hands-on Activities

1. Identify the closest nation or tribe of Native Americans to your campus, and with your instructor's help, set up a visit to their reservation or tribal council offices. (Be sure to write a letter of appreciation afterward.)

   Follow up by reading the tribe's newspaper, newsletter, or other source of current information.

2. Visit a local Native American museum or gallery, or attend an event such as a powwow or art show. You may find it helpful to check guidebooks to Indian places of interest, listed in the Sequel section at the end of this chapter (pages 57–58) under Eagle/Walking Turtle, Tiller, and Gattuso.

3. Invite a Native American artist, storyteller, or speaker to give a presentation at your school or college. Check to see if there is a fee involved.

Research Papers or Oral Reports

1. If you are an international student (or have lived for a significant period of time in another culture), research and compare the situation of an indigenous people or peoples from your home country with that of Indians in the United States. How respected is the indigenous group in your home country? What is the group's general standard of living? Are struggles for indigenous rights taking place?

2. Investigate the gender roles in some Native American tribe or tribes, making reference to the gender roles you observed in the film.

3. Investigate one or more of the religious and spiritual beliefs among the Sioux (sacred buffalo pipe, sun dance, buffalo dance), making reference to religious ceremonies you observed in the film.

4. Research the Pawnee, in particular the interactions between the Pawnee and the Sioux, and compare your findings with the depiction of the Pawnee in the film.

5. Research the hunting culture of the Great Plains Indians. Find out to what extent they depended on the buffalo for their survival and what has happened to the buffalo since the period depicted in the film.

6. Research the life and achievements of one of the legendary Sioux leaders mentioned in the history section of this chapter (pages 20–22).

7. Survey recent issues of national Native American newspapers (e.g., *Indian Country Today* or *News from Indian Country*) and/or periodicals (e.g., *American Indian Quarterly* or *Native Peoples*) and do a comparison study between the way one of the news stories is treated there and the way it is presented in the non-Native American press.

8. Compare a traditional western such as *Stagecoach* (or a non-traditional film such as *Little Big Man*) with *Dances with Wolves*.

Using Your Imagination

1. Identify the stages of Dunbar's Indianization. Describe how and when he changes.

2. Write a dialogue between Kicking Bird and Wind In His Hair after the "tatanka" (0:56:45) and/or "coffee" episodes (0:59:00). Your script should reflect how these two men initially interpret Dunbar's presence and his actions.

3. Imagine that you are Stands With A Fist. Describe your feelings and reactions when you are asked by Kicking Bird to mediate between the two languages and cultures. What does your native language mean to you? Record both your initial reactions to this request and your later thoughts as your trust for Dunbar increases.

4. Write a conversation that might have taken place between Spivey and Edwards, the two illiterate white soldiers who deny all knowledge of finding Dunbar's journal and who taunt Dunbar for being a traitor to the U.S. army.

5. Write a poem by Wind In His Hair to Dunbar beginning with:

> *I am Wind In His Hair*
> *I am not afraid of you…*

and ending with:

> *I am Wind In His Hair*
> *You will always be my friend.*

Thunderheart
Setting the Scene: Freewriting and Discussion

So the United States of America, the nation under God indivisible with liberty and justice for all—these United States were founded on stolen land.... All of what is called the United States of America, every square inch, is, was, and always will be Indian Country!

—Auntie Kie

In a book of essays on Native American life today, *Yellow Woman and a Beauty of the Spirit* (1996), Leslie Marmon Silko includes a chapter entitled "Auntie Kie Talks about U.S. Presidents and U.S. Indian Policy," from which the above quotation is taken.

Write freely of the feelings you get from Auntie Kie's statement and the content of the map below.

Land Transfers

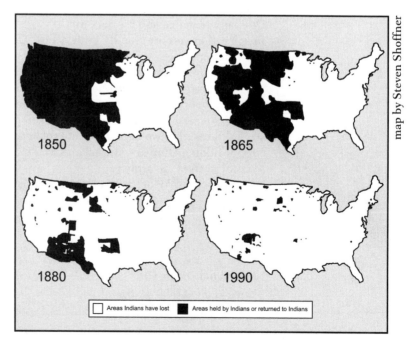

map by Steven Shoffner

1850

1865

1880

1990

☐ Areas Indians have lost ■ Areas held by Indians or returned to Indians

Wide-Angle Lens: Historical and Geographical Perspectives

Present-Day Indian Struggles

Thunderheart gives us an opportunity to pick up Indian history where *Dances with Wolves* left off. Like *Dances*, it also deals with the Lakota Sioux or, more precisely, with the Oglala, one of the Lakota tribes. Though set in the 1970s, *Thunderheart* recalls events that began in the latter half of the nineteenth century, which are critical to an understanding of the film.

The film begins with the following words: "This story was inspired by the events that took place on several American Indian reservations in the 1970s." The incident that gave impetus to *Thunderheart* was a shoot-out at the Pine Ridge Reservation in South Dakota on June 26, 1975, in which two Federal Bureau of Investigation (FBI) agents and one Indian were killed. Having launched an all-out manhunt to capture the killers, the FBI subsequently arrested four men, all members of the radical political group American Indian Movement (AIM).

Of these suspects, one was released for insufficient evidence, two others were acquitted after successfully pleading self-defense, and the fourth, Leonard Peltier, escaped to Canada. The story of Peltier's subsequent extradition (which many believe was based on fraudulent evidence), conviction on two counts of murder in the first degree, and sentencing to two consecutive life terms in the federal penitentiary has since become known worldwide (see page 53). For years Indian supporters and many other sympathizers have worked toward Peltier's release in the belief that he is innocent and may have been framed by an embarrassed and pressured FBI. Amnesty International has repeatedly expressed concerns about the fairness of his trial to the U.S. government and has advocated a new trial.

The shoot-out was in fact only one of many incidences of violence occurring on Lakota reservations at that time. More than sixty murders of AIM members and traditional Indians (those committed to preserving their culture and governing themselves) were unsolved, and firefights were commonplace. To understand why these reservations were erupting in anger, murder, and destruction, we must go back a hundred years to the roots of one of the most bitter and protracted conflicts between Indians and whites in America: the struggle for the Black Hills.

The Black Hills have long been a beloved place of spiritual significance to the Lakota. Today the meaning of the Black Hills is often expressed in terms of sacredness or holiness. The following quote by Oglala chief Luther Standing Bear illustrates what the Black Hills represent:

> *Of all our domain we loved, perhaps, the Black Hills the most. The Lakota had named these hills He Sapa, or Black Hills, on account of their color. The slopes and peaks were so heavily wooded with dark pines that from a distance the mountains actually looked black. In wooded recesses were numberless springs of pure water and numerous small lakes. There were wood and game in abundance and shelter from the storms of the plains. It was the favorite winter haunt of the buffalo and the Lakota as well. According to a tribal legend these hills were a reclining female figure from whose breasts flowed life-giving forces, and to them the Lakota went as a child to its mother's arms.*[**]

The struggle over the Black Hills coincides with the westward expansion of white settlers in the mid-nineteenth century, which caused major disruption on Sioux lands. The Sioux fought back. Their resistance to the ever-increasing encroachment was so effective and whites felt so threatened by Indians led by warriors such as Red Cloud and Sitting Bull that the government decided to make peace, resulting in the Fort Laramie Treaty of 1868. According to the terms of this treaty (see pages 44–45), the Indians agreed to cease their attacks on wagon trains and coaches and to allow the railroad to be built in exchange for "absolute and undisturbed use" of the newly created Great Sioux Reservation, a vast territory in five states with the Black Hills at its heart. The treaty clearly stipulated that no white person would be "permitted to settle upon or occupy any portion" of this territory, or to pass through it "without the consent of the Indians." Moreover, the treaty provided that no portion of the reservation lands could be ceded by further treaty unless "executed and signed by at least three-fourths of all the adult male Indians."

Within four years the treaty was a relic. Gold had been discovered in the Black Hills, and miners and settlers poured into the region. The government not only failed to protect the Sioux from intruders but also tried unsuccessfully to force them to sell or lease their lands. Clashes escalated into war. The Indians experienced momentary victory when combined Sioux, Cheyenne, and Arapaho forces, led by the

---

[**]Luther, Standing Bear, 1933. *Land of the Spotted Eagle* (Lincoln, NE: University of Nebraska Press), 43.

legendary Crazy Horse among others, annihilated George Armstrong Custer's Seventh Cavalry at the Battle of the Little Bighorn ("Custer's Last Stand") in 1876. Shortly thereafter, however, the harshness of winter and the fear of starvation—combined with the massive show of force displayed by the U.S. army to avenge the Custer "massacre"—forced the Sioux to surrender. Providing no monetary compensation, Congress simply annexed 7.7 million acres of the Black Hills in an agreement of 1877, which the Sioux refer to as the "sign or starve" treaty.

Defeated and living in dire poverty on their greatly reduced reservations, the Sioux experienced a moment of revival when a new religion began to take hold in the form of the Ghost Dance. Created by a Paiute Indian named Wovoka, who deemed himself a messiah, the Ghost Dance envisioned a world without white men, where buffalo would again roam freely and Indians would be reunited with their dead ancestors. The ceremonial ghost dances taking place on almost every Indian reservation frightened whites, who determined to halt what they perceived as a revolt. A renewed period of hostile actions against the Sioux culminated in the infamous incident at Wounded Knee creek in South Dakota (winter of 1890), where the leader Big Foot and several hundred mostly unarmed Sioux men, women, and children were slain, their bodies left to freeze in the bitter winter temperatures.

The fight for the restoration of Sioux lands continued into the twentieth century, fought increasingly in the courtroom. Numerous lawsuits filed in the 1920s and for decades thereafter finally resulted in "victory" in 1980, when the U.S. Supreme Court affirmed a lower court judgment that the Black Hills had been taken from the Sioux unconstitutionally. As a result the Court ruled that a total of $106 million (the $17.5 million judged to have been the fair market value in 1877, plus interest) was to be paid to the Sioux as compensation. To the astonishment of all concerned, the Sioux decided to refuse the money and instead to continue to press for the return of their lands. Various attempts to accomplish this, including a bill sponsored by Senator Bill Bradley in 1985, have failed, and the money is still being held in trust for the Sioux.

Discouraged with the slow pace of the courts, some Indians chose the path of political activism. AIM, founded in 1968 originally for the purpose of improving the situation of urban Indians and protecting them from police brutality, staged a number of spectacular events to raise public awareness of Indian grievances, including the occupations of Alcatraz Island (1969–1970) and Mount Rushmore (1971) and the Trail of Broken Treaties caravan to Washington, D.C. (1972).

Meanwhile on the Pine Ridge Reservation in South Dakota, traditional Indians not only faced a crisis of joblessness and extreme poverty but were also being intimidated and abused by a federally sponsored "puppet" tribal government led by one Richard Wilson. Wilson's corrupt government was backed not only by the federal government's Bureau of Indian Affairs (BIA) police and his own private police force, the GOON (Guardians of the Oglala Nation) squad, but later by a "Special Operations Group" of sixty-five specially trained U.S. marshals as well.

With support from prominent AIM members (including Dennis Banks and Russell Means), Oglala Lakota Indians from Pine Ridge decided in 1973 to take a stand at the nearby village of Wounded Knee, a site chosen for its historical significance and symbolism. Their protest was rooted most directly in grievances about the tribal government, but they also were concerned with broader issues such as sovereignty. Harking back to the Fort Laramie Treaty of 1868, the Indians believed that the promise of "absolute and undisturbed use" of the land established their rights as a separate nation. Indians had in fact always dealt with the colonial governments as independent, self-governing nations, and the treaty of 1868 only confirmed in writing the unassailable and undiminished conviction of the Sioux that they were not subject to the laws of the U.S. government.

At Wounded Knee in 1973, this conflict of views erupted into warfare. The small group of Indians (including women and children) soon found themselves surrounded by hundreds of federal agents with the most sophisticated weaponry. The armed siege, which lasted more than two months, brought national and international attention to "Wounded Knee II," as it came to be called. Why did the U.S. government respond with such a massive display of force? The reasons are complex and difficult to understand, but certainly the mood of the times—fear of Communist infiltrators, wariness of all political activism in the post-civil rights years, and the militarism of the Vietnam War era—contributed to a sense of paranoia. Moreover, the government was interested in the huge uranium deposits known to be in the Black Hills, a fact little known to the outside world at the time. The day before the two FBI agents were shot two years later, Dick Wilson signed over one-eighth of the existing mineral-rich reservation land to the U.S. government.

After Wounded Knee II the situation at the Pine Ridge Reservation only worsened. Labeled a "reign of terror" by AIM members, the following years were characterized by frequent threats, beatings, and killings. This is the setting for *Thunderheart*. In the movie the two FBI agents from the 1975 shoot-out have already been killed, and the violence continues. Still another Indian, Leo Fast Elk, has been murdered, and two other FBI agents are sent to the fictional Bear Creek reservation to investigate. The main suspect, Jimmy Looks Twice, loosely resembles Leonard Peltier, and the organization Aboriginal Rights Movement (ARM) is based on AIM.

Sioux Country

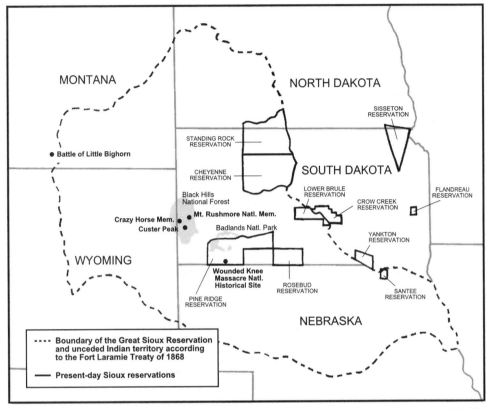

map by Steven Shoffner

Reading a Treaty

Between 1778 and 1871 the federal government signed 371 treaties with Indian nations, all of which were violated or abrogated. Today most non-Indians tend to look on treaties as relics of the past, as mere pieces of paper that were signed so far back in history that it would be absurd, not to mention highly impractical, to think of resurrecting them. To many Indians, however, the treaties are binding agreements that still stand.

In current court battles Lakota Sioux base their territorial claims on the Fort Laramie Treaty of 1868, mentioned earlier. This treaty was important to the U.S. government because Red Cloud and his followers had been waging a highly successful war against whites who continued crossing through their territories. In exchange for the promise of peace, the government established the Great Sioux Reservation where the Sioux would be able to live without intrusion as well as an "unceded" area (explained in Article 16 of the treaty) where the Sioux and Cheyenne could hunt freely (see map of reservation and unceded territory on page 43).

- Study the treaty articles one by one. If you had been a Sioux chief at the time, which of the provisions would have been advantageous for you and your tribe? Would any of the provisions have offended or alienated you? If so, why? Look for and highlight any examples of wording that suggests misperceptions or bias on the part of the federal government.
- How long do you think an agreement of this nature should be valid? If you had been a member of the U.S. Congress at the time, would you have allowed the treaty to be violated when gold was discovered in the Black Hills? Why or why not? If you were a congressperson today, would you be willing to consider returning the Black Hills to the Lakota Sioux? Explain.

Treaty of Fort Laramie

April 29, 1868

Articles of a treaty made and concluded by and between Lieutenant-General William T. Sherman, General William S. Harney, General Alfred H. Terry, General C. C. Augur, J. B. Henderson, Nathaniel G. Taylor, John B. Sanborn, and Samuel F. Tappan, duly appointed commissioners on the part of the United States, and the different bands of the Sioux Nation of Indians, by their chiefs and head-men, whose names are hereto subscribed, they being duly authorized to act in the premises.

Article 1. From this day forward all war between the parties to this agreement shall forever cease. The Government of the United States desires peace, and its honor is hereby pledged to keep it. The Indians desire peace, and they now pledge their honor to maintain it.

Article 2. The United States agrees that the following district of country[††] ...shall be...set apart for the absolute and undisturbed use and occupation of the Indians herein named, and for such other friendly tribes or individual Indians as from time to time they may be willing, with the consent of the United States, to admit amongst them; and the United States now solemnly agrees that no persons except those herein designated and authorized so to do, and except such officers, agents, and employés of the Government as may be authorized to enter upon Indian reservations in discharge of duties enjoined by law, shall ever be permitted to pass over, settle upon, or reside in the territory described in this article, or in such territory as may be added to this reservation for the use of said Indians, and henceforth they will and do hereby

[††]In the treaty a detailed description is given of the territory shown on the map on page 43.

(continued on the next page)

(continued from the previous page)

relinquish all claims or right in and to any portion of the United States or Territories, except such as is embraced within the limits aforesaid, and except as hereinafter provided....

Article 7. In order to insure the civilization of the Indians entering into this treaty, the necessity of education is admitted, especially of such of them as are or may be settled on said agricultural reservations, and they therefore pledge themselves to compel their children, male and female, between the ages of six and sixteen years, to attend school....

Article 10. In lieu of all sums of money or other annuities provided to be paid to the Indians herein named, under any treaty or treaties heretofore made, the United States agrees to deliver at the agency-house on the reservation herein named, on or before the first day of August of each year, for thirty years, the following articles, to wit:

For each male person over fourteen years of age, a suit of good substantial woolen clothing, consisting of coat, pantaloons, flannel shirt, hat, and a pair of home-made socks.

For each female over twelve years of age, a flannel skirt, or the goods necessary to make it, a pair of woolen hose, twelve yards of calico, and twelve yards of cotton domestics.

For the boys and girls under the ages named, such flannel and cotton goods as may be needed to make each a suit as aforesaid, together with a pair of woolen hose for each....

Article 11. In consideration of the advantages and benefits conferred by this treaty, and the many pledges of friendship by the United States, the tribes who are parties to this agreement hereby stipulate that they will relinquish all right to occupy permanently the territory outside their reservation as herein defined, but yet reserve the right to hunt on any lands north of North Platte, and on the Republican Fork of the Smoky Hill River, so long as the buffalo may range thereon in such numbers as to justify the chase. And they, the said Indians, further expressly agree:

1st. That they will withdraw all opposition to the construction of the railroads now being built on the plains.

2nd. That they will permit the peaceful construction of any railroad not passing over their reservation as herein defined.

3d. That they will not attack any persons at home, or travelling, nor molest or disturb any wagon-trains, coaches, mules, or cattle belonging to the people of the United States, or to persons friendly therewith.

4th. They will never capture, or carry off from the settlements, white women or children.

5th. They will never kill or scalp white men, nor attempt to do them harm.

6th. They withdraw all pretence of opposition to the construction of the railroad now being built along the Platte River and westward to the Pacific Ocean, and they will not in future object to the construction of railroads, wagon-roads, mail-stations, or other works of utility or necessity, which may be ordered or permitted by the laws of the United States....

7th. They agree to withdraw all opposition to the military posts or roads now established south of the North Platte River, or that may be established, not in violation of treaties heretofore made or hereafter to be made with any of the Indian tribes....

Article 12. No treaty for the cession of any portion or part of the reservation herein described which may be held in common shall be of any validity or force as against the said Indians, unless executed and signed by at least three-fourths of all the adult male Indians....

Article 16. The United States hereby agrees and stipulates that the country north of the North Platte River and east of the summits of the Big Horn Mountains shall be held and considered to be unceded Indian territory, and also stipulates and agrees that no white person or persons shall be permitted to settle upon or occupy any portion of the same; or without the consent of the Indians first had and obtained, to pass through the same.... ■

Lights Out: Viewing the Film

Major Characters, Locations, and Terms in the Film

Ray Levoi   Part-Indian FBI agent

Frank (Cooch) Coutelle   Legendary FBI agent

William Dawes   FBI agent who assigns Levoi to Bear Creek

Leo Fast Elk   Indian whose murder is being investigated

Walter Crow Horse   Tribal police officer

Maggie Eagle Bear   Local school-teacher and activist

Jimmy Looks Twice   Leader of ARM

Jack Milton   Leader of the tribal government and the GOONS

Grandpa Sam Reaches   Elder who is a spiritual leader of ARM

Grandma   Maggie Eagle Bear's mother

Richard Yellow Hawk   ARM member and Vietnam veteran in wheelchair

Thunderheart   Holy man killed at Wounded Knee in 1890

GOON squad   Paramilitary force terrorizing traditional and ARM Indians

Aboriginal Rights Movement (ARM)   Political group based on AIM

Red Deer Table   "The source"

Wounded Knee Memorial   Site of the 1890 massacre

the "rez"   Reservation

sweat ceremony or **lodge**   Purification ceremony

Bear Creek   Fictitious reservation modeled primarily on Pine Ridge

Ghost Dance   Religious dance dating to late 1800s

The movie *Thunderheart* appeared in 1992, produced by Robert Redford and directed by the British director Michael Apted. Interestingly, Apted had just completed a documentary entitled *Incident at Oglala* that focused on the same events. "I thought it would be fascinating," Apted says, "to look at the same historical period through two different pairs of eyes" (Cragg 1992, E4). *Thunderheart* is one of the first—and remains one of the only—films about contemporary Indians to achieve box-office success. (It has recently been joined by the Native American production *Smoke Signals*, popular among viewers and critics alike.)

The film features a splendid cast of Indian actors, including Graham Greene as Walter Crow Horse, Sheila Tousey as Maggie Eagle Bear, and Chief Ted Thin Elk as Grandpa Sam Reaches. Former AIM leader John Trudell, who has achieved recognition beyond his political activism as a poet and singer, plays Jimmy Looks Twice in a leading role, and AIM cofounder Dennis Banks plays himself in a cameo role.

Thunderheart was shot in the unusual, stark, powerful landscape of the Badlands, most of which today falls within the Badlands National Park. The southern part of the Badlands is located within the Pine Ridge Reservation (see map on page 43).

The plot, which resembles a murder mystery, is quite intricate. To ensure your comprehension, work with a partner to answer the questions on the next page.

1. Why does Ray Levoi first go out to Maggie Eagle Bear's property to investigate?
2. What is Maggie's main concern for her people?
3. Why is it important to find the Chevy belonging to Leo Fast Elk?
4. What does Grandpa Sam Reaches tell Levoi about Wounded Knee, and who was Thunderheart?
5. Who is Richard Yellow Hawk and what is his role in the crime?
6. What is the relationship between Frank Coutelle and Jack Milton?
7. What is Maggie's relationship with Yellow Hawk?
8. Why was Fast Elk killed?
9. Why does Coutelle want to frame Jimmy?
10. Who probably killed Yellow Hawk and Maggie?
11. What is happening at Red Deer Table? Why is this such a threat to the reservation?
12. What will happen at the end to Coutelle?

Answers are located on page 60.

Spotlight on Culture and Communication

In this section the spotlight is focused on values and how they may differ from one culture or subculture to another. First review the following terms in Essential Vocabulary on Cultures (page 9): *values, subculture (coculture), mainstream (dominant) culture, minority.*

Values tell us what is good, right, and important in life. Though invisible, they define, shape, and bind together the lives of people within a culture. In American mainstream culture, for example, a high value is placed on material goods, technology, youth, and individualism.

Our values give us a blueprint for our decisions, actions, and behaviors. If we value youth, for example, we will spend time and money to get rid of wrinkles and color our hair. Because our values are learned from birth and mold our identities as individuals and societies, we may not think to question them, nor can we easily imagine how anyone could reasonably hold values different from our own. Americans can be shocked, for example, to learn that some cultures revere old age rather than youth and think that elders in this country are badly treated.

The challenge for all of us in an increasingly global and multicultural society is to encounter value differences with maturity and openness. While we certainly do not have to accept or like other values, we must try to understand them. We may find that some of these differences are nonthreatening and a source of fascination and enrichment. After all, in the history of cultural contact and mixing throughout the millennia, values from outside have often been embraced. In the 1970s and 1980s, for example, many highly individualistic Americans began to learn from the Japanese to place increased value on cooperation and teamwork.

On the other hand, the encounter with differences in values, especially those that are deeply held, can also cause distress, confusion, rejection, and hatred. If there is a power differential, as in the case of minority groups within a dominant culture, the result may be suppression and subjugation of the minority.

One of the most enduring and extreme cases of this type of value clash in the United States is that between the mainstream society and Native Americans, as vividly depicted in *Thunderheart*.

 Working in small groups, select and analyze a short clip from the film that illustrates how value differences are a source of conflict. Or if you wish, show how these differences may be a source of enrichment. (Remember to note down minutes/seconds into the film for easy reference.)

Taking a Stand: Do Names and Memorials Matter?

As Indians and non-Indians alike come to terms with the past and as events are being retold today and reinterpreted from an "Indian" point of view, angry battles are raging over names and symbols. For example, in 1991 President George Bush signed legislation approving the name change from Custer Battlefield National Monument to Little Bighorn National Monument.

The issue of the Mount Rushmore and Crazy Horse Memorials, presented in the following article, is directly related to the film and vividly illustrates the type of controversy we are currently experiencing. The Mount Rushmore Memorial, located in the Black Hills, is a national site revered and visited by millions of Americans each year. Unknown to most Americans is the fact that many Lakota, Cheyenne, and other Indians consider the memorial to be a desecration. Not only are the Indians opposed to the idea of carving human faces into the landscape, but they especially object to being confronted with the likenesses of four presidents who in their view did little to stop—and often furthered—the exploitation of Indians. As a form of remedy to the Mount Rushmore Memorial, another white man, Polish-American sculptor Korczak Ziolkowski, embarked on a mission to have an image of the Lakota chief Crazy Horse carved into the Black Hills as well. Some Indians support this effort, while others are strongly opposed.

Read the newspaper article by Paul Hendrickson that begins on the next page, and then work in small groups to write a "Debate across the Centuries" in which two or three key figures from different historical periods, at least one of whom would still be living, express their views on the Crazy Horse Memorial. Make the dialogue as lively and controversial as possible.‡‡

The 1/34th scale model in the forefront is seen at a distance of one mile from the sculpture in progress.

---

‡‡Since the Hendrickson article was written, the face of Crazy Horse has been completed. On June 3, 1998, more than seven thousand people attended its official unveiling and dedication. Meanwhile, work continues on the monument itself and on a nearby orientation center, which will eventually accommodate many facilities, including two theaters and areas for educational displays, exhibitions, and workshops.

Face 9 Stories High Sculptor Began in 1948

A Dream Carved in Stone, Chief Crazy Horse Rides On

by Paul Hendrickson, Washington Post Service   © 1996

Thunderhead Mountain, South Dakota—Chief Crazy Horse, the great warrior of the Oglala Sioux, believed his bones would turn into rocks after his death. Here in the Black Hills, that conviction is coming true.

A massive statue of him is taking shape, blasted out of a mountain by a band of laborers pursuing the vision of an artist who has been dead for 14 years. Just lately the full mouth, the cleft of the chin, have begun to emerge. The face, nine stories high, is almost complete.

Various workers, led by the descendants of an obsessed Polish-American sculptor, have been toiling on Crazy Horse for almost 50 years—and have ahead of them maybe another half-century of blasting and sanding and hauling and flaking and chipping and supersonic torching. By the end, if it gets that far, Crazy Horse will be on his racing steed, arm outstretched, pointing to the lands where his beloved Sioux lie buried. It will be the largest mountain sculpture in the world.

The arm will be 263 feet (80 meters) long. The feather in his flying hair will be 44 feet high.

The original carver and presiding genius was Korczak Ziolkowski. He came to the Black Hills from New England after Chief Henry Standing Bear, a Sioux tribal elder, wrote to him and supposedly said: "My fellow chiefs and I would like the white man to know the red man has great heroes, too." This was in 1939, and Mr. Ziolkowski had just won a first prize for his marble portrait of the pianist and statesman Ignacy Paderewski at the New York World's Fair.

The self-taught sculptor answered the call, journeying to the Dakota wilderness and pitching a tent. He first began working the 600-foot-high mountain, called Thunderhead, under a special-use permit, staking a mining claim on the mountain with his own money. In the early 1950s, the Crazy Horse Memorial Foundation acquired Thunderhead and 328 acres (133 hectares) around it through a land exchange with the federal government.

By then Mr. Ziolkowski had built wooden stairs by hand, shooed away many mountain goats, begun his decades of blasting. That first explosion at the top, on June 3, 1948, took off 10 tons of granite. The blaster, the dreamer, was almost 40 years old.

For the next 34 years, Mr. Ziolkowski labored, in good weather and bad, always short of money. He began to charge admission. He endured local taunts. He found some understanding and even became a force in the community.

He fathered 10 children. He grew a mountaineer's beard. "A storyteller in stone" is how he liked describing himself. He died in 1982 at the age of 74. And ever since, his widow, Ruth Ziolkowski, and most of their children have carried on his passion.

The scoffers have mostly gone away. They can't argue with 8.5 million tons of rock, which is what has been removed from the mountain thus far.

The face alone is so big that all four presidential faces of nearby Mount Rushmore could fit inside Crazy Horse's head. They demonstrate this with superimposed artwork in a slide show at the visitors' center. If it goes all the way, the 563-foot-tall sculpture will be taller than the Washington Monument or the Great Pyramids.

The head of the beast that Crazy Horse is one day to be astride—who knows, maybe in 2051—will go 22 stories. As they say in the slide show, "One nostril could hold a five-room house."

From the beginning the work has been privately financed. The builders have been able to survive on the strength of gate ad-

(continued on the next page)

(continued from the previous page)

missions, donations, gift-shop receipts and big bank loans, with no government support. This work-in-progress is not part of the National Park Service, as Rushmore is. At the entrance, there is a large sign declaring that the nonprofit mountain carving is "to and for the Indian people of America."

There's another sign: "Never Forget Your Dreams."

Crazy Horse, that brilliant tactician, that fearless chief who helped lead the assault on General George Custer at the Battle of the Little Bighorn in 1876, a man who never signed a treaty and never surrendered in his heart, is said to have been a slim person of medium height with brown hair dropping below his belt and a scar above his lip.

No photograph or portrait painting or even true sketch of him is known to exist. Photographers, more courteous then, would beg to take a snap. "My friend," the Indian would answer, "why should you wish to shorten my life by taking from me my shadow?"

As it was he died young, in his 30s, victim of a stabbing in a white man's garrison.

Last year, according to the Ziolkowskis, 1.2 million people came to gape and marvel at Crazy Horse as he unveils himself. The gapers averaged four in a car, and paid $6 per person, or $15 a carload.

In the summer, when the gate receipts are large, the staff at Crazy Horse Memorial can swell to as many as 200 workers. Not all are engaged in chipping away at the mountain. (The core blasting and carving group, even at peak periods, seems to be no more than a dozen.) Others help out in the gift shop, staff the Laughing Water restaurant, do maintenance, conduct tours.

One Ziolkowski son, Casimir, has become an expert blaster and driller. Another, Mark, keeps the timber cleared and the roads up the mountain passable. A daughter named Jadwiga helps balance the books. At the moment seven of the 10 children work at Crazy Horse. The head of the operation is still Ruth Ziolkowski, 70.

A man once came here from the Midwest, was stunned by what he saw and donated $250,000. Just recently a woman deeded 160 acres of good Colorado grazing land to the memorial. In most cases, corporations that have given money have earmarked the funds not for the carving itself, but for the memorial's cultural center and museum.

One day the Ziolkowskis envision on these grounds, at the bottom of this mountain, a university and a medical training center for the North American Indian. Thus far, the Crazy Horse Memorial Native American Scholarship Program has awarded a total of $175,000 in educational grants.

But a question: Doesn't the whittling of a mountain into the likeness of an Indian who never allowed a picture to be taken of him represent a kind of unthinking, or at least unwitting, despoiling of the Earth? Isn't it in some sense what the Native American is against in the deepest part of his soul?

John Yellow Bird Steele is president of the Oglala Sioux Tribal Council at Pine Ridge, South Dakota. He generally supports the work. "The people all agree with the end result," he said, "especially the idea of a university and medical center someday."

Mike Her Many Horses is the legislative coordinator for the Oglala Sioux. "Historically we've been generally supportive of the work," he said. "I think the message being carved there is pride."

Lyman Red Cloud, a fifth-generation descendant of Chief Red Cloud, is a sergeant-at-arms on the reservation. "I speak for myself," he said. "I'm totally against it. Because first of all, Crazy Horse is a spiritual man. He's a sacred person. You don't carve a big statue of Jesus or God on a mountain and take money from it. No matter how you look at it, the white man is making money off the Indians. When you start carving it, you start desecrating the Black Hills and you desecrate the person. That thing is for white people." Mr. Ziolkowski, who has [sic] heard just about every criticism during his lifetime and endured them, anticipated this one.

"The purpose of Crazy Horse is noble," he wrote in 1952 to his children, some of whom had not been born yet and some of whom have the message tacked up now on their walls. "There are many people who do not see its nobility at present, and even in your time, and mayhap in your children's time, the vision of Crazy Horse might be clouded to some people, but if you so wish to dedicate your life as to carry out my dreams, and I can now say your mother's dreams too, they will then also be your dreams someday." ■

The Case of Leonard Peltier

Since 1977, people and groups from around the world have been working to free Leonard Peltier from prison. Petitions for his release have been signed by more than thirty-five million people in many countries. In France, hundreds of city and town councils have passed resolutions in support of Peltier, and in 1994 the European Council adopted a resolution urging President Clinton to grant clemency.

At the time of publication of this book, Peltier's health is failing. On June 12, 2000, he was denied parole after a hearing in Leavenworth, Kansas. His next official parole hearing will take place in 2008.

To familiarize yourself with this case, first read the article on the next page; then choose one of the following for an individual or group project:

- Find out the most recent information concerning Leonard Peltier.
- Conduct an informal survey at your school or university to find out how many students and teachers have heard of Leonard Peltier and are familiar with his case.
- Assume the role of a member of Peltier's family, and write a letter to the editor of a newspaper explaining your views.
- Assume the role of a relative of one of the FBI agents killed on the Pine Ridge Reservation, and write a letter to the editor explaining your views.
- Express your feelings about the Peltier case in a poem, poster, drawing, or button.

The Leonard Peltier Defense Committee (see address on page 59) can provide assistance with these projects. You can also use other sources found in the Sequel (pages 57–60), especially the books by Matthiessen and Messerschmidt and the film *Incident at Oglala*.

Leaders of 21 tribes demand freedom for imprisoned Peltier

At the end of a cross-country "Walk for Justice" accenting issues important to American Indians, 400 activists conduct rites at the Lincoln Memorial.

By Scott Sonner, The Associated Press   © 1994

WASHINGTON—American Indian activist Dennis Banks and 27 others celebrated the end of a five-month "Walk for Justice" across the country at the Lincoln Memorial on Friday.

The leaders of 21 tribal nations demanded that President Clinton free Leonard Peltier, a former member of the American Indian Movement, who, they contend, is innocent of killing two FBI agents in 1975 at Wounded Knee, South Dakota.

About 400 activists who joined the 3,800-mile walk along the way participated in a series of traditional sage-burning and pipe ceremonies near the memorial steps.

Twenty-eight completed the entire walk. It began February 11 at Alcatraz Island, California, in an effort to draw attention to issues ranging from treaty rights and grave desecration to nuclear waste dumping and sports team mascots.

Several thousand people participated in part of this year's spiritual trek, including walkers from Japan, Denmark, Australia, Germany, France and Great Britain.

"We knew from the beginning that we would have a hard time and that the many nations of people would help us along the way," said Banks, co-founder of the American Indian Movement.

"What we were not prepared for was the great amount of support shown to us—overwhelming."

Several tribal elders wore red T-shirts reading "Free Peltier." Others donned colorful traditional clothing, beating drums and singing as the temperatures rose into the 90s on Friday. Large black, red and yellow banners read, "Respect Mother Earth" and "The Black Hills Are Not for Sale." The latter slogan refers to efforts to keep development from the Black Hills National Forest in southwestern South Dakota. The Black Hills include lands sacred to several tribes.

Leaders said they would present a twenty-six-page document to Congress on Monday addressing topics from religious issues and land-use disputes to fishing rights and the North American Free Trade Agreement.

The position papers lead with a "demand" for executive clemency for Peltier. He has been in prison since April 1977, when a federal jury in Fargo, North Dakota, convicted him of the shootings of the two FBI agents on the Pine Ridge Indian Reservation in South Dakota.

In Portland, two dozen people gathered at Tom McCall Waterfront Park to show support for the efforts to free Peltier and to commemorate the 1993 restoration of a plaque marking the site of an American Indian trading village. "We are hoping to bring awareness to the people of the United States...and the president," said Dorothy N. Ackerman of United Indian Women.

Peltier's mother, Alvina Showers, lives in Portland.

The Supreme Court has twice denied his petitions for rehearing without comment.

FBI Director Louis J. Freeh issued a statement opposing clemency, saying, "Peltier's guilt has been firmly established."

"Leonard Peltier was convicted of grave crimes—two counts of first-degree murder in the execution-style slayings of two wounded, helpless FBI special agents—and there should be no commutation of his two consecutive terms of life in prison," Freeh said.

A group representing 15,000 past and present FBI agents ran an advertisement in the Washington Post on Friday urging Clinton to refuse requests to free Peltier.

"There are no new facts. The old facts have not changed, and Peltier is guilty as charged," said the ad by the FBI Agents Association of New Rochelle, New York, and the Society of Former Special Agents of the FBI. ∎

Where Are We Now? Indian "Nations" within a Nation

In *Thunderheart* the FBI agents Levoi and Coutelle argue with tribal police officer Walter Crow Horse about who has "jurisdiction" over what. While the federal agents have authority over the murder investigation, the tribal police has, for example, the right to issue a speeding ticket.

This wrangling over jurisdiction touches on the most significant issue facing Indians today: the question of *sovereignty* (self-determination or self-governance). Many important aspects of Indian life are linked to sovereignty, including land ownership, tax regulations, casino gambling, and fishing rights. Emphasizing their independent status, some tribes welcome visitors to their reservations with signs stating the name of the particular "nation" one is entering.

The word *nation* is not a quaint expression but an indication of monumental changes taking place in the status of Indian territories and the definition of Indian rights. Despite decades of struggle over sovereignty, many non-Indians remain unaware of the issue. Even with the current emphasis on multiculturalism, most Americans have learned little about the approximately 150 sovereign Indian "nations" now established within the United States.

Beginning with the civil rights era of the 1960s, Indians across the country began pressing for self-determination, often on the basis of rights and territory guaranteed them by treaty. The Kennedy and Johnson administrations (1960–1968) were receptive to this shift toward self-government, and in 1970 President Nixon described the new policy of self-determination in a message to Congress, stressing its key aspects: that tribal governments would be encouraged to take over the administration of federally funded programs and that tribes would be assisted to become self-sufficient economically. Nixon's message became law with the passage of the 1975 Indian Self-Determination and Education Assistance Act.

Since the 1960s other landmark legislation promoting the idea of Indian sovereignty has been passed. Examples of such legislation include the following:

Indian Civil Rights Act (1968)
Alaska Native Claims Settlement Act (1971)
Indian Education Act (1972)
Comprehensive Employment and Training Act (1973)
Indian Health Care Improvement Act (1976)
Indian Child Welfare Act (1978)
American Indian Religious Freedom Act (1978)

Archaeological Protection Resources Act (1979)
Indian Gaming Regulatory Act (1988)
Native American Graves Protection and Repatriation Act (1990)

But what does it mean for an Indian tribe to be a sovereign nation within the United States? The issues are highly complex, and there is no clear-cut answer. Moreover, the concept is undergoing constant change. In truth all of us—American Indians and American non-Indians alike—are involved in a great experiment to see if it is possible to carve out a new way of looking at our country and our government. Can there be semiautonomous units within the borders of this country—in effect, nations within a nation? Where do federal laws and tribal laws collide? What about the relationship between individual states and the Indian nations within them? Can they coexist peacefully and prosperously?

- Write about how much you personally have learned in school—or in the media—about Indian nations and the issue of sovereignty.
- Then look through local or national newspapers, Indian newspapers or periodicals, or the Internet to locate a recent article relating to Indian sovereignty (such as the right of the Makah tribe in Washington to hunt whales). Bring a copy of the article to class and be ready to summarize and discuss it.

Zoom Lens: Choosing Your Own Topic of Interest

Hands-on Activities

1. Locate one or more tribal schools or colleges, using the Internet. Learn as much as possible about each institution's mission, course offerings, and so forth. You might begin your search with Diné College (formerly Navajo Community College) in Tsaile, Arizona, or Little Big Horn College in Crow Agency, Montana (see Hirschfelder and Kreipe de Montaño in the Sequel for a more complete list).
2. Find out what courses at your school or university focus on or include Native American perspectives. Speak with a professor and/or with knowledgeable students about the extent and quality of the offerings.

3. Research and report on the recent progress of the Crazy Horse Memorial (see pages 50–51). If you wish to receive the newsletter, ask to be put on the mailing list.

Research Papers or Oral Reports

1. At the powwow in the film, Walter Crow Horse talks to Ray Levoi about the indignities he suffered in an Indian boarding school [0:56:00]. Research Indian boarding schools to expand your understanding of Walter Crow Horse's words. Possible sources include
   a. the poem "Indian Boarding School: The Runaways" by Louise Erdrich (found in her collection of poetry entitled *Jacklight* listed in the Sequel)
   b. the chapter entitled "Civilize Them with a Stick" in Mary Crow Dog's *Lakota Woman*
   c. the film entitled *Where the Spirit Lives*
2. Research the history and activities of AIM (see page 39). Read relevant sections of Russell Means' autobiography, *Where White Men Fear to Tread,* to gain an insider's perspective on the organization.
3. Religion plays an important role in the film. Explore one or more Sioux religious beliefs and practices, such as the Ghost Dance, the sweat lodge, or visions.
4. As Indians have lost their lands, they also have been deprived of important natural resources. Look into the protracted struggles over minerals and energy, including uranium. Alternatively, research the struggles over water, forests, or other natural resources. Consult especially the book by Hirschfelder and Kreipe de Montaño in the Sequel.
5. Find out more about the Native American actors in this film (as well as in *Dances with Wolves*) and the situation of Native American actors in general. You might compare Graham Greene's different roles in the two films.
6. Watch the documentary *Incident at Oglala* and compare both style and content with *Thunderheart*. What can the documentary achieve that the fictional film cannot, and vice versa?
7. Read several historical accounts of the 1973 siege at Wounded Knee. Also read Mary Crow Dog's insider's account of the happenings in her autobiographical *Lakota Woman*. What perspective does Mary Crow Dog provide that is missing in the more "objective" accounts?

Using Your Imagination

1. Imagine that Ray Levoi's father were still alive and that the two could speak with each other after Levoi leaves the reservation at the end. Write a script of their conversation.
2. As a reporter for the newspaper *Indian Country Today*, you are sent to interview Frank Coutelle about his view that, as he tells Levoi, the Indians are a "conquered people" and their "future is dictated by the people who conquered them" (1:05:00). What would you ask or tell Coutelle?
3. Imagine that Walter Crow Horse and Levoi meet ten years later. Under what circumstances might they meet? What would they discuss? Write a script of their conversation.
4. Assume that you are Maggie Eagle Bear's grandmother or Grandpa Sam Reaches. What would you like to tell Levoi about his ancestry, and why?
5. You are Jimmy Looks Twice. Explain to Levoi what you meant when you said, "It's about power, Ray," giving examples.

Sequel: Further Suggested Resources

Readings

Ballantine, Betty, and Ian Ballantine, eds. 1993. *The Native Americans: An Illustrated History*. Atlanta: Turner Publishing.

Bordewich, Fergus M. 1996. *Killing the White Man's Indian: Reinventing Native Americans at the End of the Twentieth Century*. New York: Doubleday.

Brown, Dee. 1970. *Bury My Heart at Wounded Knee: An Indian History of the American West*. New York: Henry Holt.

Costner, Kevin, Michael Blake, and Jim Wilson. 1990. *Dances with Wolves: The Illustrated Story of the Epic Film*. New York: Newmarket Press.

Cragg, Randy. 1992. "Framing Injustice." *Oregonian*, 5 July.

Crow Dog, Mary. 1990. *Lakota Woman*. New York: HarperCollins.

Eagle/Walking Turtle. 1991. *Indian America: A Traveler's Companion*. Santa Fe: John Muir Publications.

Erdrich, Louise. 1984. *Jacklight: Poems*. New York: Henry Holt.

Gattuso, John, ed. 1993. *Insight Guides: Native America*. Boston: Houghton Mifflin.

Hirschfelder, Arlene, and Martha Kreipe de Montaño. 1993. *The Native American Almanac: A Portrait of Native America Today.* New York: Prentice Hall.

Jennings, Francis. 1993. *The Founders of America: From the Earliest Migrations to the Present.* New York: Norton.

Josephy, Alvin M. 1994. *500 Nations: An Illustrated History of North American Indians.* New York: Newmarket Press.

Matthiessen, Peter. 1983. *In the Spirit of Crazy Horse.* New York: Viking.

Means, Russell. 1995. *Where White Men Fear to Tread: The Autobiography of Russell Means.* New York: St. Martin's Press.

Messerschmidt, Jim. 1983. *The Trial of Leonard Peltier.* Boston: South End Press.

Neihardt, John G. 1993. *Black Elk Speaks: Being the Life Story of a Holy Man of the Oglala Sioux.* Lincoln: University of Nebraska Press.

Niethammer, Carolyn. 1977. *Daughters of the Earth: The Lives and Legends of American Indian Women.* New York: Macmillan.

Peltier, Leonard. 1999. *Prison Writings: My Life Is the Sun Dance.* New York: St. Martin's Press.

Richardson, James D. 1896. *Compilation of the Messages and Papers of the Presidents: 1789–1897,* vol. II. Washington DC: Government Printing Office.

Silko, Leslie Marmon. 1996. *Yellow Woman and a Beauty of the Spirit.* New York: Simon & Schuster.

Tiller, Veronika E., ed. 1992. *Discover Indian Reservations USA: A Visitor's Welcome Guide.* Denver: Council Publications.

CD-ROM

Marino, Cesare (ethnohistorical consultant). *The American Indian, Version 2.0: A Multimedia Encyclopedia* (phone: 800-322-8755; fax: 800-678-3633).

Films

Geronimo: An American Legend (1993)   Story of the legendary Apache leader's resistance to the U.S. government's attempts to subdue him and his tribe. Directed by Walter Hill.

Incident at Oglala (1992)   Traces the dramatic events that occurred on the Pine Ridge Indian Reservation in the 1970s, focusing on the trial and imprisonment of Leonard Peltier. Provides fascinating insights into this period in history. Documentary, directed by Michael Apted (Facets).

Lakota Woman: Siege at Wounded Knee (1994)   Brings Indian activist Mary Crow Dog's important autobiography *Lakota Woman* and her insider's perspective on the 1973 siege at Wounded Knee to the screen. Directed by Frank Pierson.

The Last of the Mohicans (1992)   Modern retelling of James Fenimore Cooper's classic novel set at the time of the French and Indian War. Directed by Michael Mann.

Paha Sapa: The Struggle for the Black Hills (1993)   Memorable interviews with Lakota and Cheyenne shed light on their ongoing struggle to regain the Black Hills. Documentary, directed by Mel Lawrence (Mystic Fire Video; phone: 800-292-9001).

Powwow Highway (1989)   Offbeat tale of two Indian friends on the road to New Mexico in a dilapidated Buick. Based on David Seals' novel of the same title. Directed by Jonathan Wacks.

Smoke Signals (1998)   Hailed as the first full-length feature film written, directed, and coproduced by Native Americans, with a cast of Native Americans in all the major roles. Loosely based on Sherman Alexie's short story collection *The Lone Ranger and Tonto Fistfight in Heaven*. Directed by Chris Eyre.

Spirit of Crazy Horse (1990)   Correspondent Milo Yellow Horse's retelling of the proud history of the Sioux—their battles over land of the past century, their activism in the 1970s, and their present-day cultural revival. Documentary, directed by James Locker (PBS Video).

The West (1996)   Nine-part series about the American West, told through compelling firsthand accounts. Documentary series, directed by Stephen Ives and produced by Ken Burns (PBS Video).

Where the Spirit Lives (1989)   A painful story of a brother and sister kidnapped from their homes by the government that brings to life the suffering caused by the removal of Indian children to boarding schools. Directed by Bruce Pittman.

Winds of Change (1990)   Essential viewing to gain an understanding of sovereignty issues facing Indians today. The first part depicts the struggles of Onondaga, Navajo, and Lummi to become independent nations. The second part takes a personal look at the hard choices facing Hopi tribal members as to whether to live in their own nation on the reservation or in the outside world. Documentary, executive producer, Carol Cotter (PBS Video).

Websites and Mailing Addresses

AIM (American Indian Movement), 710 Clayton Street, Apartment 1, San Francisco, CA 94117 (www.aimovement.org)

Crazy Horse Memorial Committee, Avenue of the Chiefs, Crazy Horse, SD 57730-9506; phone: 605-673-4681

The Index of Native American Sources on the Internet (www.hanksville.org. NAresources)

The Leonard Peltier Defense Committee, PO Box 583, Lawrence, KS 66044; phone and fax: 913-842-5774 (www.free peltier.org)

Native American Rights Fund (www.narf.org)
Native Languages Page (www.nativeculture.com/lisamitten/natlang.html)
The Native Web (www.nativeweb.org)

Answers to quiz on page 47

1. Ray Levoi goes out to Maggie Eagle Bear's property on a tip from Walter Crow Horse.
2. Maggie's main concern is that the water on the reservation is being contaminated.
3. The discovery of the Chevy supports Crow Horse's theory that Leo Fast Elk was not killed where he was found (next to an ARM marking of an arrow in a circle), but his body was driven in his car from the river and dragged to the desert site.
4. Grandpa Sam Reaches was present at Wounded Knee as a one-year-old. He says a Lakota holy man named Thunderheart was killed there in 1890 and has passed his strength on to Levoi.
5. Richard Yellow Hawk was serving time in the federal penitentiary when the FBI convinced him to infiltrate ARM in exchange for early parole. In collaboration with the FBI and Frank Coutelle, he carried out the murder of Fast Elk.
6. Coutelle and Jack Milton were working together to destroy ARM and thwart the traditional Indians' goals.
7. Maggie, thinking that Yellow Hawk was truly an ARM member, had befriended him. When she learned that he was an FBI informant, she gave the other half of his lottery ticket to Levoi.
8. Fast Elk had learned about the FBI's interest in mining for uranium on the reservation.
9. Coutelle wanted to remove an effective leader from ARM and cover up his own involvement in the murder of Fast Elk.
10. The GOONs probably killed both Yellow Hawk and Maggie in cooperation with the FBI.
11. The FBI is supporting government efforts to prepare to mine uranium, which is already contaminating the water supply for the reservation and may have other poisonous effects.
12. Levoi and Crow Horse suspect that there will be an "internal investigation" by the FBI, which probably means Coutelle will be transferred to another position but will not be punished.

3

African American Culture: *The Long Walk Home*

Setting the Scene: Freewriting and Discussion

The photograph below shows a common sight in the Southern states prior to the civil rights movement of the 1950s and 1960s. Study the photo and freewrite your immediate reactions in your film notebook. Discuss what you wrote with your classmates.

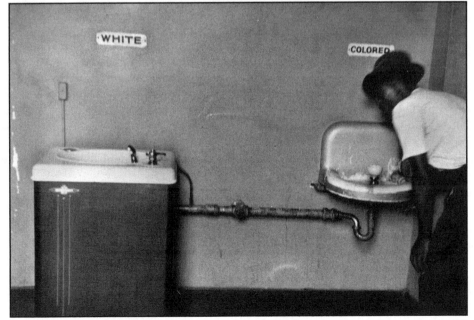

Wide-Angle Lens: Historical Perspectives

The Montgomery Bus Boycott

The 1955–1956 Montgomery, Alabama, bus boycott, which is the subject of *The Long Walk Home,* was described by Dr. Martin Luther King Jr. as a "movement that was to alter Montgomery forever and to have repercussions throughout the world" (1958, 24). This boycott can be seen as both a beginning and an end. What was coming to an end was almost a century of struggle by African Americans to overthrow rigid legal and extralegal segregation. In a country founded on the principles of democracy and equality, this segregation kept blacks apart and subjugated, denied them the basic opportunities of American society, and persecuted them in the most violent ways.

When the South lost the Civil War (1861–1865) and two centuries of slavery came to an end, an estimated four million blacks dared to believe that a new life was possible for them. Indeed, the situation for African Americans quickly began to improve, and impressive initial strides were made. But the progress during what was known as the Reconstruction period was brief. A backlash of momentous proportions on the part of primarily Southern whites, accompanied by massacres, lynchings, mutilations, rapes, and whippings, acted to replace slavery not with long-awaited equality and freedom but with a new form of oppression—the so-called "Jim Crow" segregation.

Who was Jim Crow? Some believe he was a slave or a soldier; others say the label came not from a person but from the saying "black as a crow." Whatever the case, the name was first heard by the public in 1832, when a white performer danced on the stage in a mocking imitation of blacks to a tune about one "Jim Crow." Soon a common character in minstrel shows, Jim Crow evolved into a synonym for the Negro and his "comic" way of life and, by the turn of the century, into a term referring to the near total separation of blacks and whites in the country.

While this system of *apartheid* was more open and virulent in the South, other states also segregated the races in varying degrees. Hundreds of laws, decrees, and customs kept the races apart by requiring separate rest rooms, restaurants, hotels, parks, theaters, drinking fountains, railroad cars, and schools. Blacks were to be born in Negro hospitals and buried in Negro cemeteries. In South Carolina, black and white cotton-mill workers were not allowed to look out the same window; in Oklahoma there were separate telephone booths; and in Birmingham, Alabama, blacks and whites were forbidden to play chess together. In 1896 the Jim Crow doctrine came before the U.S. Supreme Court in the infamous case, *Plessy v. Ferguson*. Despite the Fourteenth Amendment of the U.S. Constitution, which guarantees all citizens equal protection under the law, the Supreme Court upheld the states' rights to enforce segregation under the guise that facilities could be "separate but equal." In other words, according to the Court, segregation alone was not sufficient to violate the equal protection clause.

Throughout the years of Jim Crow, ongoing opposition was strong and creative. Distinguished black leaders—W. E. B. Du Bois, Ida B. Wells, William Monroe Trotter, Mary McLeod Bethune, Marcus Garvey, Asa Philip Randolph, Adam Clayton Powell Jr., Ralph J. Bunche, Reverend Ralph D. Abernathy, Charles H. Houston, Thurgood Marshall, and numerous others—devised strategies to keep the dream of equality alive against fierce opposition and the constant threat of violence by members of the Ku Klux Klan and other white militants. Moreover, countless unknown individuals stood up for their rights and worked for the cause, knowingly risking, and often sacrificing, their lives. Blacks worked through the courts, through the media, through labor unions, through national organizations, and in the military to gain their proper place in American life.

By the time of the bus boycott in Montgomery, a tradition of protest was well established in black America. Inspired by Mahatma Gandhi's philosophy of nonviolent resistance, Reverend Martin Luther King Jr., a little-known twenty-six-year-old pastor at the Dexter Avenue Baptist Church in Montgomery, led workers, common people, professionals, students, and children in a masterfully orchestrated plan of great daring that inspired a national civil rights movement.

The bus boycott was sparked by Rosa Parks, a forty-three-year-old seamstress and National Association for the Advancement of Colored People (NAACP) member, who was arrested for refusing to yield her seat on a bus to a white man. At that time, although black patrons accounted for more than three-fourths of all riders in Montgomery, black riders were forced to sit in the back of the buses—the front rows were reserved for whites—and to give up a seat to any white person who would otherwise have to stand. What was first planned as a one-day boycott of the buses in Montgomery in protest of Rosa Parks' arrest became a massive action that lasted over a year—from December 5, 1955, to December 20, 1956. As seen in *The Long Walk Home*, organized carpools were critical to the success of the protest; the sponsors of the boycott provided up to twenty thousand rides daily. The film focuses primarily on the first stage of the boycott.

After the Boycott: The Civil Rights Era and Beyond

The period immediately following the year-long boycott was a time of unprecedented citizen revolt and social change. Sparked by the boycott and similar acts of resistance, rebellion by African Americans continued for a decade in a civil rights movement that swept the nation and captured the imagination of people around the world. Newly founded organizations such as Congress of Racial Equality (CORE), Student Non-Violent Coordinating Committee (SNCC), and Southern Christian Leadership Conference (SCLC) trained their members, many of whom were students, in the philosophy and tactics of nonviolence and civil disobedience. Sit-ins, kneel-ins, and jail-ins, freedom rides and boycotts, voter registration campaigns and court battles, marches and mass demonstrations culminated in the 1963 March on Washington for Freedom and Jobs, when more than 250,000 participants converged on the Capitol and Dr. Martin Luther King delivered his now historic "I Have a Dream" speech.

To give a better idea of the phenomenal level of activism during this period, in 1963 alone—the one-hundredth anniversary of Abraham Lincoln's Emancipation Proclamation that declared the freedom of slaves in the South—more than ten thousand racial demonstrations took place. As described by Lerone Bennett Jr. in his *Before the Mayflower: A History of Black America*,

> *Blacks hurled themselves in larger and larger numbers against the unyielding bars of the cage of caste. They surged through the streets in waves of indignation. They faced police dogs and armored police tanks. They were clubbed, bombed, stoned, murdered.* (1988, 386–87)

Approximately five thousand African Americans were arrested in this one year for political activities.

In response to the pressure of ongoing black revolution on the one hand and rising white resistance and retaliatory violence on the other—and in the face of negative world opinion—the Kennedy and Johnson administrations responded with major legislation and a spate of executive orders. The Supreme Court had already handed down a landmark ruling in *Brown v. Board of Education* (1954), which effectively overturned *Plessy v. Ferguson* by determining that separate educational facilities were inherently unequal. The new ruling stated that "in the field of public education the doctrine of 'separate but equal' has no place." Although dealing only with segregation in public schools, this case laid the groundwork for the wholesale dismantling of Jim Crow through the Civil Rights Act of 1964, which was the most comprehensive civil rights bill in American history, followed by the Economic Opportunity Act (1964) and the Voting Rights Bill (1965).

While unquestionably constituting enormous victories, the legislation of the period could not alone cut through the "unyielding bars of the cage of caste." In some ways the new laws first exacerbated the tensions even as they were intended to provide a solution. For many African Americans now disillusioned with the results of nonviolent protest, an emerging vision of radical black activism, eloquently articulated by the outspoken orator and writer Malcolm X, began to take hold.

Malcolm X called for a vigorous program of revitalization, rallying African Americans to take control of their own lives and communities rather than futilely attempting to integrate into what he saw as the morally corrupt, oppressive white society. He believed fervently in self-defense, self-education, self-help, self-pride, and self-determination. Noted African American scholar Cornel West states that "Malcolm X was the first great Black spokesperson who looked ferocious white racism in the eye, did not blink and lived long enough to tell America the truth about this glaring hypocrisy in a bold and defiant manner" (West 1993, 105).

Although assassinated in 1965, Malcolm X gave inspiration and hope to large segments of the African American community. By that year the civil rights movement was losing momentum, and the concepts of *black power* and *black nationalism* were gaining credence. The Black Panther party, founded in 1966, attempted to implement the concept of black power, and new leaders such as Stokely Carmichael, Eldridge Cleaver, and H. Rap Brown gained national prominence. In a new phase of black revolt in the late 1960s, black anger erupted in a series of race riots in dozens of American cities.

Following the turbulent times of the civil rights era and black revolt, a period of relative tranquility seemed to set in. In the last three decades of the twentieth century, there were frequent isolated incidents, but the large-scale movements of the 1950s and 1960s, the daily headlines in the national press, the concerted actions of millions of people all but disappeared. What does this relative silence mean? Many whites would like to believe that the problems are over, that the legal gains of the 1960s in effect have solved the most serious problems, that African Americans now have assumed their rightful place within American society.

In truth, however, the surface calm often masks deep undercurrents of hostility, anger, and frustration. While African Americans have indisputably made significant progress toward political and economic equality—the ranks of middle-class black Americans, for example, have swelled in the past decades—many blacks remain mired in poverty and hopelessness. U.S. census population surveys from 1998 and 1999 reveal that nearly one-fourth of African Americans (compared to fewer than one-tenth of whites) live in poverty. Just as alarming, nearly one in three black children grow up in poverty, compared to one in nine non-Hispanic white children.

Some authors use the phrase "from plantation to ghetto" to describe America's failure to erase the legacy of slavery (Meier and Rudwick 1976). Another says that we are living in "two nations," one black and one white, "separate, hostile, unequal" (Hacker 1992). Despite the dreams of the 1960s for an integrated society, despite the end of Jim Crow, racial segregation continues to flourish in ways that may prove impossible to eradicate.

The most obvious of these is residential segregation. The phenomenon of "white flight" became widespread in the 1970s, when white city dwellers moved in droves to the suburbs to escape the influx of black neighbors, creating what one African American musician calls "chocolate cities and vanilla suburbs." A fast-growing trend across the country is that of "gated communities," which are generally established by whites and closed to all but residents and their guests.

Many African Americans themselves have rejected or abandoned the idea of integration, preferring to live in their own communities and attend their own schools. Whether this voluntary or self-separation is an end in itself—the best solution to the long-standing failure of American society to live up to its professed democratic ideals—or a step on the way to the type of society envisioned by Martin Luther King Jr., remains an open question.

Lights Out: Viewing the Film

The Long Walk Home (1991) provides insight into the lives of two families (one black, one white) during the 1955–1956 bus boycott in Montgomery, Alabama. The film takes a close look at the hardships people endured and the choices they had to make. The director is Richard Pearce, and Whoopi Goldberg and Sissy Spacek play the two main characters.

When the movie was first released in December, 1991, it was overshadowed by some of the holiday-season blockbusters. However, it was released again in April and achieved moderate success. One critic has referred to it as a "small picture with a large conscience."

Major Characters in the Film

Odessa Cotter (Dessie)   African American boycotter and maid in the Thompson home
Herbert Cotter   Odessa's husband
Selma Cotter   Odessa's daughter
Theodore Cotter   Odessa's older son
Franklin Cotter   Odessa's younger son
Miriam Thompson   white Southern wife and mother in the household employing Odessa
Norman Thompson   Miriam's husband
Mary Catherine Thompson (Boo Boo)   Miriam's younger daughter and narrator
Sara Thompson   Miriam's older daughter
Tunker Thompson   Norman's brother
Rachel   black maid
Martin Luther King Jr.   civil rights leader

Spotlight on Culture and Communication

This spotlight will focus on *empathy*. First review this concept from the Essential Vocabulary on Cultures, page 10. The ability to empathize requires imagination, knowledge, and compassion. To empathize, you must recognize that the other person is different from you and try to imagine what that person is feeling, *not what you would be feeling* in that situation. So an adult who sees a child lost in a grocery store can feel sympathy knowing that anyone who is lost is likely to feel confused and upset, but the adult can only feel empathy if he or she is able to imagine in particular what the lost child might be feeling. Thus empathy requires that you try to look through the other's eyes rather than looking through your own.

In cross-cultural terms this means that an American, for example, can never really know what it feels like to be Chinese, but if the American studies Chinese, travels to China, and has Chinese friends, she or he can begin to imagine observing or experiencing a situation from the "Chinese" point of view.

Working in small groups, choose a clip from the film in which a character demonstrates empathy. How does the character express this—through actions, words, nonverbal behavior? From your knowledge of the character and the situation, analyze and explain why you think the character is able to empathize in this particular scene. Finally, how do certain film techniques (see Essential Film Vocabulary, pages 11–13) heighten your impressions of the character's thoughts and behavior?

demonstrate empathy or doesn't demonstrate empathy.

Point of View: Acting as a Critic

Read the review of *The Long Walk Home* written by Coretta Scott King, the widow of Dr. Martin Luther King Jr.

Then write a one-page review in which you act as a film critic for your school, university, or city newspaper. Describe your own reactions to the film, both positive and negative, and make recommendations to others as to its value. Be prepared to share your review with other class members.

'Long Walk Home' true look at past

by Coretta Scott King   © 1991

Although Hollywood has rarely done justice to the black freedom struggle, the last two years have brought some impressive exceptions, including *Glory*, the television movie *Murder in Mississippi*, and now, *The Long Walk Home*, which has just been re-released by the film's distributor.

Starring two of the screen's finest performers, Whoopi Goldberg and Sissy Spacek, *The Long Walk Home* focuses on the relationship between a black domestic worker and her white employer during the Montgomery Bus Boycott of 1955, which launched the Civil Rights Movement. The film, which was directed by Richard Pearce, captures the feel of the segregated south of the 1950s.

The Long Walk Home opened in December to highly favorable reviews but was smothered by the attention given to such "big" Christmas movies as *The Godfather Part III* and *Home Alone*. The distributor, Miramax films, has decided that there must be more of an audience for this film, given the enormous success of *Driving Miss Daisy*, which also dealt with the growth of an interracial friendship against the background of a racist society.

The film owes much of its appeal to the fact that it focuses on average citizens instead of Martin Luther King Jr., Rosa Parks, or any of the other prominent leaders of the Montgomery bus boycott. In this way, *The Long Walk Home* better portrays the experience of the community.

The decision to make one of the central characters a domestic worker was on-target. One 1955 survey showed that 63 percent of Montgomery's black women were domestic workers.

Back then, the median annual income for blacks in Montgomery was about $970, compared to $1,730 for whites. There were about 30,000 black citizens of voting age in Montgomery County, but only about 2,000 of us were registered, and we were routinely subjected to humiliating tests and procedures.

In Montgomery in 1955, the leaders of black churches urged their congregations to love and forgive their abusers. This was no small task. Not only were the seats on the city-owned bus system segregated, but it was against the law for a white and a black person to even share the same cab.

Once the boycott started, it seemed like mass meetings were always going on in somebody's church. To this day, I have never again experienced such a community-wide family spirit.

Many of the veterans of the Montgomery movement are still alive, and a few of them have expressed disappointment about inaccuracies in *The Long Walk Home*, such as the climatic [sic] scene at the car pool headquarters, where a jeering racist mob is quieted by protesters singing a spiritual. It didn't happen quite that way in Montgomery, but similar incidents did occur in other campaigns of the civil rights movement.

The Long Walk Home also exaggerates the level of support white women gave the protesters. There were very few white women like Virginia Durr and Juliet Morgan, who worked for the Montgomery protest despite repeated threats.

Despite these minor points, *The Long Walk Home* is faithful to the spirit and history of the Montgomery story. It reveals the quiet courage and dignity of the people of Montgomery and the revolutionary power of disciplined nonviolence.

Though not as slick as *Daisy*, *The Long Walk Home* has the virtue of dealing with a historical watershed, for the victory that was won in Montgomery started a prairie fire that blazes ever more brightly in the hearts of freedom-loving people on every continent. Inspired by the same courage, determination, and commitment to nonviolence that empowered the Montgomery freedom struggle, people all over the world are singing "We Shall Overcome" in a host of languages.

As Martin Luther King Jr. said in his first speech as president of the Montgomery Improvement Association, "Our actions must be guided by the deepest principles of our Christian faith.... In spite of the mistreatment that we have confronted, we must not become bitter and end up hating our white brothers." ∎

Introducing Rosa Parks

The following passages are excerpted from Rosa Parks' book entitled *Quiet Strength* (1994, 17, 21–23).

The custom for getting on the bus for black persons in Montgomery in 1955 was to pay at the front door, get off the bus, and then re-enter through the back door to find a seat. On the buses, if white persons got on, the colored would move back if the white section was filled. Black people could not sit in the same row with white people. They could not even sit across the aisle from each other. Some customs were humiliating, and this one was intolerable since we were the majority of the ridership.

On Thursday evening, December 1, I was riding the bus home from work. A white man got on, and the driver looked our way and said, "Let me have those seats." It did not seem proper, particularly for a woman to give her seat to a man. All the passengers paid ten cents, just as he did. When more whites boarded the bus, the driver, J. P. Blake, ordered the blacks in the fifth row, the first row of the colored section (the row I was sitting in), to move to the rear. Bus drivers then had police powers, under both municipal and state laws, to enforce racial segregation. However, we were sitting in the section designated for colored.

At first none of us moved.

"Y'all better make it light on yourselves and let me have those seats," Blake said.

Then three of the blacks in my row got up, but I stayed in my seat and slid closer to the window. I do not remember being frightened. But I sure did not believe I would "make it light" on myself by standing up. Our mistreatment was just not right, and I was tired of it. The more we gave in, the worse they treated us. I kept thinking about my mother and my grandparents, and how strong they were. I knew there was a possibility of being mis-treated, but an opportunity was being given to me to do what I had asked of others.

I knew someone had to take the first step. So I made up my mind not to move. Blake asked me if I was going to stand up.

"No. I am not," I answered.

Blake said that he would have to call the police. I said, "Go ahead." In less than five minutes, two policemen came, and the driver pointed me out. He said that he wanted the seat and that I would not stand up.

"Why do you push us around?" I said to one of the policemen.

"I don't know," he answered, "but the law is the law and you're under arrest."

———

I have learned over the years that when one's mind is made up, this diminishes fear; knowing what must be done does away with fear. When I sat down on the bus the day I was arrested, I was thinking of going home. I had made up my mind quickly about what it was that I had to do, what I felt was right to do. I did not think of being physically tired or fearful. After so many years of oppression and being a victim of the mistreatment that my people had suffered, not giving up my seat—and whatever I had to face after not giving it up—was not important. I did not feel any fear at sitting in the seat I was sitting in. All I felt was tired. Tired of being pushed around. Tired of seeing the bad treatment and disrespect of children, women, and men just because of the color of their skin. Tired of the Jim Crow laws. Tired of being oppressed. I was just plain tired.

- Imagine you were a passenger on the bus on December 1 when Rosa Parks refused to move. Write an account of who you are and what you witnessed, and describe your thoughts and feelings.
- Research Rosa Parks' life and achievements subsequent to the boycott. Present your findings in a paper or an oral report.

Poetry: Dream Deferred

Read the following poem entitled "Harlem [2]" (1951) by African American poet Langston Hughes.*

Harlem [2]

What happens to a dream deferred?
Does it dry up
like a raisin in the sun?
Or fester like a sore—
And then run?
Does it stink like rotten meat?
Or crust and sugar over—
like a syrupy sweet?
Maybe it just sags
like a heavy load.
Or does it explode?

---

* Distinguished African American poet, novelist, and playwright Langston Hughes (1902–1967) produced a large body of celebrated works throughout his lifetime, including his autobiographies *The Big Sea* (1940) and *I Wonder as I Wander* (1956), the novel *Not Without Laughter* (1930), and the poetry collection *Selected Poems* (1959). In an attempt to bring recognition to African American authors and their works, he also edited several anthologies. The above poem is taken from his long poem cycle entitled *Montage of a Dream Deferred* in the *Collected Poems of Langston Hughes.*

Now consider:

- What is the effect of having this poem presented in questions?
- How do the similes (comparisons of essentially unlike things introduced by "like" and "as") convey the power of discrimination, and which simile is the most effective for you?
- Using the poet's question, "What happens to a dream deferred?" try creating several similes of your own on the theme of discrimination, following the format of the poem.

Below are two examples of student writing in response to the task on simile writing:

> *What happens to a dream deferred?*
> *Does it fall slowly like an unfueled plane?*
> *Or stop faster than the collision of two trains?*
> *Does it stay low to ground like rattle snakes?*
> *Or get psychotic like Norman Bates?*
> *Maybe it loses control like a heart attack.*
> *Or does it just turn black?*
>
> —Darryl Kelly

Following the format of the poem, I came up with three similes of my own on the theme of discrimination. The first one would read "Does it fade away, like the sun on the horizon?" My second simile would read "Would it be forgotten with time like childhood memories?" Finally, my third simile would read "Would it begin to erode like the banks of a river?" Over a period of time when no progress is made, sometimes people can lose sight of what they are trying to accomplish. The erosion of the dream refers to its meaning becoming distorted.

When pondering the poem's ending, my first interpretation was that the dream would explode in the form of violence. However, after some deeper thought, I felt that maybe the dream could explode in a positive way. This would include an acceleration in the strides made by the civil rights movement.

—Chris Dandeneau

- What kinds of explosions, emphasized in the last line, do you imagine might occur?
- In what ways does the poem apply to the situation depicted in *The Long Walk Home*?
- Read other poems by Langston Hughes and compare them with "Harlem [2]."

Freedom Songs of the Civil Rights Movement

Ain't gonna ride them buses no more,
Ain't gonna ride no more.
Why don't all the white folk know
That I ain't gonna ride no more.
            —Sung by boycotters in Montgomery,
                                1955–1956

From the earliest days of slavery, music was the African Americans' primary source of self-expression, offering some measure of solace, diversion, and inspiration in times of desperation.[†] Through their music, enslaved people could maintain ties to their former cultures, they could yearn for freedom and better lives, and they could communicate their protest and hopes to each other in masked language. A rich oral tradition of African American music evolved, including such forms as spirituals, field hollers, and work songs.

Drawing on this tradition, protesters in Montgomery and throughout the civil rights movement again turned to music to galvanize the people, reinforce their communal bonds, and lift their spirits. The music was sung everywhere: in the streets, on buses, at mass meetings and rallies, in churches, and even in police stations, jails, and cemeteries.

While some of the old songs were revived with virtually no changes, others were recast and updated. Words and lines were sometimes changed to fit the times, with singers, for example, inserting the names of white supremacists, like George Wallace, whom they opposed.

[†] For sources for compact discs of African American music, see Sequel, page 84.

Look into the songs and music widely known among the African American community at the time of the civil rights struggle.

- Study the anthem of the movement, "We Shall Overcome" (which has been adopted by people struggling for their rights worldwide), and analyze what gives it its power.
- Replay the church scenes in *The Long Walk Home* in which "We're Marching to Zion" and "Going through Jesus" are sung. What is the impact of these songs on the congregation? On you personally?
- Listen to other civil rights songs such as "O Freedom," "Ain't Gonna Let Nobody Turn Me 'Round," "Free at Last," "I'm Travelin' to Mississippi on the Greyhound Bus Line," "No More Jailhouse Over Me," "If You Miss Me from the Back of the Bus," and "Keep Your Eyes on the Prize." Play a recording of several of these songs in class. How do you feel when you hear this music? What is it about the music and lyrics that has affected people so powerfully and helped them through difficult times?

Nonviolence and Self-Defense: Martin Luther King Jr. and Malcolm X

In his leadership of the boycott and the civil rights movement, Dr. Martin Luther King Jr. was deeply influenced by the teachings of Jesus and of Mahatma Gandhi. He writes in *Stride toward Freedom,*

> I had come to see early that the Christian doctrine of love operating through the Gandhian method of nonviolence was one of the most potent weapons available to the Negro in his struggle for freedom.... Christ furnished the spirit and motivation, while Gandhi furnished the method. (1958, 85)

King was likewise guided by Henry David Thoreau's *Essay on Civil Disobedience.* He understood from Thoreau the power and righteousness of "refusing to cooperate with an evil system" (91).

King emphasized that the practice of nonviolence is never passive. Realizing that many people misunderstand nonviolent or passive resistance to be a "do-nothing method," he explained that the "method is passive physically, but strongly active spiritually" (102). As seen in *The Long Walk Home,* the boycott required planning, imagination, dedication, and bold, direct action. King knew that the way of nonviolence is not a means of avoidance but requires risk and a "willingness to suffer and sacrifice" (216).

A dynamic challenge to Dr. King's philosophy came from another daring thinker, Malcolm X. These two unsurpassed civil rights leaders found themselves in profound opposition to each other on the issue of nonviolence. While Malcolm X was not a champion of violence, as is often falsely believed, he did see it as a justifiable means of self-defense. As he explains, "If it must take violence to get the black man his human rights in this country, I'm *for* violence" (1964, 422). His often quoted and widely misunderstood statement that blacks must liberate themselves "by any means necessary" actually testifies more to his unshakable commitment to freedom than to any endorsement of violence.

In an insightful summary of the two leaders' different positions, James H. Cone, author of *Martin and Malcolm and America,* explains, "Contrary to Malcolm, who contended that nonviolence disarmed the oppressed, Martin claimed that it disarmed the oppressor" (1991, 77).

- From your knowledge of history and politics or your personal experience, make a list of examples that support one or the other of these positions.
- Think of a time in your life when you felt called upon to protest. What means did you use, and how successful were you?

Black English

Many African Americans speak a language or dialect that is distinctly their own, variously labeled "Black English," "Ebonics," "Black English Vernacular," and "Black Dialect." There are many misconceptions about, and biases against, Black English—namely, that it is an error-ridden, sloppy, lower-class way of speaking. Recent research by linguists linking Black English with languages spoken in West African countries from which the enslaved Africans were brought substantiates that it is none of these but rather a linguistic system with its own unique grammar, pronunciation, vocabulary, and idiomatic expressions.

As with most other languages, Black English is not the same everywhere; it exists in a variety of forms around the world and within the United States. A particularly fascinating form is Gullah, a Creole language preserved in nearly original form and spoken by more than two hundred thousand blacks on the Sea Islands off the coast of South Carolina. (A Creole is formed when two languages form a hybrid that eventually becomes a mother tongue passed from one generation to the next.)

To provide an idea of some of the features of Black English, here are a few of the patterns of grammar and pronunciation that distinguish it from so-called "Standard" English:

1. nonexistence of the final s in the third-person singular of the present tense, for example, He walk
2. no use of the verb form of *be* as a linking verb in the present tense, for example, *She real pretty*; *if you angry*
3. use of *d, t,* or *f* pronunciation where Standard English uses *th*, for example, *dis* for *this*; *wif* for *with*; *toof* for *tooth*
4. use of multiple negatives for emphasis, for example, *Don't nobody know dat story*; *Nobody never done dat before*
5. use of *do* in cases where Standard English uses *if*, for example, *I ask Gloria do she want to dance*
6. stress on the first syllable of some words that are stressed differently in Standard English, for example, PO-lice, DEE-troit, MO-tel

Black English has features that are nonexistent in Standard English. For example, the use of *be* or *bees* signifies a stable or habitual condition. Thus "This food too spicy" means it's too hot now, whereas "This food bees too spicy" means it's too spicy all the time. A familiar expression is "It bees dat way," meaning "It's always like that."

As linguistic scholar Geneva Smitherman explains, "Black English consists of both language and style" (1997, 16). What is this style? It has to do with the sounds, cadences, and intonation of the language, along with its unpretentious, vivid vocabulary. It also has to do with a long tradition of respect for the word and belief in its power. This tradition reaches back to the *griots* (storytellers) of Africa and extends to the great African American orators of the past two centuries, such as Frederick Douglass, Martin Luther King Jr., and Jesse Jackson as well as to the street rappers in today's cities. Even the short segments of speeches by Martin Luther King Jr. heard in *The Long Walk Home* reveal the uniqueness and beauty of the rhythms of this "speech-music" (134).

Furthermore, Black English is characterized by special modes of discourse such as *call-response*. This is a dynamic exchange between speaker and listener common, for example, in black church services. You can hear call-response in church scenes in *The Long Walk Home*, especially during the sermon interrupted by the news that Reverend King's house has been bombed. Call-response includes both verbal comments and exclamations ("Yeah!" "I hear you!" "Yessuh!") and nonverbal affirmation (nodding head, stomping feet, clapping hands).

It is a way of looking at communication that places considerably more emphasis on ongoing interaction and group unity than is customary among whites.

Another form of discourse observable in the film is *frontin*, which is a way of avoiding confrontation by masking one's true emotions. Odessa is frontin when she serves the Christmas dinner and in the following kitchen scene with Mr. Thompson, when she evades his questions and reveals little. Such behavior has often characterized black exchanges with whites, especially when there is an unequal power situation, lack of trust, and perceived risk. In this case Odessa's anger and frustration do not surface until she is able to talk freely with Rachel at the end of the workday.

Still another important verbal pattern of Black English, though not evident in *The Long Walk Home*, is *signifyin*. This animated form of discourse has to do with exchanging insults, often in a clever and humorous way. For example, when blacks engage in a form of signifyin called "playing the dozens," competitors hurl insults at each other, often by making negative references to each other's mothers (these insults must *never* be true). Usually, the opponents are inspired to greater feats by crowds that soon surround them, adding their own comments. Though violence is always a possibility when the dozens is played, the true test of skill is to maintain one's cool. Interestingly, whites often misinterpret the aggressive verbal exchanges as being meant to lead to a physical fight, whereas the real purpose is quite the opposite. Among the various theories about the origins of the term "playing the dozens" (the game itself can be traced back to Africa) is that it derives from the degrading practice of slave auctioneers selling sick or older slaves in lots of twelve. Some believe that the dozens functions as a way for blacks to learn and practice how to maintain calm in the face of verbal abuse and humiliation from whites.

Other modes of discourse include *rappin, lyin, testifyin, shuckin,* and *woofin*. Each of these has its own rules and traditions and requires verbal sophistication and agility.

To many African Americans, Black English is important as a link to their past, as a means of showing and maintaining solidarity, as an expression of their culture, and in some cases, as a refusal to adopt white man's speech. Because speakers of Black English may regard it as their right to use their own language, furious debates have raged over the education of black children. In a 1996–97 battle over Ebonics in Oakland, California, for example, African American educators claimed that Ebonics should be taught as a separate language rather than as a bridge to Standard English. They were forced to retreat from this stance by an outcry against it, including opposition from some blacks who argued that an emphasis on Black English would place their children at a disadvantage.

Many words, phrases, and proverbs from Black English have "crossed over" to Standard English. This adoption of Black English terminology by nonblacks is controversial, since some African Americans feel their language should not be taken out of its context—a context associated with oppression and protest—and simply used, or even exploited, by whites to whom it may seem colorful or *hip* ("with it," "in style").

Examples of words and phrases from Black English are given on the next page. Some are outdated and seldom used in everyday speech, but many are current. A number of terms have crossed over to general usage.[‡]

- If you are an African American familiar with Black English, help your classmates to understand more about it. If there are no speakers of Black English in your class, see if you might invite a guest to provide explanations and information.
- Listen to examples of Black English from the film (such as in the church scenes or when Odessa and Claudia leave the Thompson home after the Christmas dinner) or from other sources (recorded speeches, music, friends talking). How would you describe the style, sounds, and flow of the language?
- Have you ever been discriminated against because of your own language, dialect, or accent? If so, when, where, and how did this happen? Why do you think it happened? How did it make you feel, and how did you react?
- Do you ever find yourself discriminating against others because of their language or accent?

[‡] We are indebted to Geneva Smitherman (*Talkin and Testifyin; Black Talk*) for the explanations of many of the terms. We also thank Barry Tucker and Darryl Kelly for their assistance.

Some examples of words and phrases from Black English

4–1–1   The information, the story, as in *Give me the 4–1–1.*

attitude   An arrogant, defiant air.

bad   Very good, as in *He's a bad dude* (pronounced "baaaad").

the bomb   The best, highest quality; the height of something.

case   A person's business, affairs, situation (*to be on somebody's case, git off my case*).

chillin or **chilling**   Relaxing, taking it easy.

cut somebody some slack   Take it easy on a person; give a person a break.

def   Great, wonderful, cool, hip.

dis   Show disrespect; insult or put someone down.

get ghost, do a ghost   To leave.

high five   Slapping of palms with hands held in the air (both the phrase and the ritual have crossed over).

hood   Neighborhood (especially one's own).

jammin   Having a good time.

keep on keepin on   Keep struggling despite the odds.

kick it   To have fun.

like white on rice   Sticking closely to someone or something.

live   Good, exciting; updated form of *all the way live.*

mean   Good, positive, as in *He's a mean dude.*

member   Any black person.

no count   Useless, no good.

off the hook   Very good; e.g., *The party was off the hook.*

on a mission   Committed to achieving a goal.

Oprah   Get someone to reveal private matters, intimacies.

outta here   Gone, leaving, not staying any longer.

phat   Fine, good-looking, sexy (usually referring to a woman).

rags   Fine clothes.

slam-dunk   From basketball to mean accomplishing a task with authority.

soul shake   Complicated handshake to show bond among blacks.

sprung   Desperately in love; out of control emotionally.

wack   Bad (e.g., that idea is *wack*).

wannabe   An African American who strives to be (and acts) white; thus, any person who tries to be someone else.

white white   A white person who acts very white or who is racist.

word!   Response of affirmation.

Yo!   Greeting meaning hey, hello.

Z's   Sleep.

Zoom Lens: Choosing Your Own Topic of Interest

Hands-on Activities

1. Watch the documentary *Eyes on the Prize: America's Civil Rights Years,* especially the first episode, entitled *Awakenings (1954–56).* What insights do you gain about the struggle in Montgomery?
2. Contact one or more of the following organizations to find out about its purpose, programs, and efforts to combat racism (contact information is provided in the Sequel).

   - Martin Luther King Jr. Center for Nonviolent Social Change
   - Southern Poverty Law Center (especially the "Teaching Tolerance" program)
   - NAACP
   - National Urban League

3. Examine the offerings in African American Studies at your school or university. Interview professors to learn about individual courses or about the program and its goals. If you haven't already taken a course, consult the list of offerings. Explain which courses most interest you and why.
4. Learn more about African American organizations on campus, and attend a meeting or event. If you are African American and know about events that might interest your class, provide relevant information.

Research Papers or Oral Reports

1. Although African American women played an instrumental role in the organization and success of the Montgomery bus boycott, their contributions are often unrecognized in history books. Explore the work of Jo Ann G. Robinson, president of the Women's Political Council, and other key black figures such as Claudette Colvin, Mary Fair Burks, Johnnie Carr, and Irene West. White women who supported the boycott included Virginia Durr and Juliet Morgan. Consult especially the books by Crawford, Curry, Olson, and Robinson (listed in the Sequel).

2. Study the philosophy and operation of the Montgomery bus boycott in more detail. Include information on the leaders, the car pools, the financing of the movement, and the methods for maintaining momentum. Consult especially the books by Crawford and King listed in the Sequel as well as the video series Eyes on the Prize.

3. Research the activities of the Ku Klux Klan and the White Citizens Council during the period of the Montgomery bus boycott.

4. The black churches in Montgomery served as the spiritual and organizational heart of the boycott. Research the history of black religion and churches in America and explain how this history sheds light on the role of the churches during the boycott.

5. Investigate the life and contributions made to the advancement of blacks or to the civil rights movement by W. E. B. Du Bois, Thurgood Marshall, or one of the other black leaders listed in the history section of this chapter (pages 62–67).

6. Read and if possible listen to at least one speech by Dr. Martin Luther King Jr. (At the church rally in the film, you hear a part from his "First Address at Mass Meeting," held on December 5, 1955, at the Holt Street Baptist Church.) Also, read his "Letter from a Birmingham Jail." What effect do his spoken and written words have on you?

7. Read at least one biography of Martin Luther King Jr. and one of his own books to see what factors caused him to emerge as such a charismatic leader in 1955.

8. How integrated or segregated is the neighborhood where you grew up or currently live? Investigate the ethnic and racial makeup of one or more nearby communities, of your state, or of your homeland if you are from another country.

9. Find out about the nation's historically black colleges and universities (HBCUs). In your judgment, what unique role do these institutions play? Be sure to examine factors such as mission, history, enrollment, and alumni. You might wish to begin with the renowned institutions Spelman College and Morehouse College, both located in Atlanta, Georgia.

Using Your Imagination

1. Imagine you could have dinner with one of the characters in the film. With whom would you most like to have a conversation, and why? Write the conversation.

2. Imagine you are Mary Catherine as an older woman looking back on her life. Explain if and how your mother and father ever recon-

ciled their differences. Or give your views as to whether the civil rights movement fulfilled its promises.

Sequel: Further Suggested Resources

Readings

Bennett, Lerone Jr. 1988. *Before the Mayflower: A History of Black America.* 6th ed. New York: Penguin Books.

Branch, Taylor. 1998. *Pillar of Fire: America in the King Years, 1963–65.* New York: Simon and Schuster.

———. 1988. *Parting the Waters: America in the King Years, 1954–63.* New York: Simon and Schuster.

Carson, Clayborne, et al., eds. 1991. *The Eyes on the Prize Civil Rights Reader.* New York: Penguin Books.

Chideya, Farai. 1995. *Don't Believe the Hype: Fighting Cultural Misinformation about African-Americans.* New York: Penguin Books.

Cone, James H. 1991. *Martin and Malcolm and America: A Dream or a Nightmare.* Maryknoll, NY: Orbis Books.

Crawford, Vicki L., et al., eds. 1990. *Women in the Civil Rights Movement: Trailblazers and Torchbearers, 1941–1965.* Brooklyn: Carson Publishing.

Crum, Robert. 1986. *The Story of English.* New York: Viking.

Curry, Constance, et al. 2000. *Deep in Our Hearts: Nine White Women in the Freedom Movement.* Athens, GA: University of Georgia Press.

Gates, Henry Louis Jr., and Kwame Anthony Appiah, eds. 1999. *Africana: The Encyclopedia of the African and African American Experience.* New York: Basic Civitas Books.

Gates, Henry Louis Jr., and Nellie Y. McKay, eds. 1997. *The Norton Anthology of African American Literature.* New York: W. W. Norton.

Hacker, Andrew. 1992. *Two Nations: Black and White, Separate, Hostile, Unequal.* New York: Scribner's.

Henderson, George. 1999. *Our Souls to Keep: Black/White Relations in America.* Yarmouth, ME: Intercultural Press.

Kasher, Steven. 1996. *The Civil Rights Movement: A Photographic History, 1954–68.* New York: Abbeville Press.

King, Martin Luther Jr. 1958. *Stride Toward Freedom: The Montgomery Story.* New York: Harper and Brothers.

Kochman, Thomas. 1981. *Black and White Styles in Conflict.* Chicago: University of Chicago Press.

Malcolm X. 1964. *The Autobiography of Malcolm X,* edited by Alex Haley. New York: Ballantine Books.

Massey, Douglas S., and Nancy A. Denton. 1993. *American Apartheid: Segregation and the Making of the Underclass.* Cambridge: Harvard University Press.

Meier, August, and Elliott Rudwick. 1976. *From Plantation to Ghetto.* 3d ed. New York: Hill and Wang.

Oates, Stephen B. 1982. *Let the Trumpet Sound: The Life of Martin Luther King, Jr.* New York: Harper and Row.

Olson, Lynne. 2001. *Freedom's Daughters: The Unsung Heroines of the Civil Rights Movement from 1830 to 1970.* New York: Scribner's.

Parks, Rosa. 1994. *Quiet Strength.* Grand Rapids, MI: Zondervan.

Robinson, Jo Ann Gibson. 1987. *The Montgomery Bus Boycott and the Women Who Started It.* Knoxville: University of Tennessee Press.

Smitherman, Geneva. 1994. *Black Talk: Words and Phrases from the Hood to the Amen Corner.* Boston: Houghton Mifflin.

———. 1977. *Talkin and Testifyin: The Language of Black America.* Detroit: Wayne State University Press.

Swanson, Meg, with Robin Murray. 1999. *Playwrights of Color.* Yarmouth, ME: Intercultural Press.

West, Cornel. 1993. *Race Matters.* Boston: Beacon Press.

Williams, Juan. 1987. *Eyes on the Prize: America's Civil Rights Years, 1954–65.* New York: Penguin Books.

Films

Amistad (1997)   A story of the little-known successful mutiny of Africans being transported to the New World aboard the slave ship *Amistad* in 1839. Directed by Steven Spielberg.

Boyz 'N the Hood (1991)   Focuses on a group of teenagers growing up in a tough neighborhood of South Central Los Angeles. Directed by African American John Singleton.

Do the Right Thing (1989)   Set in a primarily black neighborhood in Bedford Stuyvesant (Brooklyn), where the local pizzeria is owned by Italian Americans, this disturbing look at urban street life and racial violence foreshadows the 1992 Los Angeles riots. Written and directed by African American Spike Lee.

Eyes on the Prize: America's Civil Rights Years (1986)   Six-part series. The story of the civil rights struggle between 1954 and 1965 comes alive through news footage, photographs, and personal recollections. Winner of dozens of national awards. Directed by Henry Hampton (PBS Video).

Eyes on the Prize II: America at the Racial Crossroads (1989)   Eight-part series. This continuation of the first documentary series traces the civil rights movement from 1965 to 1985. Directed by Henry Hampton (PBS Video).

Ghosts of Mississippi (1996)   Thirty years after the murder of civil rights leader Medgar Evers, his case is reopened in a search for justice. Directed by Rob Reiner.

Glory (1989)   Unforgettable epic film about the little-known Massachusetts 54th Colored Infantry, an all-black unit that served heroically during the Civil War. Directed by Edward Zwick.

Hoop Dreams (1994)   The compelling story of two African American teenagers living in urban Chicago who dream of becoming professional basketball stars. Documentary, directed by Steve James.

Malcolm X (1992)   A powerful version of the life of Malcolm X (Denzel Washington), from his early days as a street hustler to his emergence as a brilliant orator and revolutionary leader to his assassination. Directed by Spike Lee.

Mississippi Burning (1988)   The FBI investigates the disappearance of three white civil rights workers in Mississippi during the summer of 1964. Directed by Alan Parker.

Separate but Equal (1991)   Traces events leading to the landmark Supreme Court ruling in the *Brown v. Board of Education* case. The hero, Thurgood Marshall, is played by Sidney Poitier. Directed by George Stevens.

To Kill a Mockingbird (1962)   Classic film about a lawyer in a small Southern town who defends a black man accused of raping a white woman. Based on the novel by Harper Lee. Directed by Robert Mulligan.

Compact Discs

African American Spirituals: The Concert Tradition (Wade in the Water Volume I). Smithsonian/Folkways Recordings and National Public Radio, 1994; phone: 301-443-2314.

Negro Spirituals (Osceola Davis, Jorma Hynninen, and Ilmo Ranta). Ondine Oy, 1988.

Voices of the Civil Rights Movement: Black American Freedom Songs 1960–1966. Smithsonian/Folkways. 1997.

Websites and Mailing Addresses

Archives of African American Music and Culture (www.indiana.edu/~aaamc)

Black History Links (www.webcom.com/cjhook/bhistory/html)

Historically Black Colleges and Universities (www.webcom.com/cjhook/hbcu/html)

International Black Index Source Directory (IBIS) (www.blackindex.com)

Martin Luther King Jr. Center for Nonviolent Social Change, 449 Auburn Avenue, NE, Atlanta, GA 30312; phone: 404-524-1956 (www.theKing center.com)

NAACP (National Association for the Advancement of Colored People), 4805 Mt. Hope Drive, Baltimore, MD 21215; phone: 410-358-8900 (www.naacp.org)

National Urban League, 120 Wall Street, New York, NY 10005; phone: 212-558-5300 (www.nul.org)

San Diego BLAACK Pages (www.sdbp.com)

Southern Poverty Law Center, 400 Washington Street, Montgomery, AL 36104; phone: 334-264-0286 (www.splcenter.org)

Universal Black Pages (www.ubp.com)

4

Chinese American Culture:
The Joy Luck Club

Setting the Scene: Freewriting and Discussion

At the very beginning of the film, you will hear the following fable:

The old woman remembered a swan she had bought many years ago in Shanghai for a foolish sum. "This bird," boasted the market vendor, "was once a duck that stretched its neck in hopes of becoming a goose, and now, look, it is too beautiful to eat."

Then the woman and the swan sailed across an ocean many thousands of li wide, stretching their necks toward America. On her journey, she cooed to the swan, "In America, I will have a daughter just like me, but over there nobody will say her worth is measured by the loudness of her husband's belch. Over there, nobody will look down on her because I will make her speak only perfect American English. And over there, she will always be too full to swallow any sorrow. She will know my meaning because I will give her this swan, a creature that became more than what was hoped for."

But when she arrived in the new country, the immigration officials pulled the swan away from her, leaving the woman fluttering her arms and with only one swan feather for a memory. For a long time now, the woman had wanted to give her daughter the single swan feather and tell her, "This feather may look worthless, but it comes from afar and carries with it all my good intentions."

Freewrite your initial reactions to the fable in your film notebook. Then make a prediction as to what you think the film will be about.

Wide-Angle Lens: Historical Perspectives

Set in the present day, *The Joy Luck Club* tells the tale of four Chinese women immigrants and their four American-born daughters. The lives of these eight women are part of a history of Asian immigration that reaches back to the late 1840s. To understand the historical background of the film, two distinct strands of immigration must be examined, one of men and one of women, keeping in mind the extent to which gender has influenced the lives and experiences of the generations of Chinese who first left their homeland more than 150 years ago to seek a better life.

White Americans do not usually think of these Chinese or of other Asians when they express pride in their country as a land of immigrants. What they understand by the term *immigration* is usually limited to the influx of millions of Europeans since colonial days. The two renowned landmarks of this immigration, the Statue of Liberty and Ellis Island—where new arrivals were detained before they were admitted or sent back—are both on the Atlantic Ocean.

The "other" immigration, that of Asians who came across the Pacific Ocean and landed on the West Coast after detainment at places such as Angel Island, located in San Francisco Bay, has often been forgotten or ignored. Recent important scholarship, including Ronald Takaki's *Strangers from a Different Shore*, records the accounts of those who came with the same dreams as the Europeans but were afforded little opportunity to realize these dreams. In addition to the Chinese, who are the focus of this chapter, these immigrants include Japanese, Koreans, Asian Indians, Filipinos, and Southeast Asians.

The first Chinese venturers to the United States were almost exclusively men. Yearning to escape poverty as well as political and social upheaval, tens of thousands of peasants, mostly young married men from the southeastern province of Guangdong, left to seek their fortunes in Hawaii and in the gold fields of California (a place the Chinese called *gam saan,* or "Gold Mountain"). As the first Asians to arrive in large numbers in the U.S., these sojourners generally expected to stay only a few years—long enough to pay back their passage and save enough to return home to their families as wealthy, respected men.

The women at that time stayed at home, not only because of the anticipated rigors of the journey but also because their traditional role in a feudal, patriarchal society precluded lives of equality and independence. The stories of the grandmothers in *The Joy Luck Club* provide some insight into Chinese women's situations in the nineteenth and early twentieth centuries. Following the Confucian social order, women were destined to assume roles subservient to men. The Confucian "three obediences" prescribed a lifetime of obedience, first to the father, then to the husband, and finally to the eldest son. Girls were usually betrothed at a young age by matchmakers and had to leave their homes to serve their husbands and in-laws. Their worth depended primarily upon their ability to manage the household and produce male heirs. While men could divorce, remarry, commit adultery, and keep concubines and mistresses, female adulterers were punished, and widowed women were not expected to remarry.

For decades the lives of the Chinese male immigrants to the U.S. mainland were marked by the absence of women and families. (The situation was different in Hawaii, where women were encouraged to settle.) Dedicating themselves to their work, these solitary men became a vitally important part of the workforce in California and nearby states, contributing not only labor but also expertise and entrepreneurship. They are acknowledged for their essential roles in the mining industry and later in the building of the nation's transcontinental and western railroad networks. As experienced farmers, they also helped to develop California's agriculture. They reclaimed farmland from swamps, became skilled fruit packers, developed the shrimp industry in the San Francisco Bay area, worked in vineyards, and became tenant farmers and truck gardeners. Their contributions extended beyond California: in Oregon, Ah Bing bred the famous Bing cherry, and Lue Gim Gong in Florida developed the frost-resistant orange so vital to that state's citrus industry.

Though the Chinese men eventually found success in various other areas of employment (they established restaurants and laundries and worked in construction and factories), they led hard lives characterized by backbreaking, sometimes dangerous work and meager incomes. Speaking little English, facing frequent insults and prejudice, and planning to stay for only a limited time, they generally lived in separate Chinese neighborhoods called "Chinatowns." At the same time that religious, political, and social organizations provided support for residents of Chinatowns, many of the lonely, desperate men sought recreation in gambling parlors, opium dens, and houses of prostitution. Gradually, most of the men came to realize that they were trapped on the "Gold Mountain" with no way to pay for their family's passage over or even for their own return trip home.

Asian American Broad label used to refer to Americans from more than twenty Asian nations. Many Asian Americans prefer specific names, such as Filipino, Hmong, or Korean American.

Chink, coolie, slanteye Derogatory terms for Chinese.

Oriental Previously used to refer to Asian Americans but now widely rejected as having negative connotations as exotic and alluring. Today it is used to refer to carpets or other objects but generally not to people.

yellow Derogatory term referring to people of Asian descent, in spite of the fact that their skin is more tan or brown than yellow. The term is universally rejected as having associations with cowardice. "Yellow menace" and "yellow peril" have been used to incite fear that America will be overrun by people from Asia.

The few women who managed to immigrate in the early decades also experienced lives of great hardship, often being forced into prostitution. Those who married usually lived in rural areas, performing household duties as well as fishing, mining, laundering, and other hard labor. Viewing them as curiosities, the whites often gave them generic names, such as "China Mary." Though most of their stories remain unknown, some do survive, providing fascinating glimpses into these women's strength and adaptability. Among the figures known today are Polly Bemis and China Annie of Idaho City, both of whom won their freedom from involuntary prostitution, and the China Marys of Sitka, Alaska; Evanston, Wyoming; and Oakdale, California.

As the number of both Chinese men and women grew (reaching more than one hundred thousand by 1880) and as an economic depression in the West caused growing unemployment, anti-Chinese sentiment increased and turned more often to violence. Ironically, the Chinese workers' reputation for dedication, speed, and reliability on the job worked to their detriment when whites claimed they could not compete fairly with the Chinese. Prompted by fear and outright racism, anti-Chinese activities became widespread, including mob violence, attacks by the press, and highly discriminatory laws such as the foreign miner's tax (1852), a penalty aimed at the Chinese that required foreign miners to pay a heavy monthly tax.

The anti-Chinese movement culminated in the infamous Chinese Exclusion Act (1882), which prohibited Chinese laborers from entering the country and made it illegal for those already here to become citizens or to bring their wives. This law marks the first time that this "land of immigrants" acted to ban potential newcomers of a specific nationality. Ironically, the fears that led to the Exclusion Act—that "hordes" of Chinese were entering the country and threatening the American way of life—were completely unfounded in terms of actual population statistics. At that time only two in every one thousand people in the United States were Chinese. But the anxieties persisted. The original 1882 exclusion legislation was later broadened and renewed, remaining in effect for more than half a century before finally being repealed in 1943. Even then, the number of legal entrants from China was limited to a token annual quota of 105.

The Second World War proved to be a turning point for Chinese Americans. Wartime labor shortages opened new opportunities for skilled and technical workers, and many Chinese served in the military. In fact, Chinese heroism in the face of Japanese wartime aggression in their country shifted the public mood from hostility to one of greater sympathy. (In the film it is during the Japanese bombing of Guilin in southern China that the film character Suyuan flees with her twins to join her husband in Chongqing.)

The War Brides Act of 1946 was an important step in reversing discrimination against men of Asian and other descent who had not been able to bring their Asian families to this country (see description of the film *Sayonara* on page 119). This legislation permitted Asian wives and children of all U.S. servicemen to enter as nonquota immigrants (not subject to the restriction of 105 legal entrants each year), making possible the arrival of nearly eight thousand Chinese women between 1946 and 1950. The four Chinese mothers in the film emigrated during this post-war period.

With the takeover of mainland China by the Communists in 1949 and the establishment of the People's Republic of China, large numbers of Chinese migrated to the United States. In particular, many who fled to the then-British colony of Hong Kong eventually made their way to America. The number of legal entrants remained small, however, because of the above-mentioned quota of 105.

This changed dramatically when Congress reformed immigration law in 1965. With the passing of the Immigration and Nationality Act of 1965, government policy, which had long favored northern and western Europeans, began to allow immigrants from other parts of the world to compete on a more equal basis. After the 1965 law went into effect, the number of Chinese immigrants from Taiwan and Hong Kong, including many students, increased substantially. The normalization of relations between the United States and mainland China in the late 1970s, coupled with the liberalization of China's emigration policy, led to a large growth in immigrants from the mainland.

Since 1965 a new class of Chinese Americans has emerged, as upwardly mobile second- and third-generation professionals have been joined by many highly educated immigrants entering the ranks of white-collar employment. In recent decades both Chinese and Japanese Americans' phenomenal success in achieving the American Dream has led to the stereotype of Asian Americans as the "model minority": hardworking, uncomplaining, brilliant in school, and highly accomplished in their professions.

Though a positive stereotype, this concept of the model minority is harmful nonetheless, partly because it creates a backlash of jealousy and resentment. Having endured years of prejudice when they were on the bottom of the social and economic ladder, many successful Chinese Americans now face discrimination again as they climb upward. The stereotype also prevents help from reaching many Chinese Americans—and other Asian Americans such as Vietnamese and Laotian refugees—who are living below the poverty level and clearly not succeeding. Moreover, the stereotype sets an unrealistic standard for all Asian Americans and can be a disguised way of criticizing African Americans and Latinos, who by implication should follow the Asian example.

Lights Out: Viewing the Film

The Joy Luck Club (1993), based on Amy Tan's 1989 best-selling novel of the same name, contrasts the lives of four mothers who grew up in China under harsh circumstances with the lives of their four Chinese American daughters, who were born into privilege and prosperity. It is the classic story of the conflicts—and the bonds—that exist between first- and second-generation immigrants. Widely seen and discussed, it bears the distinction of being one of the first films to bring Chinese American family life before the general public. Amy Tan, who cowrote the script, is herself Chinese American, and director Wayne Wang was born in Hong Kong.

Main Characters and Stories in the Film

Story One	**Mother Suyuan** **Daughter June**
Story Two	**Mother Lindo** **Daughter Waverly**
Story Three	**Mother Ying Ying** **Daughter Lena**
Story Four	**Mother An Mei** **Daughter Rose**

The film is also credited with portraying Chinese American women as real people with individual personalities. In the history of American film, Asian women have generally been stereotyped either as subservient to males or as coy, alluring temptresses. Moreover, roles of Asian women have often gone to Caucasian actresses, usually heavily made up and even wearing tape on their eyes to look the part. *The Joy Luck Club* features an almost all Asian or Asian American cast of sterling actors, including Kieu Chinh (Suyuan) and Tsai Chin (Auntie Lindo), celebrated actresses in Vietnam and China; France Nuyen (Auntie Ying Ying), known for her performance in *South Pacific*; Rosalind Chao, whose credits include *A Thousand Pieces of Gold*; and Tamlyn Tomita from *Come See the Paradise*. Amy Tan appears in a walk-on role as one of the first guests to appear at the farewell party in the opening scene.

 After viewing the film, make your own chart of each mother-daughter relationship.

	Important fact about her past life	*Important fact about her present life*
Mother Suyuan		
Daughter June		
Mother Lindo		
Daughter Waverly		
Mother Ying Ying		
Daughter Lena		
Mother An Mei		
Daughter Rose		

Spotlight on Culture and Communication

This spotlight will help illuminate the concept of *internalized oppression** among nondominant minority groups (see definition in Essential Vocabulary on Cultures, page 10). Research over the past decades has shown that many members of marginalized groups not only experience assaults on their self-worth and dignity from the society as a whole but (to the extent that they themselves begin to believe the negative stereotypes about them) they may also actually participate in their own subjugation. Women, for example, who have been told for centuries that they are not as smart as men, may actually think of themselves as less intelligent and behave accordingly. Or blacks who have been made to feel that their skin color is ugly and dirty may actually begin to see themselves as less beautiful than whites. As these examples demonstrate, the damage that results from internalized oppression, ranging from mild self-doubts to extreme insecurities and even self-hatred, can be enormous.

In *The Joy Luck Club*, four Chinese women who were oppressed in their homeland dream of a more dignified life for themselves and their daughters in their adopted country. But in America they and their daughters are "twice a minority" (Takaki 1993)—as Asian Americans and as females—and thus have an especially difficult and complicated struggle to prove their worth to themselves and to the world around them.

In small groups choose a clip that you feel illustrates the struggle of one of the women characters to achieve self-worth and dignity. What are the pressures on the character, and how does she cope? What stereotypes about herself has she internalized?

In your presentation be sure to mention relevant nonverbal communication and film techniques in your clip.

---

* Researcher Claude Steele describes a similar phenomenon among African Americans, which he calls *stereotype vulnerability*.

Point of View: Interview with Wayne Wang

Film director Wayne Wang, born in Hong Kong in 1949, grew up in a bilingual home and is familiar with both the Chinese and the American worlds. After graduating from a Jesuit high school in Hong Kong, Wang moved to California, where he earned a bachelor's degree in painting and a master's degree in film and television from the California College of Arts and Crafts. His first commercially successful film, the low-budget *Chan is Missing* (1982), deals in a humorous way with a search for a missing man in San Francisco's Chinatown. While remaining dedicated to Chinese American and Chinese themes in subsequent films such as *Dim Sum* (1984), *Eat a Bowl of Tea* (1989), and *Chinese Box* (1998), Wang does not wish to restrict himself to this genre, as evidenced by films such as *Slamdance* (1987) and *Smoke* (1995). As he says, "I will go off and do something that has nothing to do with China, like *Smoke*, but I think I will always come back to it" (Faison 1997, B7).

During Wang's 1993 international media tour to promote *The Joy Luck Club,* he gave the interview that follows.

- After reading the interview, what do you now understand better about the film and/or the filmmaking process?
- What further question(s) do you wish Tibbets had asked Wang?

A Delicate Balance: An Interview with Wayne Wang about *The Joy Luck Club*

by John C. Tibbets © 1994

WANG: Although I speak Mandarin, I had lots of problems communicating with the people there. But at the same time, I understand the Chinese culture. It's part of my consciousness, part of my history. If anybody else had wanted to do this, he would have had to spend a lot of time researching the subject, and even then the subtleties of the culture would have been too confusing.

QUESTION: *This isn't your first film to deal with several generations of Chinese and Chinese Americans, is it?*

WANG: *Dim Sum*, obviously, comes to mind, because that one's also about a mother-daughter relationship. There's one other film that I completed in 1989 called *Eat a Bowl of Tea*, which is about a father-son relationship, set after the war in 1949. That one is in some ways also very much related to *The Joy Luck Club*, because it's about a generation gap, the Chinese-American culture, the particular period where actually the Chinese were not allowed to bring their wives over. It wasn't until after the war that the GIs could use the GI Bill to bring their wives over. And that was the introduction to the Chinese-American families. In that sense it's related to the roots of *The Joy Luck Club*.

QUESTION: *Do you see recent Asian-American films, like* Joy Luck *and Ang Lee's* The Wedding Banquet, *especially, becoming as popular as the martial arts and ghost-story genres?*

WANG: It's true the family genre seems to be very popular now. I guess the American audience is becoming interested in seeing movies about Chinese Americans—although elsewhere in the world the ghost stories, the action films, and the kung fu films seem to be more popular.... I think we're still pretty much a country of immigrants, some older and some newer than others. Stories about immigrants and the different generations and how the parents may be closer to their roots in their own history, and the kids are not. These things concern all of us and are very strong, universal themes that way.

QUESTION: *Tell me how you came to [the] project in the first place.*

WANG: I was given Amy Tan's book, read it, and found it very moving. It was familiar in the sense that the stories reminded me of stories I heard while growing up. And yet at the same time it was very universal. Not just about Chinese, but about all immigrants. I also liked a lot of the details in the book that were true and visually oriented. I called up Amy—we both live in San Francisco. We got together informally, got to know each other, and formed a relationship and eventually a partnership.

QUESTION: *Was the task of telling so many interlocking stories at all intimidating?*

WANG: Yes, actually. And don't forget there are not just eight characters telling a story, but that each story has its own past and present. Sixteen stories! At first I was very worried about that, that it was very complicated; that it would be very tough to pull off. But we also connected up with a very experienced screenwriter, Ron Bass, who won an Academy Award for *Rain Man*, and he came in and had good ideas about how it would work: Using the simple structure of a dinner party to see one of the daughters off to China to visit her twin sisters. Using that to introduce all the mothers and daughters. And also to use narration to bridge things and get more information across.

QUESTION: *It's dazzling. But as easy as it is to watch, it must have been terribly complex to write the script.*

WANG: Yes it was. I think we took a long, long time trying to figure out how many stories we were going to tell and what kind of emphasis we wanted in the sixteen stories. And how to get into the stories in an elegant and simple way. That was the major part of the first step in the scripting process. Later on, in the cinematic sense, we had to

(continued on the next page)

(continued from the previous page)

make sure that each story had a different look; that the flashbacks to the near past and far past had a different look. Those were all things that were very important. They may not be obvious to the viewer, but subconsciously it will make a difference to them.

QUESTION: *And there's such a delicate balance you maintain between the tragic and the comic elements. Everybody talks about it as an "eight-handkerchief movie," but it really is quite funny in places.*

WANG: I especially like the scene where Andrew McCarthy goes to have dinner with the parents of his girl friend [Rosalind Chao as Rose]. He doesn't understand anything about their customs and the affair is a disaster! Ms. Tan told me that scene grew out of experiences she had had. And when I read it I remembered different things in my own background where a Caucasian had to cope with the Chinese "Emily Post" kind of things. It's funny how such small details of table etiquette can create such serious problems!

QUESTION: *On the other hand, other scenes are heartbreaking, like the drowning of Ying Ying's baby.*

WANG: Forgive me if I laugh when I think about it, but we found a baby who actually loved the water very much. The mother was great and we used her hands as doubles. And it worked out nicely, the baby was so natural it was amazing. This baby really loved the water. It was a tough scene to film, though.

One of the saddest scenes, though, was June's reunion in China with her two older sisters. When we were filming the scene, what was amazing was that during the rehearsal the whole row of extras could hear the dialogue. They were completely in tears. An older woman came up to me later and told me she had had to leave her baby during the war and had never found it again. She really broke down. There's a lot there that the Chinese can identify with. Chinese Americans in their own way can identify with this daughter, June, because her story is going back to your own roots, going to your home, and finally doing something for your mother. In another sense, for any daughters watching the film, I think they would be moved by it: because in the end it's about fulfilling your mother's wish. That's what that scene is all about.

QUESTION: *The problems of the daughters don't seem particularly serious, after all, when they are compared to what their mothers had to go through.*

WANG: I'm forty-four years old and my genera-

tion has been very lucky. We haven't been through major wars or major tragedies, so to speak, in terms of having been bombed by another country, having to escape from our own country, having lost family members, giving up babies—all that kind of stuff. And we live in a way a very self-centered life, our generation. And our problems are quite minor compared to what my parents in China have gone through. And I feel like sometimes I forget about that. And through this film I feel there's a lot we can learn from the dramas, tragedies, and sufferings that our parents have gone through. And what they've gone through to get us to this country and bring us up and all that. On the one hand, it's a burden, their expectations on us; on the other hand, we need to learn from their history and past, because that's where our roots are.

QUESTION: *What a contrast this strikes with some of the pictures by a filmmaker like, say, John Hughes, where the parents are idiots. Where the teenagers deride their elders.*

WANG: That goes back to my own generation being so self-centered. I think a lot of films actually serve to please that in a sense—we look at our parents and we laugh at them because they're so old-fashioned. They have certain ideas that seem very strict. We've lost the value of trying to understand where all that has come from. Some of it is old-fashioned, but if you understand the essence and where they come from, there is a lot of value to them. Take for example a scene in the movie where the daughter has to cut her own flesh to make a soup for her mother who's dying. I think I could in a sense say that's a stupid ritual; but in another sense, I look at it and can say that's a really strong thing about how much respect you show for your parents, which doesn't exist anymore.

QUESTION: *Do you feel sometimes like your characters, poised between generations, between the Old and New World? Is that a potentially tragic dilemma?*

WANG: I think my parents definitely fit that description. My dad has always wanted to become an American. And he finally became an American just a couple of years ago. And now he's kinda— he doesn't feel like he belongs here, either. He's a big baseball fan, football fan, all that good American stuff; but he feels there's something that's not his home here. He wants to move back to China, now that it's opened up. It's very strange to be caught between those two poles. ∎

Amy Tan's (and Our Own) Many Englishes

In *The Joy Luck Club*, each of the four Chinese mothers speaks her own unique form of English. Having learned English as adult immigrants, these women speak with accents, and their mastery of the grammar and vocabulary is imperfect. Nonetheless, their English is fluent, vivid, and colorful. They use the language in creative ways and are able to express their ideas and personalities.

In an essay entitled "Mother Tongue,"[†] Amy Tan speaks of her own mother's English with respect and admiration. Though Tan herself has thoroughly adopted forms of English used in academic and literary circles, she finds herself slipping into familiar patterns of Chinese immigrant English when she is with her mother. For example, when she and her mother are discussing the costs of new and used furniture, Tan finds herself saying "Not waste money that way." One of her goals in the film, she explains, was to capture "what language ability tests can never reveal": her mother's "intent, her passion, her imagery, the rhythms of her speech and the nature of her thoughts." It bothers her to think of her mother's English as "broken" or "limited"; rather, as she hears it, it is "vivid, direct, full of observation and imagery."

 Divide into small mixed-language groups—as much as possible, try to distribute among the groups students who

- speak a first language other than English
- come from an English-speaking country other than the U.S.
- are bilingual
- speak Black English
- come from various parts of the U.S. and have a regional dialect and accent

To guide your discussion, try the following.

- Begin by identifying the different languages, vernaculars, or dialects each of you speaks.
- Then think about how you use English. List, for example, some of the situations or settings in which you adjust your style of speech. When, how, and why do you do so?
- Finally, talk about which forms of English are considered "superior" to others. When are particular usages of English looked down upon?

---

† In *Making a Difference: A Reader for Whites*, edited by Trudy Smoke. Boston: Houghton Mifflin, 1994 (53–58).

Time permitting, analyze the varieties of English used by the mothers in the film and show the clips in class.

Zoom Lens: Choosing Your Own Topic of Interest

Hands-on Activities

1. Visit a Chinatown nearby and explore not only its streets and souvenir shops but also its grocery stores, herbal medicine shops, and bookstores. If possible, have a *dim sum* ("small delicacies") meal in which you can sample a variety of foods, often offered by waiters pushing food carts.
2. If there is a Chinese or Chinese American organization on your campus or in your community, find out if you might attend a meeting or event.
3. Find out what program or courses your school offers in Asian American studies. Analyze the offerings and speak with professors and students to obtain their views and evaluations.

Research Papers or Oral Reports

1. Prepare a paper or oral report on one of the following:
   a. the history of Chinatowns in America
   b. Angel Island (see book by Lai, Lim, and Yung listed in the Sequel)
   c. the Chinese Exclusion Act of 1882 (and/or other anti-Chinese legislation)
   d. the immigration of Chinese women to America (see books by Chang, Ling, Peffer, and Yung listed in the Sequel)
2. Read Maxine Hong Kingston's *The Woman Warrior* or Jade Snow Wong's *Fifth Chinese Daughter*. Compare their depiction of Chinese American women with that of Amy Tan's in the film.
3. Read Amy Tan's novel *The Joy Luck Club* and compare the novel with the film. Or read one of the author's other novels (*The Kitchen God's Wife, The Hundred Secret Senses, The Bonesetter's Daughter*) and compare it with *The Joy Luck Club*.

4. Read *China Boy* by Gus Lee, *Typical American* by Gish Yen, or *Rice Room* by Ben Fong-Torres. Compare the experiences of Chinese men in these books with those of Chinese women as portrayed in Amy Tan's book or film.

Using Your Imagination

1. Imagine that you are taking a friend from a different cultural background to your home for dinner. First determine your friend's culture, and then describe how you would prepare both your friend and your family for any cultural differences they might encounter.
2. Imagine that you could have coffee (or dim sum) with one of the characters in the film. Whom would you like to meet and why? What would you like to talk about? (Or imagine you could interview Amy Tan or one of the actors or film crew.) Write the conversation (or interview).
3. Design a poster to be hung in movie theaters to advertise the film.

Sequel: Further Suggested Resources

Readings

Asian Women United of California, eds. 1989. *Making Waves: An Anthology of Writings by and about Asian American Women.* Boston: Beacon Press.

Bruchac, Joseph, ed. 1983. *Breaking the Silence: An Anthology of Contemporary Asian American Poets.* New York: Greenfield Review Press.

Cao, Lan, and Himilce Novas. 1966. *Everything You Need to Know about Asian American History.* New York: Penguin.

Chang, Leslie. 1999. *Beyond the Narrow Gate: The Journey of Four Chinese Women from the Middle Kingdom to America.* New York: Dutton.

Chen, Jack. 1980. *The Chinese of America.* San Francisco: Harper and Row.

Chin, Frank. 1991. *Donald Duk.* Minneapolis: Coffee House Press.

Faison, Seth. 1997. "Casting Hong Kong as a Drama-Filled City." *New York Times,* 1 July, B7.

Fong-Torres, Ben. 1995. *Rice Room.* New York: Penguin Books.

Kingston, Maxine Hong. 1977. *China Men.* New York: Ballantine.

———. 1975. *The Woman Warrior: Memoirs of a Girlhood among Ghosts.* New York: Vintage.

Lai, Him Mark, Genny Lim, and Judy Yung, eds. 1980. *Island: Poetry and History of Chinese Immigrants on Angel Island, 1910–1940*. Seattle: University of Washington Press.

Lee, Gus. 1991. *China Boy*. New York: Dutton.

Ling, Huping. 1998. *Surviving on the Gold Mountain*. Albany: State University of New York Press.

Mah, Adeline Yen. 1997. *Falling Leaves: The True Story of an Unwanted Chinese Daughter*. New York: Broadway Books.

Peffer, George Anthony. 1999. *If They Don't Bring Their Women Here: Chinese Female Immigration before Exclusion*. Urbana, IL: University of Chicago Press.

Takaki, Ronald. 1993. *A Different Mirror: A History of Multicultural America*. Boston: Little, Brown.

———. 1989. *Strangers from a Different Shore: A History of Asian Americans*. Boston: Little, Brown.

Tan, Amy. 2001. *The Bonesetter's Daughter*. New York: Putnam.

———. 1995. *The Hundred Secret Senses*. New York: Ballantine Books.

———. 1991. *The Kitchen God's Wife*. New York: Putnam.

———. 1989. *The Joy Luck Club*. New York: Ballantine Books.

Wong, Jade Snow. 1945. *Fifth Chinese Daughter*. New York: Harper.

Yen, Gish. 1991. *Typical American*. New York: Penguin Books.

Yung, Judy. 1999. *Unbound Voices: A Documentary History of Chinese Women in San Francisco*. Berkeley: University of California Press.

———. 1995. *Unbound Feet: A Social History of Chinese Women in San Francisco*. Berkeley: University of California Press.

———. 1986. *Chinese Women of America: A Pictorial History*. Seattle: University of Washington Press.

Films

Carved in Silence (1988)   Poignant story of potential Chinese immigrants detained for up to three years on Angel Island. The title refers to poems the Chinese carved into the stone of their prison walls. Directed by Felicia Lowe (NAATA).

Dim Sum (1984)   Portrayal of a Chinese American mother and daughter, considered a breakthrough in creating three-dimensional Asian women characters. Directed by Wayne Wang.

Double Happiness (1994)   Charming portrait of a Chinese Canadian woman caught between her dream to become an actress and her parents' wish that she marry and have children. Directed by Mina Shum.

A Great Wall (1986)   Story of a Chinese American family's first trip to visit relatives in the People's Republic of China, filled with opportunities for culture clash and humor. Directed by Peter Wang.

Pushing Hands (1992)   Early film about marital tensions that ensue when a Taiwanese American man brings his aging father, a tai chi master who speaks no English, from Taiwan to live with his Anglicized suburban family. Directed by Ang Lee.

A Thousand Pieces of Gold (1991)   Young Chinese woman escapes from her homeland only to be trapped in the harsh life of a prostitute in a small frontier mining town. Based on a true story. Directed by Nancy Kelly.

Who Killed Vincent Chin? (1988)   Disturbing account of a brutal hate crime that occurred in Detroit in 1982 and resulted in the death of twenty-seven-year-old Chinese American Vincent Chin. Documentary, directed by Christine Choy (Filmakers Library).

Websites and Mailing Addresses

Asian American Legal Defense and Education Fund, 99 Hudson Street, New York, NY 10013; phone: 212-966-5932

Chinese for Affirmative Action, 17 Walter U. Lum Place, San Francisco, CA 94108; phone: 415-274-6750 (www.caasf.org)

5

Japanese American Culture:
Come See the Paradise

■ ■

Setting the Scene: Freewriting and Discussion

■ ■

> *I wanted to be an American. I wondered why God had not made me an American. If I couldn't be an American, then what was I? A Japanese? No. But not an American either. My life background is American.... [But] my looks made me Japanese.* (Takaki 1989, 225)

 The conflict described by this second-generation Japanese immigrant in a 1924 oral interview is true for many Asian Americans, especially those born in the United States. Think about these words and freewrite your initial reactions. Then discuss your ideas with your classmates.

Wide-Angle Lens: Historical and Geographical Perspectives

The Japanese American Internment

The persecution of American residents of Japanese ancestry in the 1940s, as depicted in the film *Come See the Paradise*, has its roots in the first Japanese immigration to the United States. Following in the footsteps of the Chinese, the Japanese began to migrate to the mainland and Hawaii in significant numbers toward the end of the nineteenth century. At first the arrivals were mostly young, single males hoping to make their fortunes and eventually return home. They provided cheap labor in farming, fishing, railroad construction, lumbering, and mining. After accumulating savings, many were able to start small businesses, such as groceries, barbershops, and restaurants.

Before long the men were joined by increasing numbers of women. Markedly different from the situation for women in China, liberal policies in Japan under the Meiji government encouraged the education and employment of women. Thus, less confined to the home and domestic work than women in China, thousands of Japanese women were able to leave, mostly under a form of arranged marriage called the "picture bride" system. Having received little more than photos of their prospective husbands, they set out for Hawaii and the mainland with dreams that seldom turned out to match the realities they would find.

Despite their hard work and contributions, these immigrant men and women met with strong anti-Japanese sentiment. Laws and policies of "exclusion" kept them locked in the status of strangers and prevented them from assimilating into the new society. To give a few examples: first-generation Japanese (*Issei*) were declared ineligible for citizenship; a decision was made by the school board in San Francisco in 1906 to segregate Japanese into Oriental schools; the infamous Gentleman's Agreement was signed by Japan and the United States in 1906, dramatically reducing Japanese immigration by specifically excluding all laborers (although a loophole allowed immediate family members to join laborers already here); the Alien Land Bill was passed in California in 1913 and was soon followed by similar legislation in other states, preventing Issei from leasing land for longer than three years and thus forcing them to relocate again and again; and the

Immigration Act of 1924 barred Japanese immigration completely and remained in effect until 1952.

In their personal lives the Japanese in America faced decades of hostility and indignities from those who considered them inferior or even subhuman. Whites often gave vent to deeply held prejudices, as evidenced by the widespread use of epithets such as *Jap* (also *dirty Jap, yellow Jap*), *gook, nip,* and *slant-eye.* The stereotype prevailed that people from Japan were crafty, devious, and cowardly, and fears of a "yellow peril" and "silent invasion" persisted, despite the fact that the Japanese presence was always small. (Approximately 127,000 people of Japanese ancestry lived on the U.S. mainland in 1940, just one tenth of one percent of the nation's population.)

The worst period in Japanese American history began when the Japanese attacked the American naval base at Pearl Harbor, Hawaii, on December 7, 1941, whereupon the United States declared war on Japan and entered World War II. Reaction against Japanese Americans, 90 percent of whom lived on the West Coast, was immediate. Daily life for those of Japanese heritage became more dangerous than ever, with stores on the West Coast boasting signs reading "We kill rats and Japs here." The most rabid exclusionary groups, such as the Native Sons of the Golden West, declared bluntly that "The Japs must go!" Politicians and the press joined in, inciting further hysteria (see example on page 112).

The government acted quickly to restrict Japanese Americans from traveling and to freeze their bank accounts. More than two thousand teachers, priests, and other community leaders (like Mr. Kawamura in the film) were detained and arrested by the FBI as enemy aliens. The most drastic measure came two months after Pearl Harbor, in February, 1942, when President Franklin D. Roosevelt signed Executive Order 9066. This order gave the military the power to arrest, transport, and detain in prisonlike conditions—without hearing or trial—all people considered a threat to security on the Pacific Coast. Although German and Italian Americans were also subjected to violations of their civil rights and internment (much long-neglected information about these groups has recently begun to emerge), they did not undergo the same prolonged, extensive suspicion and mistreatment as those of Japanese ancestry.

Although three-fourths of the approximately 110,000 men, women, and children interned were second-generation *Nisei* and therefore American citizens (as is the case with Lily and her siblings in the film), the Supreme Court upheld the constitutionality of the executive order in several court challenges. In a rare dissenting opinion, Justice Frank Murphy stated that this decree bore a "melancholy resemblance to the treatment accorded to members of the Jewish race in Germany" (Daniels 1971, 135). The Supreme Court did not reverse its decision until 1944.

Related Terms

—————————

Issei First-generation Japanese immigrants.
nip, gook, Jap Derogatory racist terms.
Nisei Second-generation Japanese born in the U.S. and thus American citizens.
Sansei Third-generation Japanese Americans.

For additional Related Terms, see page 90.

The process of evacuation began with orders to sell, dispose of, or store (usually within a week) all belongings other than those that could be carried. The Japanese Americans were taken first to temporary "assembly centers" such as fairgrounds, stockyards, or racetracks (the Kawamura family sleeps in racetrack stables) and moved later to one of ten more permanent "relocation" camps, which are often described today as prison or concentration camps (see map on page 108). Most of these hastily constructed camps, designed for an average of 10,000 people each, were located in remote, semi-desert areas unsuitable for human habitation. The uniform, sparse barracks had no running water. Flight was virtually impossible, since the camps were patrolled by armed guards and surrounded by barbwire fences and sentry towers. Many Japanese remained imprisoned behind the fences for three years.

Firsthand accounts of life in the detention camps reveal the harshness of the physical conditions. The internees were unaccustomed to and unprepared for the extreme temperatures (such as 130 degrees Fahrenheit in the Arizona summer), and they could not escape from the dust and sand blowing constantly through the cracks of their barracks. The crowding, rigid regimentation, unsanitary latrines, and lack of privacy along with the unpalatable and sometimes spoiled food contributed to illness and malaise. For many, even worse than the physical hardships was the emotional distress—the humiliation of imprisonment, the fear of their uncertain future, and the justified anxiety over the dissolution of their close-knit families.

Although the camps remained relatively peaceful, resistance and uprisings were not uncommon. The main forms of protest were work slowdowns, strikes, and noncompliance with regulations. Major demonstrations and riots also occurred, such as the Manzanar Riot of 1942. The most widespread rebellion came in 1943 after the government required the completion of a questionnaire by internees in order to establish eligibility for some types of leave clearance and to secure recruits for a special Nisei combat unit. Great turmoil, confusion, and resentment were created, especially by the two so-called "loyalty questions." Question 27 asked, "Are you willing to serve in the armed forces of the United States on combat duty, wherever ordered?" And Question 28 asked, "Will you swear unqualified allegiance to the United States of America and faithfully defend the United States from any or all attack by foreign or domestic forces, and forswear any form of allegiance or obedience to the Japanese emperor, or any other foreign government, power or organization?"

Understandably, most Issei felt they could not renounce their allegiance to Japan, where they were citizens, in favor of allegiance to the United States, where they were not allowed to become citizens. And the Nisei did not know if their affirmative responses could be interpreted as a wish to volunteer for military service. Many did not think it fair to be expected to serve in the military at the same time that their citizenship rights—and constitutional rights—were being violated.

Eventually, more than twelve hundred of those who answered yes to the loyalty questions (including Harry in the film) volunteered to serve in the military with thirty thousand other Nisei, many from Hawaii, who were determined to prove their loyalty to the United States. In combat Nisei units distinguished themselves; for example, the 442nd Regimental Combat Team, an all-Nisei unit, was the most highly decorated of the war and suffered the highest percentage of casualties and deaths. President Harry Truman welcomed the Nisei of the 442nd home with the words, "You fought for the free nations of the world...you fought not only the enemy, you fought prejudice—and you won" (Tanaka 1982, 171). Other Nisei served in military intelligence as translators, interpreters, and interrogators, also demonstrating exceptional capability and loyalty. General Charles Willoughby, chief of intelligence in the Pacific, estimated that Nisei military contributions considerably shortened the war.

Many of those who answered no, including Charlie in the film, were sent to the Tule Lake Segregation Center in northern California. These so-called "No-No Boys" and other "disloyals," many of whom requested repatriation to Japan or renounced their American citizenship (twelve thousand disloyals in total), were subjected to especially repressive conditions at Tule Lake.

After the war, those freed from the camps struggled to rebuild their lives. Some stayed in their new locations, but most returned to their former communities, where the Issei in particular found it difficult to reestablish themselves, having lost their homes, property, jobs, and businesses. Overall, however, postwar Japanese Americans have shown unusual determination and resourcefulness in recovering from their tragedy and reestablishing themselves in American society.

In hindsight it seems important to note that the fears that led to such a dark chapter in American history were not borne out in fact, for not a single Japanese American resident or citizen was ever indicted for wartime espionage or sabotage.

How much of this history is new to you? Reflect on what you have read and describe your initial reactions in your film notebook. If you are Japanese or Japanese American, you may wish to recount personal stories you have heard about the internment.

Map Exercise: Study the map below and compare the locations of the assembly centers with those of the relocation centers. Why do you think these places were chosen and what do they seem to have in common? Discuss with your classmates.

Internment Camps

● ASSEMBLY CENTERS

Puyallup, Wash.
Portland, Ore.
Marysville, Calif.
Sacramento, Calif.
Tanforan, Calif.
Stockton, Calif.
Turlock, Calif.
Merced, Calif.
Pinedale, Calif.
Salinas, Calif.
Fresno, Calif.
Tulare, Calif.
Manzanar, Calif.
Santa Anita, Calif.
Pomona, Calif.
Mayer, Ariz.

◇ RELOCATION CENTERS

Manzanar, Calif.
Tule Lake, Calif.
Poston, Ariz.
Gila, Ariz.
Minidoka, Ida.
Heart Mountain, Wyo.
Granada, Colo.
Topaz, Utah
Rohwer, Ark.
Jerome, Ark.

map by Steven Shoffner

Lights Out: Viewing the Film

 Set in the Little Tokyo section of Los Angeles in the 1930s and 1940s, *Come See the Paradise* (1991) deals with a period of American history that until recently had been given little attention: the illegal internment of Japanese Americans in prison camps during World War II. British director and screenplay author Alan Parker, who had previously addressed another controversial racial subject in his widely known film *Mississippi Burning*, brings his story to life by focusing on one family, the Kawamuras. The immigrant parents and their six children cope with both the political events of their time and the personal turmoil caused by the appearance on the scene of daughter Lily's determined white suitor, Jack McGurn. Lily's father, Mr. Kawamura, initially treats Jack with disdain and is unable to accept him into the family.

In addition to the Japanese American theme, Parker takes a hard look at a different type of discrimination: the oppression of the working class. As a labor union organizer, Jack McGurn struggles to achieve gains in employment conditions and to enhance the status of powerless blue-collar workers in the harsh post-Depression years.

The fine cast of Asian American actors includes Tamlyn Tomita as Lily, Sab Shimono as Mr. Kawamura, and Stan Egi as Charlie.

Major Characters in the Film

Lily Kawamura   Nisei woman and seamstress

Jack McGurn   Irish American labor union organizer and projectionist

Mini   Daughter of Lily and Jack

Mr. Hiroshi Kawamura   Lily's father

Mrs. Kawamura   Lily's mother

Charlie, Harry, Dulcie, Joyce, Frankie   Lily's siblings

Gerry McGurn   Jack's brother

Marge McGurn   Jack's sister-in-law

Mr. Fujioka   Lily's Japanese suitor

Mr. Ogata   Film projectionist

Spotlight on Culture and Communication

This spotlight addresses the process of assimilation among immigrants to the United States, as experienced in the film by three generations of the Japanese American Kawamura family.

After reviewing the concept in Why American Cultures? (pages 1–4) and Essential Vocabulary on Cultures (page 9), work in small groups to choose a character from this family whom you find interesting. Examine the assimilation issues of this character as an Issei, Nisei, or Sansei, considering the following points:

- To what extent is the character Japanese, and to what extent is he or she American in behavior and attitudes?
- What internal and external barriers exist to the character's assimilation, including reasons why he or she might consciously choose not to assimilate?
- What might this character lose if he or she is able to totally assimilate? In other words, what is the price of total assimilation?
- How are the character's relationships with others affected by the degree to which that character has assimilated?

Select a film clip that demonstrates an important point related to your character's assimilation, and be prepared to show and explain it. As usual, look for nonverbal behavior and film techniques in your clip.

Poetry: Best Friends Separated

Read the following poem by Dwight Okita, a Japanese American whose mother was interned shortly after the outbreak of World War II.

In Response to Executive Order 9066: All Americans of Japanese Descent Must Report to Relocation Centers

Dear Sirs:

Of course I'll come. I've packed my galoshes
and three packets of tomato seeds. Janet calls them
"love apples." My father says where we're going
they won't grow.

I am a fourteen-year-old girl with bad spelling
and a messy room. If it helps any, I will tell you
I have always felt funny using chopsticks
and my favorite food is hot dogs.
My best friend is a white girl named Denise—
we look at boys together. She sat in front of me
all through grade school because of our names:
O'Connor, Ozawa. I know the back of Denise's head very well.
I tell her she's going bald. She tells me I copy on tests.
We are best friends.

I saw Denise today in Geography class.
She was sitting on the other side of the room.
"You're trying to start a war," she said, "giving secrets away
to the Enemy. Why can't you keep your big mouth shut?"
I didn't know what to say.
I gave her a packet of tomato seeds
and asked her to plant them for me, told her
when the first tomato ripened
she'd miss me.

- How do the title and salutation of the poem contrast with what follows?
- Imagine Denise could write a letter to her Japanese friend several months (or several years) later. Write the letter. Or imagine the Japanese girl writes a letter to Denise either from the internment camp or after returning home.

How to Tell Your Friends From the Japs

© 1941

There is no infallible way of telling [Chinese and Japanese people] apart, because the same racial strains are mixed in both. Even an anthropologist, with calipers and plenty of time to measure heads, noses, shoulders, hips, is sometimes stumped. A few rules of thumb—not always reliable:

- Some Chinese are tall (average: 5 ft. 5 in.). Virtually all Japanese are short (average: 5 ft. 2 1/2 in.).

- Japanese are likely to be stockier and broader-hipped than short Chinese.

- Japanese—except for wrestlers—are seldom fat; they often dry up and grow lean as they age. The Chinese often put on weight, particularly if they are prosperous (in China, with its frequent famines, being fat is esteemed as a sign of being a solid citizen).

- Chinese, not as hairy as Japanese, seldom grow an impressive mustache.

- Most Chinese avoid horn-rimmed spectacles.

- Although both have the typical epicanthic fold of the upper eyelid (which makes them look almond-eyed), Japanese eyes are usually set closer together.

- Those who know them best often rely on facial expression to tell them apart: the Chinese expression is likely to be more placid, kindly, open; the Japanese more positive, dogmatic, arrogant.

In Washington, last week, Correspondent Joseph Chiang made things much easier by pinning on his lapel a large badge reading "Chinese Reporter—NOT Japanese—Please."

- Some aristocratic Japanese have thin, aquiline noses, narrow faces and, except for their eyes, look like Caucasians.

- Japanese are hesitant, nervous in conversation, laugh loudly at the wrong time.

- Japanese walk stiffly erect, hard-heeled. Chinese, more relaxed, have an easy gait, sometimes shuffle. ■

Racism in the Media

On December 22, 1941, two weeks after the bombing of Pearl Harbor, *Time* magazine published the above article. Read it and examine the methods used to bias the reader against the Japanese.

Interestingly, *Time* decided to make known its regret at having published the 1941 article much later, in its "75th Anniversary Issue" dated March 9, 1998.

Regrets, We Have a Few

As with most publications, *Time*'s approach to questions of ethnicity and gender wasn't always what it should have been.

There is no infallible way of telling [Chinese and Japanese people] apart. Even an anthropologist, with calipers and plenty of time to measure heads, noses, shoulders, hips, is sometimes stumped. A few rules of thumb—not always reliable... Japanese—except for wrestlers—are seldom fat; they often dry up and grow lean as they age. The Chinese often put on weight. The Chinese expression is likely to be more placid, kindly, open; the Japanese more positive, dogmatic, arrogant. Japanese walk stiffly erect, hardheeled. Chinese, more relaxed, have an easy gait, sometimes shuffle.

- How do you react to this form of an apology? Is it praiseworthy? Appropriate? Necessary? Sufficient?
- If you were the editor-in-chief of the magazine, would you have approved this apology? Why or why not? If not, try to describe or write a better alternative.

Where Are We Now? Further Thoughts on Apologies and Reparations

How does a nation makes amends for injustices of the type perpetrated against the Japanese Americans during World War II? After a long period of silence about the shameful events, the U.S. government created the Commission on Wartime Relocation and Internment of Civilians (CWRIC) in 1981 to determine whether wrongs had been committed as a result of Executive Order 9066 and to recommend "appropriate remedies."

The Commission's report, *Personal Justice Denied*, issued after testimony was heard from more than 750 witnesses, condemned the wartime treatment as a "grave personal injustice" done to Americans of Japanese ancestry. According to the report, Executive Order 9066 and the ensuing actions were not justifiable on military grounds but were driven by "race prejudice, war hysteria and a failure of political leadership" (1983, 5). In 1983, the Commission recommended that Congress allocate $1.5 billion to provide personal redress to former internees.

After much debate and controversy, the enactment of the American Civil Liberties Act in 1988 offered the Japanese Americans an apology and provided a payment of twenty thousand dollars for each of the approximately sixty thousand survivors of the internment, to be paid over ten years, beginning in 1990. This act also provided for the establishment of the Civil Liberties Public Education Fund, which received an appropriation of five million dollars to embark in 1997 on grant projects designed to promote education and research related to the exclusion and detention of Japanese Americans during World War II.

A further development in the attempt to recognize the wrongs committed was the establishment of Manzanar as a state and national historical landmark (1985) and a national historic site (1992). The preservation of this site was due largely to lobbying by Japanese Americans, who began making annual pilgrimages to the site in 1969. Today Manzanar serves as a vivid reminder of the past and as a center for historical interpretation.

Some cities and towns have also erected monuments and memorials to the Japanese internment, as depicted in the photographs shown below and on the following page of the Japanese American Historical Plaza in Portland, Oregon.

Rounded up

In the sweltering yard.

Unable to endure any longer

Standing in line

Some collapse.

Think about the issue of making reparations and correcting historical wrongs. In *Personal Justice Denied,* the Commission recognizes that "history cannot be undone" but states that "nations that forget or ignore injustices are more likely to repeat them" (1983, 8).

- How do you feel about attempts to make amends as described in the above reading? Is it ever too late to offer apologies and/or try to make reparations?
- What is the importance of sites and memorials of remembrance or apology such as Manzanar and the historical plaza in Portland, Oregon? Are you aware of any such sites (not only Japanese American) in this country or abroad? If you have visited them, what were your reactions?

Zoom Lens: Choosing Your Own Topic of Interest

Hands-on Activities

1. Conduct an informal survey of fellow students, friends, or relatives to see how much they know about the period of Japanese internment. Be sure to inquire sensitively, especially if you are not Japanese American but your interviewees are.
2. Contact social studies teachers in local high schools to find out whether and how the Japanese internment is taught. Review this period in history in some high school textbooks to see how the topic is addressed.
3. If you live nearby, arrange a visit to Manzanar or contact the Manzanar National Historic Site for information on its philosophy and projects.

Research Papers or Oral Reports

1. Choose one of the following topics for a research paper or oral report.
   a. The "No-No Boys" (consult Okada's book listed in the Sequel)

b. The military achievements of Nisei units in World War II
c. The situation in Hawaii during the war for those of Japanese ancestry
d. Anti-Japanese groups such as the Native Sons of the Golden West
e. The Alien Land Laws
f. The activities of labor unions during the post-Depression years
g. "Picture brides"

2. Read *Farewell to Manzanar*, an insider's view of life in a prison camp, written by Jeanne Wakatsuki Houston and James D. Houston. Compare the book to the film, especially from the point of view of historical accuracy.

3. Study some of the paintings and drawings, photographs, or poems that focus on the internment (consult books by Armor, Gesenway and Roseman, Inada, and Okihiro, listed in the Sequel). Report on your findings.

Using Your Imagination

1. Imagine that you are one of the characters in the movie and write as suggested:
    a. Mini, in her thirties, writing a reflective piece on her mother's and father's experiences
    b. Charlie, writing a letter to his mother, sisters, and younger brother from Japan after the war
    c. Mr. Kawamura, shortly before his death, writing a letter to Jack
    d. Another character of your choice

2. Assume the persona of a Japanese American at the time of the internment. First tell who you are and then explain how you would have answered the loyalty questions, giving your reasons.

3. Imagine that within a single week you had to get rid of all of your belongings except what you could carry. What would you keep? How would you dispose of the rest? How would you feel?

4. If the United States were to be at war with the country of your ancestry or nationality, where do you think your own loyalties would be, and why?

Sequel: Further Suggested Resources

Readings

Armor, John, and Peter Wright. 1988. *Manzanar=Ringoen*. Commentary by John Hersey and photographs by Ansel Adams. New York: Times Books.

Asian Women United of California, eds. 1989. *Making Waves: An Anthology of Writings by and about Asian American Women*. Boston: Beacon Press.

Bruchac, Joseph, ed. 1983. *Breaking Silence: An Anthology of Contemporary Asian American Poets*. Greenfield Center, NY: Greenfield Review Press.

Chan, Jeffrey Paul, Frank Chin, Shawn Wong, and Lawson F. Inada, eds. 1991. *The Big Aiiieeeee!: An Anthology of Chinese American and Japanese American Literature*. New York: Penguin Books.

Commission on Wartime Relocation and Internment of Civilians. 1983. *Personal Justice Denied Part II: Recommendations*. Washington, DC: U.S. Government Printing Office.

———. 1982. *Personal Justice Denied Part I*. Washington, DC: U.S. Government Printing Office.

Daniels, Roger. 1971. *Concentration Camps USA: Japanese Americans and World War II*. New York: Holt, Rinehart and Winston.

Gesenway, Deborah, and Mindy Roseman. 1987. *Beyond Words: Images from America's Concentration Camps*. Ithaca, NY: Cornell University Press.

Hagedorn, Jessica, ed. 1993. *Charlie Chan Is Dead: An Anthology of Contemporary Asian American Fiction*. New York: Penguin Books.

Houston, Jeanne Wakatsuki, and James D. Houston. 1973. *Farewell to Manzanar*. New York: Bantam.

Inada, Lawson Fusao. 1992. *Legends from Camp: Poems by Lawson Fusao Inada*. Minneapolis: Coffee House Press.

Levine, Ellen. 1995. *A Fence Away from Freedom: Japanese Americans and World War II*. New York: G. P. Putnam.

Okada, John. 1990. *No-No Boy*. Seattle: University of Washington Press.

Okihiro, Gary Y. 1996. *Whispered Silences: Japanese Americans and World War II*. Seattle: University of Washington Press.

Takaki, Ronald. 1994. *Issei and Nisei: The Settling of Japanese America*. New York: Chelsea House.

———. 1993. *A Different Mirror: A History of Multicultural America*. Boston: Little, Brown.

———. 1989. *Strangers from a Different Shore: A History of Asian Americans*. Boston: Little, Brown.

Tanaka, Chester. 1982. *Go For Broke: A Pictorial History of the Japanese American 100th Infantry Battalion and the 442nd Regimental Combat Team*. Richmond, CA: JACP.

Weglyn, Michi Nishiura. 1996. *Years of Infamy: The Untold Story of America's Concentration Camps*. Seattle: University of Washington Press.

Films

The Color of Honor (1988)   Vivid documentary looks at the exceptional contributions of Japanese American men who served in the military during World War II, in both combat and intelligence. Also tells the story of those who chose to resist military service. Directed by Loni Ding (NAATA).

Family Gathering (1988)   Chronicles the effect of the Japanese American internment on one family, as captured by director Lise Yasui, granddaughter of interned community leader Masuo Yasui (NAATA).

Picture Bride (1994)   Emotional tale of a young Japanese woman who leaves home in the early 1900s to find a better life by marrying an unknown man in Hawaii. Directed by Kayo Hatta.

Sayonara (1957)   Classic film set in postwar Japan during the period of American occupation. Deals with a forbidden love affair between an American pilot (Marlon Brando) and a beautiful Japanese entertainer. Directed by Joshua Logan.

Slaying the Dragon (1988)   Thought-provoking documentary exposes stereotypes of Asian women by using clips from television and films and by interviewing Asian American actresses. Directed by Deborah Gee (NAATA).

Snow Falling on Cedars (1999)   Set in 1954 on San Piedro Island in the Pacific Northwest, the film deals with events surrounding the suspicious drowning death of a German American fisherman. With postwar anti-Japanese sentiment still running high, a Japanese American fisherman is charged with the murder. Based on the novel by David Guterson and directed by Scott Hicks.

Unfinished Business (1986)   Award-winning film tells the stories of three Japanese Americans—Fred Korematsu, Gordon Hirabayashi, and Minoru Yasui—who challenged the constitutionality of Executive Order 9066. Directed by Steven Okazaki (NAATA).

Websites and Mailing Addresses

Japanese American National Museum (www.janm.org)

Manzanar National Historic Site, PO Box 426, Independence, CA 93526; phone: 760-878-2932; fax: 760-878-2949 (www.nps.gov/manz)

National Clearinghouse for U.S.-Japan Studies (www.indiana.edu~ japan)

National Japanese American Historical Society (NJAHS) (www.nikkeiheritage.org)

Oregon Nikkei Legacy Center, 117 NW 2nd Avenue, Portland, OR 97209; phone: 503-224-1458; fax: 503-224-1459

6

Mexican American Culture:
Lone Star

Setting the Scene: Freewriting and Discussion

Study the following two cartoons and write your interpretation and reactions.

"La Cucaracha," by Lalo Alcaraz from POCHO Magazine, 1993.

Wide-Angle Lens: Historical and Geographical Perspectives

Mexicans as Early Americans

"Some of the oldest and the newest Americans are from Mexico" (1981, 244). This statement by Thomas Sowell, author of *Ethnic America*, may seem simple, but it illuminates the source of the deep-seated ethnic conflict in the fictitious Texas border town of Frontera depicted in the film *Lone Star*.

While it is common knowledge in this country that the American Indians were here first and that the British were among the original colonizers, the early presence of the Mexicans is rarely understood and infrequently acknowledged. To appreciate this history we must go back to the early 1500s, when the first Spanish conquistadores landed in the New World. They eventually claimed for Spain one of the largest empires in world history, including most of present-day Central and South America and the American Southwest. By the time the British established their first permanent colony in Jamestown in 1607, the Spanish had been maintaining a strong presence in the hemisphere for almost a century.

Spanish rule over the area that is now Mexico began with Hernan Cortes' landing on the Mexican coast in 1519. At that time many different groups of indigenous Indian peoples lived in the region, including members of the highly advanced civilizations of the Aztecs and Mayans. Cortes was at first received by the Aztec emperor Moctezuma as the god Quetzalcoatl, whose return at this time in history had been prophesied in Aztec religion. Taking advantage of the misplaced reverence shown by the Aztecs, Cortes was able to conquer their large and powerful empire within only two years.

Cortes' expedition and those of other Spaniards established a pattern of conquest and settlement vastly different from that followed by the British on the North Atlantic seaboard. Because the Spanish came in smaller numbers and mostly without women, a population of mixed offspring of Spanish and Indian blood, called *mestizos*, began to flourish. The mestizos eventually outnumbered not only the peninsular Spaniards (those born in Spain) but even the indigenous Indians. While today relatively few North Americans are of dual European and Indian heritage, most Mexicans are mestizos. African strains are also present in Mexican heritage as a result of the colonists' importation into this territory of as many as two hundred thousand black slaves.

Missionaries, explorers, and settlers from Mexico gradually began to move northward, conquering local Indians and expanding the colony of New Spain into present-day California, Texas, New Mexico, and beyond. The Spanish government devised an ingenious dual approach to conquest, establishing both missions to convert the natives to Catholicism and *presidios*, or forts, to control them militarily. Indians brought to live in the missions were virtual slaves, denied freedom of movement, stripped of their culture and religion, and compelled to perform agricultural and other labor.

Mexican Independence from Spain and Loss of Territory to the United States

After enduring three centuries as a Spanish colony, Mexico won an eleven-year war for independence (1810–1821).* During this conflict the northernmost region of New Spain (in today's American Southwest) was left much to its own devices. In the territory that is now Texas, for example, the Spanish-Mexican population felt distanced physically and psychologically from its own government in Mexico City and was drawn into interactions with Anglo-American explorers and traders. Initially, the new Mexican government even encouraged Anglo immigration to the sparsely settled region, primarily to fuel the economy and to help provide a buffer against the Comanche Indians. The first American *empresario* (land agent) was Stephen F. Austin, who in 1823 received a territory of eighteen thousand square miles in exchange for agreeing that he and his colonists would adopt the Catholic religion and Mexican citizenship.

But these promises were not fulfilled by Austin's colonists or by most of the others who subsequently received large tracts of land from the Mexican government. And before long the area was filling up with Americans, including many cotton farmers who brought slaves into the region in violation of Mexico's prohibition against slavery. Consequently, the Mexican government stopped promoting Anglo settlement, but its efforts to inhibit further immigration and to hinder trade met with little success.

---

*Although the terms *Mexico* and *Mexicans* are often used to refer to the territory and people of the region prior to the war, historically speaking the terms are only accurate when referring to the period after independence was gained in 1821.

The uprising that changed the history of the Southwest took place in Texas, where by 1830 more than twenty thousand Anglos significantly outnumbered the Mexican population. Upset at attempts by the Mexican government to exert control, a volunteer army of both Anglo and Mexican Texans staged the Texas Revolt in 1835, seizing garrisons and capturing San Antonio, the most important city in Texas. Believing the struggle to be over, the rebel army was caught off guard on March 6, 1836, when Mexican president and general Antonio López de Santa Anna attacked the Alamo, a fortified mission near San Antonio. Greatly outnumbered, all 187 defenders were killed, including well-known Anglos Jim Bowie and Davy Crockett. Enraged by the loss of the Alamo, Sam Houston's volunteer army attacked and defeated Santa Anna's troops at the San Jacinto River on April 26, claiming independence for Texas with the famous cry of "Remember the Alamo."

The freestanding Lone Star state of Texas, now unattached to a country, immediately requested annexation to the United States. It was not admitted to the Union until 1845, however, the delay resulting primarily because of Northerners' reluctance to admit a slave state to the union and thus destroy the balance of thirteen slave and thirteen free states. The Mexican government, which had never accepted the independence of Texas, now viewed its annexation by the U.S. as an insult to Mexico's national honor.

Tensions between the two countries were exacerbated by newly elected President James Polk, a firm believer in the concept of Manifest Destiny (see page 21), who unsuccessfully pressured Mexico to sell lands in what are now New Mexico and California to the United States. In 1846 Polk called on Congress to declare war on Mexico. The hard-fought two-year Mexican American War (1846–1848) did not end until General Winfield Scott's army penetrated deep into Mexican territory, ultimately taking the capital, Mexico City, and raising the U.S. flag over Mexico's National Palace. The ensuing Treaty of Guadalupe Hidalgo (1848) established the Rio Grande as the new boundary between the countries and determined that California, New Mexico, Arizona, Nevada, Utah, and parts of Colorado, Kansas, Wyoming, and Oklahoma be incorporated into the U.S., representing a loss to Mexico of *nearly half* of its territory. (The final acquisition, a strip of land south of the Gila River measuring thirty thousand square miles, was obtained in the Gadsden Purchase of 1853.)

In Texas the approximately eighty thousand *tejanos* (Texan residents of Mexican descent) were given the choice by the U.S. government of leaving for Mexico or becoming U.S. citizens. About 80 percent stayed in the state, where they constituted a minority population with deep ties to the land. The postwar period was marked by the Anglos' widespread and often flagrant violations of tejanos' rightful claims to their property. The tejanos were gradually dispossessed of their land and deprived of their civil rights. Like the American Indians, they became a conquered people in their own land. (Not to be forgotten is the fact that throughout the struggle for the Southwest between the United States and Mexico, the rights of the original inhabitants, including Apache, Comanche, and other Indians, were ignored by both sides.)

Migrant Labor

At the present time the proud heritage of Mexican Americans as descendants of some of the "oldest Americans" is overshadowed by the issues surrounding the numerous Mexicans who are crossing the border every day, fleeing poverty and seeking work. Even the most cursory study of U.S. policy and practice concerning Mexican immigration in the twentieth century reveals that whenever Mexicans were needed as cheap labor, they were either allowed in legally or simply permitted to work illegally. And whenever they became superfluous, they were expelled.

In the early part of the twentieth century, when the two-thousand-mile-long border was virtually unpatrolled, American employers actively recruited Mexican laborers to work on the railroads and in the agricultural fields. These Mexicans were generally welcomed, especially since restrictive legislation such as the Chinese Exclusion Act (see page 90) had virtually stopped the influx of workers from Asia. Encouraged by these circumstances, approximately one million Mexicans immigrated between 1900 and 1930, bringing the total Mexican American population to three million.

From the beginning these immigrants established or were confined in provisional, often seasonal settlements, living separately from the rest of American society. This isolation contributed to their becoming an invisible minority, stereotyped as agricultural laborers. Their work was long and hard, their pay minimal, and their living conditions deplorable; still, Mexicans could earn considerably more in American fields and orchards than they could at home. They were able to send money to their families in Mexico and to dramatically improve their own standard of living if they themselves returned there.

The warm welcome extended to these immigrants turned cold during the Great Depression of the 1930s. Suddenly Mexicans were seen as taking jobs from needy Americans such as the poverty-stricken people from the Oklahoma dust bowl who left their homes for the Southwest in search of jobs. By 1940 nearly half a million people of

Mexican descent, some of whom were U.S. citizens, had been deported or pressured into leaving.

The pattern of exploitation repeated itself when World War II labor shortages brought a renewed demand for agricultural laborers. A federally organized project called the *bracero* program ("arm" in Spanish, meaning "hired hand" in this context) was set up in 1942 by the American and Mexican governments to allow certain numbers of seasonal workers to enter the United States legally. In reality the bracero program brought little improvement to Mexicans who continued to work under much the same desperate conditions, albeit legally.

Nor did the program serve to halt illegal immigration, which continued in massive proportions. Mercedes' crossing of the Rio Grande in the film is an example of what was occurring at the time. Like Mercedes, people could simply wade or swim across the shallow river (hence the term *wetbacks* from the Spanish *mojados,* or "wet ones") and then blend easily into Mexican communities on the U.S. side. To curb the influx, the U.S. government implemented another extensive deportation program, called Operation Wetback, in 1954. Once again illegal resident workers were treated badly, and the civil rights of many Mexican American citizens were violated.

Demand for Civil Rights

Resistance to this type of oppression and humiliation and to miserable working conditions became central issues in the Chicano movement (*el movimiento*) of the 1960s. The use of the name "Chicano" differentiated this more activist, militant group from other Mexican Americans. As James Banks makes clear in his book *Teaching Strategies for Ethnic Studies,* this protest movement did not suddenly spring into existence in the 1960s. To understand it more fully, he explains, "we must view it as an important link in the long range of resistance activities in which Chicanos have been involved since 1848" (1997, 348). Inspired by the civil rights movement of the decade, Chicanos developed a broad agenda of goals toward securing their rightful place in American society.

Of the many prominent Chicano leaders, the most well known was César Chávez, a modest yet charismatic figure who rose from the poverty of migrant labor to found the nation's first successful union of farm workers in 1965. Using nonviolent tactics such as boycotts, strikes, and fasts, Chávez captured the attention of the media and involved Americans nationwide in the struggles of the laborers he represented. His 1968 campaign against California's San Joaquin Valley

Related Terms

brown people   Can be considered offensive but can also be used neutrally. "Brown power" was a slogan popularized during the civil rights movement. Today social scientists use the term "the browning of America" to indicate that people of color may outnumber whites by midcentury.

Chicano/Chicana   Terms used by Mexican American activists in the late 1960s as a label of pride and rebellion. The word itself probably derives from the Spanish *mexicano* (Mexican), in which the *x* is pronounced as *sh* in some regional dialects. Today it is accepted by some as a generic term for Latinos but is scorned by others who regard it as pejorative and militant.

gringo/a   Term used originally by Mexicans (but now becoming more common throughout Latin America) to refer to white people, especially those who speak English. Often derogatory.

Hispanic   Considered a term of respect by some Latinos but rejected by others because it recalls the colonization by Spain, ignoring Indian and African roots of many people; also omits Portuguese and Brazilian Americans. Many Hispanics/Latinos prefer to be called by their country of origin (Cubans or Cuban Americans, Dominicans or Dominican Americans, Puerto Ricans, etc.).

La Raza   Literally meaning "the race." The term is used to refer to Latinos, but in more a cultural than a racial sense.

Latino/Latina   Terms preferred to *Hispanic* by many of Latin American descent to describe Americans who trace their roots to approximately twenty-four different countries in Central and South America and the Caribbean. The term refers to cultural background, not to race, as Latinos (males) and Latinas (females) can be white, black, brown, of Asian descent, or mestizo.

spic, greaser, wetback   Derogatory terms for Latin Americans, particularly those from Mexico.

undocumented workers   Refers to Mexicans and others who are employed in this country but have not obtained the necessary legal documents from the Immigration and Naturalization Service; preferred to the widely used term *illegal aliens*.

grape growers, who opposed union contracts, proved an enormous success when millions of Americans stopped buying grapes in their local supermarkets. Even though much that Chávez fought for was not achieved, his union, the United Farm Workers of America, helped to improve the lot of impoverished agricultural laborers who previously had no employment benefits, seniority rights, or grievance procedures.

The Chicano movement and its aftermath have contributed significantly to the improved situation of many Mexican Americans in the United States today. A growing number are now successfully employed in a wide range of occupations. Although Mexican Americans still reside predominantly in the Southwest, others have settled throughout the country and have become increasingly urbanized. Many are assuming local and national leadership positions in business, government, and education. Their contributions to American culture in areas such as cuisine, language, the arts, and architecture are becoming increasingly apparent and appreciated.

But these gains cannot erase the fact that grave and persistent problems remain. The plight of migrant agricultural laborers nags at the nation's conscience, though not sufficiently to stimulate legislation or another remedy. In 1960 CBS news correspondent Edward R. Murrow produced a landmark documentary, *Harvest of Shame*, which exposed the injustices faced by migrant workers. Thirty years later, in a follow-up documentary entitled *New Harvest, Old Shame*, CBS showed that little had changed.

The border also continues to be a source of constant conflict and dispute. Mexican author Carlos Fuentes tells us that some who cross the border say it "is not really a border but a scar" (1992, 342). Chicana writer Gloria Anzaldúa echoes these sentiments when she calls the area *una herida abierta*, "an open wound." The U.S. government's position is, in fact, precarious. Although it does not want to lose control of illegal immigration, neither does it want to spend too much money or appear too heavy-handed. And as mentioned before, the economy is dependent on the presence of these workers. New, often elaborate measures to slow the influx are constantly being proposed, devised, and revised. The primary tool is legislation, such as the Immigration Reform and Control Act of 1986, which imposes penalties on employers who knowingly hire illegal workers. Measures taken along the border include helicopters, motion-sensor systems, and night-vision devices. Recently a type of high-tech visa with digital fingerprints was introduced.

And, of course, there are walls. Currently, fences and walls run across sixty miles of the border at the most heavily trafficked spots. Many Mexicans and some Americans strenuously oppose having this type of physical barrier in the post-Berlin Wall era. The presence of walls is also seen as inconsistent with NAFTA, the North American Free Trade Agreement. Other Americans, including former presidential candidate Pat Buchanan, believe the wall should be extended across the entire border.

Meanwhile, illegal crossings such as those shown in the film continue unabated at rates that are estimated at three hundred thousand per year. Because of the fences and patrols, attempts have become more dangerous, and uncounted numbers of Mexicans are dying, often anonymously, from drowning or exposure. The millions of so-called "undocumented workers" who successfully cross the border find themselves caught in a painful trap. The unofficial policy of their employers, and to some extent of the U.S. government, is to rely on them as a source of cheap, unskilled labor. Officially, though, they are here illegally, possessing few rights and living in constant fear of being caught by immigration officials—*la migra*. In *Lone Star* we see such workers in the kitchen of Mercedes' cafe.

Heated debates over immigration policy, border policy, and related controversial topics continue, both regionally and nationally. Should bilingual education be expanded or terminated? What is the proper place of Chicano studies in universities? Should the public support the English Only movement, which could prohibit languages other than English from being used in hospitals, public schools, and elsewhere? Should history textbooks be rewritten and taught in a way that reflects the Mexican American experience more accurately? Should we support legislation aimed at denying benefits such as schooling and nonemergency medical care to undocumented workers and their families?

These policy controversies are fueled by persisting stereotypes and prejudice, causing many Mexican Americans to feel they are treated as second-class citizens. Interestingly, discrimination exists even within the Mexican American community: some "old," more established residents show bias toward lower-class newcomers.

Currently, Mexican Americans are the third largest ethnic group in the nation after whites and African Americans. They also represent well more than half of all Latinos in this country; Puerto Ricans and Cuban Americans are the next largest groups, together representing somewhat more than 20 percent of the Latino population. As the numbers of Mexican Americans and other Latinos continue to grow, it is in everyone's interest to find new and creative solutions to problems whose roots are older than the nation itself.

Map Exercise: Write in your film notebook a chronology of historical events to explain the boundary changes depicted on the three maps below. Then create a title to link all three maps thematically.

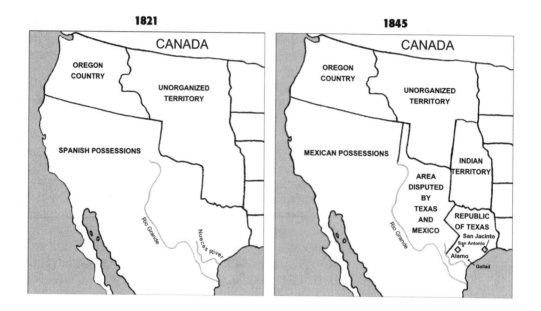

maps by Steven Shoffner

Lights Out: Viewing the Film

 The backdrop for *Lone Star* (1996), directed by John Sayles, is the fictitious border town of Frontera, through which the Rio Grande flows. In Frontera nineteen out of every twenty inhabitants are Mexican, yet their lives are controlled by the wealthy, powerful, property-owning Anglos. The plot revolves around three generations of the town's sheriffs: Charlie Wade, an incorrigible racist (played by Kris Kristofferson) who disappeared suddenly; Buddy Deeds, his much-liked successor, now deceased; and Sam Deeds, Buddy's son and the current sheriff. A murder mystery begins when a skull and a sheriff's badge are found on an old rifle range. Sam Deeds believes that the skull is that of Charlie Wade and suspects his father, Buddy, of Wade's murder. As Sam investigates the case, the story of racial and political entanglements in Frontera's history is revealed, and Sam discovers startling information about his own past.

Sayles achieves authenticity by shooting the movie on location in Eagles Pass, Texas, and its sister town, Piedras Negras, Mexico, and also by selecting well-respected Latino actors. Especially notable among these are Miriam Colon (Mercedes), who was founder of the Puerto Rican Traveling Theatre in New York, and Elizabeth Peña (Pilar), who comes from a Cuban family of actors, writers, and directors. Accomplished African American actors Ron Canada and Joe Morton play the roles of Otis and Delmore Payne, and professional dancer Carmen de Lavallade plays Otis' wife.

Major Characters in the Film

Cliff and **Mickey**   Two officers from Fort McKenzie

Charlie Wade   Deceased former sheriff of Frontera

Buddy Deeds   Wade's successor

Sam Deeds   Buddy's son and current sheriff

Pilar Cruz   Widowed schoolteacher and Sam's high school girlfriend

Mercedes Cruz   Pilar's mother and Mexican American restaurateur

Eladio Cruz   Mercedes' murdered husband

Otis Payne   African American bar owner

Delmore Payne   Colonel at Fort McKenzie and Otis' estranged son

Chet Payne   Delmore's teenage son

Hollis   Charlie Wade's former deputy and mayor of Frontera

Mrs. Roderick Bledsoe   Elderly African American widow of Roderick Bledsoe, who formerly owned the bar now operated by Otis Payne

Private Johnson   Young, female African American army recruit

With its many subplots and flashbacks, the story presented in *Lone Star* is quite intricate. Answer the questions below to piece together the elements of the story. (This may be most effectively done working in pairs or in small groups.)

The Wade Case

1. Why does Sam interview Mrs. Roderick Bledsoe?
2. Why does Sam continue to question Hollis about the murder?
3. What further clues do Cliff and Mickey provide in solving the murder?
4. What wrong assumption does Sam make about the murder?

The People of Frontera

1. What is the cause of friction between the parents and teachers?
2. What are the views of the white bartender on the future of Frontera?
3. What are some of the political forces behind the proposal for building a new jail?
4. What is Mercedes' role and image in Frontera?
5. Why are some Frontera people upset with Buddy Deeds?

The Buddy Deeds Legend

1. What disagreement did Buddy Deeds and Charlie Wade have shortly before Wade's death?
2. How does Otis Payne praise Buddy Deeds?
3. How did Buddy Deeds use his position as sheriff to his own advantage?
4. How do the Anglos honor Deeds?

The Cruz Family

1. What is Pilar's job?
2. What trouble is Pilar's son Armando in?
3. What source of friction exists between Pilar and Mercedes?
4. What demand does Mercedes make on her employees?
5. What is Mercedes' attitude toward "wetbacks"?
6. What happened to Eladio Cruz?

The Paynes

1. Why is Colonel Delmore Payne in Frontera?
2. How does Chet Payne first meet his grandfather?
3. What is Otis' nickname, and why?
4. What causes the cold relationship between Otis and Delmore?
5. Which of Otis' actions surprises Delmore?

Sam and Pilar

1. Under what circumstances do Sam and Pilar meet again after several years?
2. How does Sam learn about his father's relationship with Mercedes? What does he find in the garage of his ex-wife's house?
3. What misbelief has Pilar lived with regarding her father's death and his identity?

———————

Answers are located on page 145.

Spotlight on Culture and Communication

John Sayles once described *Lone Star* as a "film about borders." Working in small groups, identify various cultural borders you observe in the film. From your list, select a clip to illustrate the cultural conflicts that define one of these borders.

Bring the clip to class and be prepared to lead a discussion in which you explain the various points of view held by people on either side of the border. You may wish to mention how specific film techniques are used to highlight the cultural differences.

Try to relate your clip to something you may have experienced yourself as you encountered another culture.

Poetry: The Latino Experience

"I Too, America..." was written by Leo Romero, who grew up in New Mexico. Read the poem on the next page and respond in your film notebook to one or more of the following:

- How does the poem compare with what you read in Wide-Angle Lens?
- Select and explain any parts of the poem that remind you of scenes you observed in *Lone Star*.
- Do you perceive any changes of tone in the poem? If so, where do they occur and how does Romero create them?
- Notice any words or lines that really stand out. Copy them into your film notebook and explain why they affected you.
- Study the shape of the poem on the page. Why do you think Romero chose this form?
- Write the line, "I Too, America..." in your film notebook. Step inside Romero's skin and continue writing in poetry or prose. Or write from your own perspective or another besides Romero's.
- Locate Langston Hughes' poem "I, Too," and compare it with this one. Why do you think Romero chose a similar title?

I Too, America . . .

America
blue eyes and blond hair
America from England
Protestant America
pilgrims
Dutch New York
America of George Washington
on every dollar
and Lincoln
on every penny
America of shells
exploding in the air
and in every elementary school
from the Atlantic to the Pacific
children are taught
about Daniel Boone
and Davy Crockett
remember the Alamo
kill the dirty Mexicans
America of North
and South
marching into Santa Fe
in the name
of the United States of America
we are taking away your land
we respect your quaint customs
and picturesque
way of living
but if you oppose us
you will be hung
America of Thoreau
in New England
pleading civil disobedience
while the American army
marches into Mexico City
and children throw themselves
from Aztec pyramids
against the invading Americans
their pulsating hearts
in their hands
the heroes of Mexico
and President Polk
smiling wryly
at a freshly painted map
of an expanded America...

America of United Rubber
Shell and Coca-Cola
America sending Rockefeller
on a goodwill tour of South America
as a representative
of the capitalistic-enterprise system
so that the sandaled peasants
will gawk at him
and want to be Americanos
Viva Americanos
Hell no
Yankee Go Home
Yankee Go Home
Yankee Go Home
and take Coca-Cola with you
and take your blood men with you
who have been bleeding us
like monstrous mosquitoes
who have been like leeches
take them away
or we will handle them our own way
America that imprisons
César Chávez
because of grapes and lettuce
America that wants cheap labor
America of profit
at the expense of others
America who imprisoned Reies Tijerina
for attempting to lawfully
secure wrongly taken lands...
America I too
live on this continent
and in this country
I too am an American
and my eyes are brown and my hair
obsidian black
America from Spain
Catholic America
conquistadores
Sur América
mestizo Méjico
Simón Bolívar los Incas
los Aztecas
Juárez y Villa y Zapata

Spanish—An American Language?

"In English, Enrique. This is the United States. We speak English," says Mercedes Cruz in *Lone Star* as she admonishes one of her employees. A former "wetback" herself, Mercedes disdains her Mexican background and is proud of her proficiency in English. But how true is her claim that in the United States "we speak English"?

Within our national borders more than seventeen million people identify themselves as Spanish speakers, making them the largest linguistic minority group in the country. Indeed, the language is flourishing in the United States, especially in New York (the home of many Puerto Ricans), in Florida (the adopted state of large numbers of Cubans), and in Southern border states, where many Mexican Americans live. A former Spanish-speaking mayor of Miami once said of his city:

> You can be born here in a Cuban hospital, be baptized by a Cuban priest, buy all your food from a Cuban grocer, take your insurance from a Cuban broker, and pay for it all with a check from a Cuban bank. You can get all the news in Spanish—read the Spanish daily paper, watch Spanish TV, listen to Spanish radio. You can go through life without having to speak English at all. (Crawford 1992, 91)

While most Spanish speakers do not "go through life without having to speak English at all," they do have ample opportunities to retain their native language. Throughout the U.S. there are more than eight hundred Spanish-language radio stations. Regular network television programs as well as cable networks such as Univision and Telemundo bring Spanish-language broadcasts into millions of homes. Periodicals such as *Hispanic* and *Latina* and newspapers such as *La Opinion* (in Los Angeles) and *El Nuevo Herald* (in Miami) are widely read. Spanish-language music is hugely popular, and theater companies in many cities present plays in Spanish.

Why does Spanish continue to be used so widely when so many other immigrant languages die out after a few generations? Are Spanish speakers not learning English? Studies demonstrate that they are indeed learning English basically in accordance with acculturation patterns of other immigrants. That is, first-generation immigrants tend to learn English imperfectly, second-generation children are fluent in English while still maintaining some knowledge of Spanish, and third-generation children often lose their grandparents' language altogether.

Despite this loss over the generations, Spanish persists as a vibrant language, mainly because of the proximity of Spanish-speaking countries to the United States. There is first of all an ongoing flow of new immigrants who keep the language alive; and then there is travel back and forth by individuals and their families, especially to Mexico, providing opportunity and incentive to use the language. Other factors such as pride in their language and even resistance to being "taken over" by the more powerful English speakers may play a role. Also not to be forgotten is the fact that the first language of Puerto Rico, a U.S. commonwealth territory, is Spanish.

How are English speakers reacting to such a strong second-language presence within U.S. borders? In a country that has long seen itself as a melting pot, many non-Latinos perceive Spanish as a threat. They are offended that some immigrants do not achieve fluency in English, which they interpret as a lack of respect for, or gratitude to, the adopted country. They resent hearing conversations they do not understand in supermarkets, in the workplace, or on the airwaves. They may fear for the unity of a country that does not have one common language.

Those who wish to ban and restrict the use of languages other than English have joined together in a strong and well-financed movement known as English Only. A primary political goal of English Only is to pass an amendment to the U.S. Constitution making English the "official language" of the country. Currently, the Constitution does not address the subject of language, a silence interpreted by some as the wisdom of our forefathers but by others as a major oversight. Thus far, English Only adherents have been successful in passing official-English legislation in various states, but not at the national level.

If members of English Only have their way, languages other than English could be prohibited on signs, driver's license regulations and tests, radio and television broadcasts, transportation schedules, and voting materials as well as in public schools and hospitals. Taken to an extreme, languages other than English could be banned in workplaces, even among employees having private conversations.

Opponents of Spanish and other languages are also fighting a heated, controversial battle against bilingual education. The theory underlying the bilingual approach is that students receive instruction in their native language while learning English, thus allowing them to learn the content of their schoolwork without the difficulty of having to do so in a foreign language. In the process they become bilingual rather than neglecting or forgetting their first language. Some innovative two-way programs allow native English-speaking students to learn Spanish, Japanese, or another second language while their classmates are learning English.

Bilingual education originated during the civil rights era and finds legal grounding in Title VI of the Civil Rights Act of 1964, which prohibits denial of equal educational opportunity on the basis of race, language, or national origin. The Bilingual Education Act of 1968 and the 1974 Supreme Court decision *Lau v. Nichols* gave further legal backing and monetary support to the concept. Now, however, this legislation has been challenged by voters in states such as California and Arizona who believe bilingual education to be a failure. Even some Latino parents have joined the opposition to bilingual education in the belief that it holds their children back and does not prepare them quickly enough to enter American society (surely this would be Mercedes' view). At present the future of bilingual education nationwide is uncertain and depends very much on initiatives taken in individual states.

Of course not all English-speaking Americans oppose other languages. In fact many have joined together to found English Plus, an organization favoring bilingualism and multilingualism for all Americans. Members of English Plus and many other Americans view languages as a source of enrichment and opportunity. Especially in our increasingly interdependent world, they see the many advantages of fostering rather than suppressing Spanish and other "minority" languages.

While the debates rage in the schools, the media, and the courtrooms, the number of Spanish speakers continues to grow. Already, the Hispanic population in the United States is one of the largest in the world, and soon it is expected to be second only to Mexico. In U.S. schools and universities, Spanish study is growing rapidly in popularity, outpacing all other foreign languages. It seems that the survival of Spanish is not in question; what remains to be seen is whether the language, and what it represents, will be welcomed or rejected by non-Latino Americans.

- If Spanish is your native language, explain to your classmates your personal experiences learning and using both Spanish and English.
- If you are not a native Spanish speaker but have studied or are studying Spanish now, explain your reasons for doing so.
- If you are a native speaker of a language other than Spanish or English, what are your views on the debate over whether Spanish should be recognized as a U.S. language?
- If you are a native English language speaker and have never learned Spanish, what are your views on the debate?

The "Latin Wave": Young, Hip, and Successful

The Mexican characters in *Lone Star,* from Mercedes to Pilar to Enrique, are all confronted with negative stereotypes that have long pervaded American life. Only very recently has a new trend begun to make itself felt, a sudden and astonishingly rapid rise in popularity of Latin culture and Latin images. As *Newsweek* magazine put it in a cover story (12 July 1999), "Hispanics are hip, hot, and making history" (48). In its own cover story (24 May 1999), *Time* magazine featured sensation Ricky Martin and other performers who are part of the new pop Latin wave.

Of course Latin music and rhythms have been around for a long time, and names such as Xavier Cugat and Tito Puente were familiar nationwide as early as the 1940s. Later artists such as Julio Iglesias and Gloria Estefan also achieved huge "crossover" success, reaching both Latino and non-Latino audiences. But the recent stardom of heartthrob Ricky Martin and of artists like Marc Anthony, Jennifer Lopez, and Shakira seems to have a new and different quality. Having captured the attention and imagination of America's youth, this generation of artists has suddenly made it acceptable—even cool—to be Latin. In August 2000 nearly a dozen Latino and Latina artists received Grammy Awards. Notably, the winners included both established and newer names; Carlos Santana, for example, who first made his mark in the 1960s, won nine awards.

In many other areas, young Latinos and Latinas are making a similar mark on American life. Sports stars like Samuel Sosa, Rebecca Lobo, and Oscar De La Hoya are widely known and are seen as role models by their fans. Actors Benjamin Bratt and Salma Hayek reach large viewing audiences. And writers such as Esmeralda Santiago and Junot Diaz join more established authors (Sandra Cisneros, Rudolfo Anaya, Oscar Hijuelos) in giving voice to the experiences of biculturalism and promoting Hispanic literature to a recognized position in American literary life.

The *Newsweek* cover story proclaims that the new Latin wave "will change how the country looks—and how it looks at itself" (48). Certainly the coming decade will be a critical time, as Latinos become the largest U.S. minority and as sparkling new images confront what seem to be age-old stereotypes.

- If you are Latino or Latina, how do you feel about the "new Latin wave"? Does it affect you personally?
- Locate and read the *Time* or *Newsweek* cover story cited above. Based on the information presented, do you think the "Latin wave" is here to stay?
- Choose one of the people named above or another Latino or Latina figure with whom you are familiar, and explain how that person has influenced your ideas of Latino life and culture.

Zoom Lens: Choosing Your Own Topic of Interest

Hands-on Activities

1. Visit your local community center, chamber of commerce, library, or newspaper office to learn about programs organized by and with Latinos in your community. Select one program that interests you, contact the organizer, and ask if you can attend a meeting or program.
2. Consult one or more of the Latino Websites listed in the Sequel to explore current topics of interest to this population.
3. Locate issues of Latino/Latina magazines such as *Hispanic* or *Latina*. What insights do you gain from these publications about the situation and concerns of Hispanics in the U.S. today?

Research Papers or Oral Reports

1. Research the life and works of one Latino or Latina author or poet. As part of your project, read one or more of the author's works. (If the work was originally written in Spanish and you are sufficiently proficient in the language, read it in the original.)
2. Research bilingual education, beginning with the Bilingual Education Act of 1968 and including the more recent Proposition 227 in California (1998). What progress and changes have been made since 1968, and what are the main points of contention today? Contact your local school district to find out what types of bilin-

gual education programs exist in your state. You may wish to contact the National Association for Bilingual Education (see Sequel).

3. Research life along the U.S./Mexican border. You may wish to focus on border crossings (see Conover and Urrea in the Sequel). Or you may choose another focus, such as the factories called *maquiladoras* that flourish along the border.

4. Outline the debate over the English Only and English Plus movements. Summarize the salient arguments on both sides of the issue, and try to draw your own conclusions (see Baron and Crawford in the Sequel).

5. Learn more about César Chávez's life, or select another Chicano or Chicana activist such as Dolores Huerta (organizer and vice president of United Farm Workers), Reies López Tijerina (organizer of the Federal Alliance of Land Grants), Rodolfo "Corky" Gonzales (founder of the Crusade for Justice in Denver), or José Angel Gutiérrez (founder of the Mexican American Youth organization and La Raza Unida).

6. What is El Teatro Campesino, started by Luis Valdez? Find out how this theater company began and how it has progressed since its inception in 1965.

Using Your Imagination

1. Why do you think John Sayles chose the title *Lone Star* for his film? Consider the places, characters, and themes to which the title could apply.

2. You have been asked to design a statue or plaque as an alternative to that of Buddy Deeds, to be erected in front of the Frontera Courthouse. Who or what will it commemorate or represent? Either describe or illustrate this commemorative piece, and write the speech that will be given when it is unveiled.

3. Imagine that you overheard a conversation between Otis and Hollis right after they realized that Sam Deeds was investigating the death of Charlie Wade. Given that they are the only two people who knew what really happened on the night of Wade's death, what might they have said to each other? Write the conversation.

4. You are a journalist for the local Frontera newspaper. Either write an article on the discovery of Wade's body and the ongoing inquiry into his death, or write an obituary for Charlie Wade or Buddy Deeds.

5. You are Delmore Payne the evening after you have interviewed Private Johnson. Reflect on your reasons for joining the army compared with Johnson's rationale.
6. You are Chet, the teenage son of Delmore Payne. Write a letter to your father in which you explain that an army career is not for you. Or, given your talent for drawing, express in a sketch or illustration your feelings toward your grandfather Otis Payne, whose acquaintance you have just made and whom you would like to know better.
7. You are Pilar or Sam. Continue your dialogue from the closing scene of the movie. If you are Pilar, explain what you mean by "Forget the Alamo!" If you are Sam, try to interpret Pilar's words.

Sequel: Further Suggested Resources

Readings

Anzaldúa, Gloria. 1999. *Borderlands/La Frontera.* 2d ed. San Francisco: Aunt Lute Books.

Banks, James A. 1997. *Teaching Strategies for Ethnic Studies.* 6th ed. Boston: Allyn and Bacon.

Baron, Dennis. 1990. *The English Only Question.* New Haven: Yale University Press.

Cisneros, Sandra. 1984. *The House on Mango Street.* New York: Random House.

Conover, Ted. 1987. *Coyotes: A Journey through the Secret World of America's Illegal Aliens.* New York: Random House.

Crawford, James. 1992. *Hold Your Tongue: Bilingualism and the Politics of "English Only."* Reading, MA.: Addison Wesley.

———. 1992. *Language Loyalties.* Chicago: University of Chicago Press.

Faragher, John Mack, Mary Jo Buhle, Daniel Czitrom, and Susan H. Armitage. 1994. *Out of Many: A History of the American People.* Englewood Cliffs, NJ: Prentice Hall.

Fuentes, Carlos. 1992. *The Buried Mirror: Reflections on Spain and the New World.* New York: Houghton Mifflin.

Galarza, Ernesto. 1971. *Barrio Boy.* Notre Dame, IN: University of Notre Dame Press.

Gonzales, Juan. 2000. *Harvest of Empire: A History of Latinos in America.* New York: Viking.

Kanellos, Nicolás. 1998. *Thirty Million Strong: Reclaiming the Hispanic Image in American Culture.* Golden, CO: Fulcrum Publishing.

LaFeber, Walter. 1989. *The American Age: United States Foreign Policy at Home and Abroad since 1750.* New York: W. W. Norton.

Meier, Matt S., and Feliciano Ribera. 1994. *Mexican Americans/American Mexicans: From Conquistadors to Chicanos.* New York: Hill and Wang.

Novas, Himilce. 1994. *Everything You Need to Know about Latino History.* New York: Penguin Books.

Ortego, Philip D. 1973. *We Are Chicanos: An Anthology of Mexican American Literature.* New York: Washington Square Press.

Rodriquez, Richard. 1982. *Hunger of Memory: The Education of Richard Rodriquez.* Boston: D. R. Godine.

Rosales, Arturo F. 1997. *Chicano! The History of the Mexican American Civil Rights Movement.* Houston: Arte Publico Press.

Shafer, Robert Jones. 1978. *A History of Latin America.* Lexington, MA: D. C. Heath.

Sowell, Thomas. 1981. *Ethnic America: A History.* New York: Basic Books.

Stavans, Ilans. 1995. *The Hispanic Condition: Reflections on Culture and Identity in America.* New York: HarperCollins.

Suro, Robert. 1999. *Strangers among Us: Latino Lives in a Changing America.* New York: Vintage Books.

Urrea, Luis Alberto. 1993. *Across the Wire: Life and Hard Times on the Mexican Border.* New York: Doubleday.

Films

Ballad of Gregorio Cortez (1982) Intriguing film about turn-of-the-century Mexican American folk hero Gregorio Cortez, who was accused of murder under dubious circumstances. Convinced he would not receive a fair trial, Cortez managed to elude numerous Texan posses for hundreds of miles in a daring attempt to escape across the Mexican border on horseback. Directed by Robert Young.

Born in East L. A. (1987) Comic adventures of a third-generation Mexican American who is mistaken for an illegal immigrant and deported to Tijuana. Directed by Cheech Marin.

Chicano! (1996) Excellent four-part history of the Mexican American civil rights movement. Produced by José Luis Ruiz. (NLCC Educational Media; phone: 213-953-2928).

El Norte (1983) Heartbreaking story of a brother and sister from Guatemala who travel north to Los Angeles in hopes of realizing their dreams. Shows the harsh realities of border crossings and immigrant life. Directed by Mexican American Gregory Nava.

La Bamba (1987) Story of Mexican American popular singer Ritchie Valens' rapid rise to fame. Directed by Luis Valdez.

Mi Vida Loca/My Crazy Life (1994) Daily life of Latina gang girls in Echo Park area of Los Angeles. Directed by Allison Anders.

My Family/Mi Familia (1995)   Generational saga of a Mexican American family that emigrates to Los Angeles in the 1920s. Featuring Latino actors Edward James Olmos and Jimmy Smits and directed by Gregory Nava.

Selena (1997)   Biography of tejana singer Selena. Wildly popular among Southwest Latinos, Selena was poised to achieve crossover success when she was murdered under mysterious circumstances. Starring Jennifer Lopez and directed by Gregory Nava.

Stand and Deliver (1987)   Celebrates the achievements of students from an East Los Angeles barrio who come to score among the highest in the nation on the Advanced Placement Calculus test. Based on the true story of a Hispanic teacher named Jaime Escalante (Edward James Olmos). Directed by Ramon Menendez.

Websites and Mailing Addresses

Bilingual Education (www.csulb.edu/~clmer/pswrtc/biled.htm)

Center for Immigrants' Rights, 48 St. Marks Place, New York, NY 10003; phone: 212-505-6890

English Plus Information Clearinghouse (EPIC), 200 I Street NE, Berkeley, CA 94710; phone: 415-644-2555

Hispanic (www.hisp.com)

Hispanic Page in the United States (www.coloquio.com/index.html)

LatinoWeb (www.latinoweb.com)

League of Latin American Citizens (LULAC), 221 N. Kansas, Suite 1211, El Paso, TX 79901; phone: 915-577-0726 (www.mundo. com/lulac.html)

Mexican American Legal Defense and Education Fund, 634 S. Spring Street, 11th Floor, Los Angeles, CA 90014; phone: 213-629-2512 (www.maldef. org)

National Association for Bilingual Education, Union Center Plaza, 810 1st Street NE, 3d Floor, Washington, DC 20002 (www.nabe.org)

National Association for Chicano Studies (NACS), 14 East Cuche LaPoundre, Colorado Springs, CO 80903; phone: 509-359-2404

National Council of La Raza, 20 F Street NW, Washington, DC 20001; phone: 202-289-1380 (www.nclr.org)

Answers to quiz on pages 132–33

The Wade Case

1. Sam interviews Mrs. Bledsoe to find out if Charlie Wade went to the club on the night of his murder.
2. Hollis was Wade's deputy, so Sam believes he knows about the murder.
3. Cliff and Mickey find a pistol shell among the rifle shells.
4. Sam assumes his father, Buddy Deeds, killed Wade.

The People of Frontera

1. The Anglo mother wants the history of Texas to be taught from the Anglo viewpoint.
2. The white bartender thinks Deeds will be the last white sheriff in Frontera. He is worried the Mexicans will take over.
3. Fenton is pushing the construction project and Jorge, who is a candidate for mayor, thinks the jail will provide jobs and will therefore win him more votes in the next election.
4. Mercedes is a Mexican American of Spanish descent. She has become a respected bilingual businesswoman in Frontera.
5. Buddy Deeds is known to have split up a Mexican community in Frontera in order to build his own house on coveted lakeside property.

The Buddy Deeds Legend

1. Wade wanted Buddy to pick up illegal immigrants ("wetbacks") and send them back.
2. Otis tells Sam that no Mexican had died in Buddy Deeds' custody and that no man regardless of race would have hesitated to enlist Deeds' help.
3. Buddy used county funds for his own betterment.
4. They name the courthouse after Buddy Deeds and erect a statue of him in front of it.

The Cruz Family

1. Pilar is a schoolteacher.
2. Armando was caught installing car radios that he did not know were stolen.
3. Mercedes never liked Pilar's deceased husband.
4. Mercedes requires her employees to speak English.
5. Mercedes disdains wetbacks and reports them to immigration.
6. Eladio Cruz was murdered by Charlie Wade.

The Paynes

1. Colonel Payne has been transferred to Fort McKenzie.
2. Chet meets Otis in the bar on the night of the shooting of a young African American.
3. Otis is called "the mayor of Darktown" because he runs the only bar where black people can drink and feel welcome.
4. Delmore resents the fact that his father abandoned the family when Delmore was young.
5. Delmore is surprised that his father has kept all the photos and articles about his son's achievements.

Sam and Pilar

1. Sam and Pilar meet at the police station. Pilar is looking for her son.
2. Sam learns about Buddy's relationship with Mercedes from the old Indian. Sam probably found the photo of Mercedes and Buddy in his father's papers. He also found a handwritten letter, presumably from Mercedes, beginning "My Dearest Buddy."
3. Pilar thought her father was killed only a couple of months before her birth. She also believed that Eladio Cruz was her father.

7

Mainstream White Culture: Film of Your Choice

Setting the Scene: Freewriting and Discussion

Give me your tired, your poor,
Your huddled masses yearning to breathe
*   free,*
The wretched refuse of your teeming
*   shore.*
Send these, the homeless, tempest-tossed
*   to me,*
I lift my lamp beside the golden door!

 Read these lines from *The New Colossus*, a sonnet inscribed on a tablet mounted at the base of the Statue of Liberty. The sonnet was written in 1883 by Emma Lazarus, a Jewish woman born in New York City. Now look at the cartoon printed in *The New Yorker* magazine a century later. Freewrite your reactions in your film notebook.

"Well, it all depends. Where are these huddled masses coming from?"

Wide-Angle Lens: Historical Perspectives

White America: Immigration and Influence

By this point in the course you may be asking yourself about the group of Americans we have only briefly referred to from time to time— white (or mainstream, dominant, Anglo, European, Caucasian) Americans. In some ways it hardly seems necessary to focus on them, since they already receive so much attention. After all, we can find literally thousands of books on white American history (which was virtually the only type of American history written for a long time). And we hear from white America all the time, since whites still overwhelmingly possess the wealth, control the resources, and shape the policies of this country.

While it is true that whites have traditionally been in positions of relative power and control with ample opportunity to have their voices heard, white culture has not necessarily been well understood. Recent scholarship reveals many misconceptions that nonwhites have about whites and that whites have about themselves.

One of the most pervasive misconceptions is that whites, like their skin, are bland and colorless, with no real culture to speak of. In truth no human being exists without culture. Culture is a way of life including tangibles such as dress, food, and customs and intangibles such as values and beliefs. White culture is as complex, intriguing, rich, and real as any other, but it often seems invisible. The reason it is less obvious than other cultures is that it predominates: it is everywhere. If everyone wears jeans, for example, then jeans do not seem as distinctive as the "colorful" dress of Laotian or Guatemalan Americans. If most people are Christians, then Christianity does not seem as noteworthy as the less common and therefore more "exotic" Buddhism. And if most people speak English, this language does not seem as interesting as the Hungarian spoken by recent immigrants from eastern Europe.

Another misconception is that we actually know what *white* means. Throughout the history of this country the definition has frequently changed, and it remains unclear. How dark can a person be and still qualify as white? Are Italians and Greeks white? Are Jews and Arab Americans? According to founding father Benjamin Franklin, the English were the most desirable Americans. Why, he asked, should the country "darken its people," when there was, as he described it, "so fair an opportunity, by excluding all Blacks and Tawnys, of increasing the lovely White" (Franklin 1959, 234)?

According to Franklin's definition of the "lovely White," many white Americans of today would not qualify. Because the English and northern Europeans have intermarried for generations with darker-skinned Europeans and people of color, American whites now assume many different shades of color. Thus the term *white* itself must be used with an awareness of its limitations.

A third mistaken notion about whites is that they are all alike. In fact they come from widely diverse backgrounds and heritages, speak different languages, practice different religions, and cut across all socioeconomic classes. The differences are often most apparent in the cases of new immigrant groups, who tend to cling for some time to the cultures of their homelands, perhaps settling in their own ethnic communities and speaking their own languages. But other white ethnic groups that were thought to have blended into the melting pot long ago, such as Poles, Italians, Irish, and Greeks, are only recently beginning to rediscover their ancestral identities, celebrating a revival of customs, languages, and values.

So who are the white Americans? Since at one time they were all newcomers to this continent, how did they get here? How have they shaped this country in accordance with the ways of life and values they brought from their original homelands?

The group that has had the most decisive influence on this country's direction is the English, also known as Anglos or Anglo-Saxons. The United States began, after all, as a group of thirteen English colonies that were settled along the eastern seaboard during the seventeenth century. Although people from other countries also lived in these colonies, the English were predominant, shaping the new nation's identity and future course. Foremost, they gave the country the English language, which carries with it an entire way of thought and life. In America's formative decades the English also left their indelible stamp on its government, laws, churches, literature, and customs.

The English emerged victorious among the original colonial rivals and thus were able to give the new nation its basic imprint; nevertheless, other European powers and peoples also contributed to the molding of America. Spain, whose conquistadores arrived first in the Americas and long claimed a huge land mass in what is now the southwestern United States, has left its own unmistakable mark on that region and on the country as a whole, influencing everything from architecture to food to western ranching life.

Other European groups lived their own stories and made their own distinctive contributions. If the English arrived in the largest numbers in the seventeenth and eighteenth centuries, it was the Irish and Germans who predominated in the first half of the nineteenth century, to

Related Terms

Anglo (Anglo-Saxon), European American Widely used synonyms for whites.

Caucasian Anthropological term for whites that is now discredited but still seen on some questionnaires.

Eurocentrism, Anglocentrism Philosophy that places Europe at the heart of world history and civilization. Eurocentric views and curricula have been challenged by Afrocentrists, among others.

paleface, honky, white trash, cracker Derogatory terms for whites.

WASP Acronym for White Anglo-Saxon Protestant; often used to criticize whites of privilege who are seen as smug and bigoted, but can also be used without apology by self-identified WASPs.

white Most widely accepted term for those of European descent and skin color that approximates, though is not truly, white.

be followed by Italians and eastern Europeans in the last half of the nineteenth and early twentieth centuries.

What all of these non-English European groups had in common was their struggle to find a place and create an identity for themselves as they increased their presence in the country. Because the basic norms of the society were already established, many white newcomers had to either fit in or fight for changes, just as nonwhites have always had to do.

Let's look briefly at the case of just one white immigrant group, the Irish, as an example of the experiences shared by many other non-English whites. While both Catholic and Protestant Irish had come to America in small numbers from the 1600s onward, a mass migration of Irish Catholics took place in the nineteenth century as a result of the potato blight of 1845–1851. Prior to the Great Irish Famine caused by the failure of this staple crop, the Irish people, many of whom were rural farmers, had already suffered from severe poverty and centuries of British subjugation. The Great Famine, however, caused unequaled devastation: of an estimated eight million people in Ireland in 1840, more than one million perished of hunger and disease, and an estimated three million survivors immigrated to America in the following decades. Among these immigrants came many families, but so did large numbers of single women, an unusual occurrence at the time.

As destitute, unskilled workers and as Catholics, the Irish who arrived in America at this time in history were made universally unwelcome. Negative stereotypes of brutish, violent, drunken men prevailed, and discrimination was rampant. Want ads and signs proclaiming "No Irish Need Apply" were everywhere. The lives of the newcomers were marked by extreme hardship and sacrifice. Living in urban slums in abject poverty, the Irish found jobs as manual laborers, often in dangerous, toilsome work such as coal mining and the construction of railroads, canals, and roads. The women generally worked as domestic servants or in the sewing trades. Even in these undesirable jobs, the Irish had to compete with the Chinese and blacks, resulting in ugly animosities and rivalries. In an unfortunate chapter of Irish American history, the Irish generally used their whiteness against those in their same economic class rather than joining forces with them.

Several decades of struggle to achieve the American Dream gradually bore fruit; the Irish improved their lot, becoming respected especially as municipal employees (the "Irish cop" and "Irish fireman" were fixtures in major cities), playing an important role in the American Catholic Church, and achieving particular success in politics. The Irish political tradition reached its pinnacle when John F. Kennedy became the first Irish Catholic to be elected president of the United States.

As the Irish rose from the bottom economic and social rung, other new immigrant groups—Poles, Italians, Jews, and Greeks—quickly took their place, beginning their own arduous climb upward. Interestingly, the more recent waves of newcomers often settled in the same neighborhoods the previous groups had vacated. In various forms this pattern has repeated itself over and over in American immigrant history.

The Irish, English, and many other peoples who uprooted their lives to face the unknown in America were motivated by a complex of factors. Certainly the promise of freedom, whether religious, political, or social, inspired many. Other reasons such as curiosity, lust for adventure, and desire for land must also be taken into account. The most compelling attraction for five centuries, however, has been economic. America has been seen as a land of opportunity, of wealth, of streets paved with gold. Generations of immigrants have come here in the belief that anyone can rise to the top and live in luxury. Although the American Dream has been unrealized for most, especially for first-generation immigrants, it continues to maintain a powerful grip on the minds of both Americans and millions of people worldwide.

Today, at the beginning of the twenty-first century, non-Hispanic whites are estimated to number nearly two hundred million people, or about 70 percent of the country's population. Although this percentage is steadily diminishing, whites still predominate in terms of number and influence. The variety of white ethnic groups in the U.S. population is astonishing: the *Harvard Encyclopedia of American Ethnic Groups* contains entries for literally dozens of groups ranging from Canadians and New Zealanders to Luxembourgers, Romanians, and Ukrainians.

To some extent the people from these groups have lost much of their ancestral national and ethnic identities, becoming simply white Americans or European Americans. As Mary C. Waters explains in *Ethnic Options: Choosing Identities in America,* many families are so mixed that ethnic identity becomes more of a choice than a reality. To illustrate, a young woman whose great-grandparents emigrated from Italy and France may identify with both of her ethnic backgrounds. If she is closer to the Italian side of the family and can speak some Italian, she may consider herself Italian American. Or she may choose to see herself simply as an American.

What all Euro-Americans share, however, is their whiteness, which in this society carries with it privilege and opportunity not necessarily granted to nonwhites. Regardless of education, abilities, and financial means, whites have traditionally had a much easier climb up the ladder of success and wealth than people of color. One of the crucial tests of the twenty-first century is the extent to which white Americans can work with Americans of color to create a society that more nearly approximates the ideals of equality and justice expressed when this nation was created more than two hundred years ago.

Spotlight: Presenting Your Film Choice

Because there are so many films that focus on white Americans, we decided not to pick one film for you to view as a class. Rather, we would like you to choose a film that you feel represents, illustrates, or gives cultural insights into white America. Work in small groups to select a feature film; each group may choose its own film. You may wish to select from the suggestions given in the Sequel or you may instead decide on another film of the group's choosing.

After viewing the film with your group, prepare a presentation for the class in which you explain why you chose this particular film and why you think it says something culturally significant about white mainstream America. Plan to show a clip from your film to illustrate one or two of your main points. Be sure to give a short plot summary so that the students who have not seen the film will understand your presentation.

Remember that you should not try to speak about *all* of white America. Your film, after all, takes place at a particular time and unfolds under particular circumstances. It will be sufficient for you to uncover one or more "truths" about white America rather than to try to be comprehensive. When you give your presentation, explain to the class what particular slice of white America you looked at; for example, you may choose to analyze religious values in the film *A River Runs Through It* and the extent to which they influence styles of parenting.

Below are some of the questions that can guide you in preparing your presentation. Don't limit yourself to these questions, but do try to address one or two of them. They will help you learn not only about white American culture, but about any cultural group.

1. What are the visible aspects of the segment of white culture depicted in your film, for example, dress, foods and eating habits, architecture and public spaces, customs?
2. How do people in the film relate to time, and how do they spend their time? Look at occupations, leisure activities, and daily schedules.
3. How is religion viewed and practiced in the film?
4. How important are modernization and technology?
5. What languages are spoken?
6. How do people relate to nature?
7. How do people relate to health, to aging, to sickness and dying?
8. How important are the arts? What forms of art are respected and cultivated?
9. How materialistic is the segment of the culture that is portrayed? How important are money and property? What types of possessions are valued?
10. What are the roles of men, women, family, parents, and children?
11. What values can you discover and describe (work values, family values, historical values, social values, moral values)?

When you watch other groups' presentations, jot down some notes in your film notebook in response to the following questions:

1. If you have already seen the film, what points presented by the group do you agree or disagree with?
2. If you have not seen the film, are you inspired to see it? If so, why?

Alexis de Tocqueville's America

Alexis de Tocqueville (1805–1859), a French aristocrat and writer, traversed the eastern United States for nine months in 1831–32 at the request of his government for the purpose of reporting on certain aspects of American society. His resulting two-volume work, *On Democracy* (*De la Démocratie en Amérique,* 1835), is recognized as one of the most thoughtful, insightful analyses of American life, democracy, and society ever written. Many of de Tocqueville's observations seem as valid today as they were in his time. His work clearly demonstrates the worth of an outsider's perspective in understanding a people, country, or culture.

Fascinated and inspired by much of what he saw, de Tocqueville often wrote with admiration, but he did not hesitate to express his criticisms and reservations. Read the following translation of an excerpt from *On Democracy* to get a glimpse of de Tocqueville's view of the mainstream values that have shaped this country.

As you read, keep the following questions in mind. Then, after you finish reading, respond to them in your film notebook as preparation for class discussion:

- If you are American, do any of de Tocqueville's claims—made more than 150 years ago—apply to you personally or to your family? If so, copy those lines in your film notebook and give an account of a personal experience as an illustration.
- If you are not American, do you agree with de Tocqueville's statement that Americans are "restless in the midst of abundance"? Select a passage from the text that concurs with your observations of Americans today, or select one that you find to be untrue. Copy it into your film notebook and include an example to illustrate your point. Add questions that may have occurred to you while reading the passage, and see if other members of your group can answer them.

Why the Americans Are So Restless in the Midst of Their Prosperity

by Alexis de Tocqueville

I have witnessed in America some of the most enlightened men, free to think as they please in the happiest of situations. Yet, in this seemingly desirable state, they appeared serious and sad as if a cloud perpetually hung over them.

It was strange to observe these Americans pursuing their prosperity with a sort of feverish ardor. They seemed to be endlessly troubled by a fear that they had not chosen the quickest route to their well-being.

The American is attached to worldly goods as if he could keep them forever. He seizes everything within his grasp, fearing that he will die at any moment before having a chance to relish his bounty. He grabs everything, yet holds on to little, leaving what he has behind in order to search for new delights.

A man in the United States carefully builds a house in which he will spend his later years; yet he sells it before the construction is complete. He plants a garden and then leaves it to someone else before even tasting the fruits of his labor. He clears a field and relinquishes to others the task of reaping the harvest. He embarks on a career, then leaves it. He plants himself in one area and within a short time deserts it to follow his fancy elsewhere. No sooner has his private business given him some momentary relief, than he throws himself into the whirlpool of politics. And when, at the end of a labor-intensive year, there remains a little free time for pleasure, his curiosity drives him to travel the length and breadth of the vast U.S. territory. In just a few days, he will traverse five hundred miles as a distraction from his perpetual search for happiness.

Death finally overtakes the American and prevents him from ever completing this endless search for a happiness that continually evades his grasp.

At first it seems astonishing to see so many fortunate men seemingly restless in the midst of their abundance. However, this sight is as old as the world; what is new is to see a whole people so engaged.

Poetry: Immigrant Dreams and Realities

The poem on the next page, "Public School No. 18: Paterson, New Jersey," was written by Maria Mazziotti Gillan, the daughter of immigrant parents from southern Italy.

- Read the poem aloud in class or at home and describe in your film notebook the insights it gives you into the immigrant experience.
- Write the name of your primary or secondary school at the top of a page in your film notebook. Freewrite about cultural memories from when you were growing up and attending this school. If you wish, turn the freewrite into a poem.

Public School No. 18: Paterson, New Jersey

Miss Wilson's eyes, opaque
as blue glass, fix on me:
"We must speak English.
We're in America now."
I want to say, "I am American,"
but the evidence is stacked against me.

My mother scrubs my scalp raw, wraps
my shining hair in white rags
to make it curl. Miss Wilson
drags me to the window, checks my hair
for lice. My face wants to hide.

At home, my words smooth in my mouth,
I chatter and am proud. In school,
I am silent, grope for the right English
words, fear the Italian word
will sprout from my mouth like a rose,

fear the progression of teachers
in their sprigged dressed,
their Anglo-Saxon faces.

Without words, they tell me
to be ashamed.
I am.
I deny that booted country
even from myself,

want to be still
and untouchable
as these women
who teach me to hate myself.

Years later, in a white
Kansas City house,
the Psychology professor tells me
I remind him of the Mafia leader
on the cover of Time magazine.

My anger spits
venomous from my mouth:

I am proud of my mother,
dressed all in black,
proud of my father
with his broken tongue,
proud of the laughter and noise of our
house.

Remember me, ladies,
the silent one?
I have found my voice
and my rage will blow
your house down.

Sequel: Further Suggested Resources

Readings

Babb, Valerie. 1998. *Whiteness Visible: The Meaning of Whiteness in American Literature and Culture*. New York: New York University Press.

Bailey, T. A. 1961. *The American Pageant: A History of the Republic*. Boston: D. C. Heath.

Daniels, R. 1990. *Coming to America: A History of Immigration and Ethnicity in American Life*. New York: HarperCollins.

Franklin, Benjamin. 1959. "Observations Concerning the Increase in Mankind." *The Papers of Benjamin Franklin*. Vol. 4. Edited by Leonard W. Labaree. New Haven: Yale University Press.

Gillan, Maria Mazziotti, and Jennifer Gillan, eds. 1994. *Unsettling America: An Anthology of Contemporary Multicultural Poetry*. New York: Penguin.

Glazer, Nathan, and Daniel Patrick Moynihan. 1963. *Beyond the Melting Pot: The Negroes, Puerto Ricans, Jews, Italians, and Irish of New York City*. Cambridge: MIT Press.

Handlin, Oscar. 1951. *The Uprooted: The Epic Story of the Great Migrations that Made the American People*. New York: Grosset and Dunlop.

Hill, Mike, ed. 1997. *Whiteness: A Critical Reader*. New York: New York University Press.

Jones, M. A. 1992. *American Immigration*. Chicago: University of Chicago Press.

Kennedy, John F. 1965. *A Nation of Immigrants*. New York: Harper and Row.

Martin, Judith N., and Thomas K. Nakayama. 1999. *Whiteness: The Communication of Social Identity*. Thousand Oaks, CA: Sage Publications.

Miller, Kirby, and Paul Wagner. 1997. *Out of Ireland: The Story of Irish Emigration to America*. Niwot, CO: Roberts Rinehart.

Novak, Michael. 1971. *The Rise of the Unmeltable Ethnics: Politics and Culture in the Seventies*. New York: Macmillan.

Roediger, David R., ed. 1998. *Black on White: Black Writers on What It Means to Be White*. New York: Schocken Books.

Steinberg, Stephen. 1989. *Race, Class, and Ethnicity in America*. Boston: Beacon Press.

Thernstrom, Stephan, ed. 1980. *Harvard Encyclopedia of American Ethnic Groups*. Cambridge: Bellknap Press of Harvard University.

Tocqueville, Alexis de. 1990. *Democracy in America*. Translated by Henry Reeve. Revised by Frances Bowmant. New York: Vintage.

Waters, Mary C. 1990. *Ethnic Options: Choosing Identities in America*. Berkeley: University of California Press.

Weatherford, Doris. 1995. *Foreign and Female: Immigrant Women in America, 1840–1930*. New York: Facts on File.

Films

American History X (1998) Brutal story of a young man's seduction by a neo-Nazi skinhead gang and subsequent attempt to free himself and his brother from racist ideology. Directed by Tony Kaye.

Angela's Ashes (1999) Sensitive young boy experiences desperate poverty in Depression-era Ireland. At the end of the film, he decides to leave his troubled family and follow his dreams in the United States. Based on the best-selling novel by Frank McCourt. Directed by Alan Parker.

Apollo 13 (1995) Inspiring, suspenseful story of the Apollo 13 moon mission. Directed by Ron Howard.

Big Night (1996) Two immigrant brothers open their own Italian restaurant in the 1950s. Slow-paced, charming story. Directed by Campbell Scott and Stanley Tucci.

Broadcast News (1987) Behind-the-scenes look at the personalities and pressures of network news. Directed by James L. Brooks.

Country (1984) An Iowa farm family faces foreclosure on their property when they cannot repay their government loans. Directed by Richard Pearce.

Fame (1980) Students at New York High School of the Performing Arts prepare for future stardom. Directed by Alan Parker.

Far and Away (1992) Two young Irish immigrants—a spirited farmer and boxer (Tom Cruise) and a well-to-do aristocrat's daughter (Nicole Kidman)—make their way in America at the time of the 1893 Oklahoma land rush. Directed by Ron Howard.

Hoosiers (1986) Small-town Indiana high school basketball team sets its sights on the state championship. Directed by David Anspaugh.

Kramer vs. Kramer (1979) Inexperienced father (Dustin Hoffman) learns to care for his son when his wife (Meryl Streep) leaves to pursue her own goals. Directed by Robert Benton.

A League of Their Own (1992) Story of a professional women's baseball league that came into being during World War II. Based on actual sports history. Directed by Penny Marshall.

Moscow on the Hudson (1984) Russian musician (Robin Williams) defects following a performance in New York. Funny, insightful film about the immigrant experience. Directed by Paul Mazursky.

Mystic Pizza (1988) Small-town romance as experienced by three young women working at a pizzeria in Mystic, Connecticut. Directed by Donald Petne.

Places in the Heart (1984) Determined widow (Sally Fields) fights to keep her farm and support her family through hard times. Directed by Robert Benton.

A River Runs Through It (1992) Tragic tale of two brothers whose love for fly fishing is shared by their father, a Presbyterian minister. Directed by Robert Redford.

Rocky (1976)   Rousing story of a gutsy Philadelphia boxer's (Sylvester Stallone) chance for fame and glory in a championship bout. Followed by four sequels. Directed by John D. Avildsen.

Rudy (1993)   Young man from a working-class family in a mill town refuses to give up his dream to win a place on the Notre Dame football team. Based on a true story. Directed by David Anspaugh.

Searching for Bobby Fischer (1993)   Brilliant young chess hopeful is thought to be the next Bobby Fischer. A wonderful film based on a true story. Directed by Steve Zaillian.

Spitfire Grill (1996)   Young woman who wants to start over after her release from prison goes to a small town in Maine and accepts a job at the local grill. Directed by Lee David Zlotoff.

Stand by Me (1986)   Adventures of four boyhood friends in rural Oregon in the 1950s. Directed by Rob Reiner.

What's Eating Gilbert Grape (1993)   Poignant story of a young man who looks after his mentally handicapped brother, obese mother, and troubled sisters in a dead-end town. Directed by Lasse Hallstrom.

8

Gay Culture:
The Wedding Banquet

Setting the Scene: Freewriting and Discussion

Perhaps you are familiar with the "Safe Zone" triangle represented below. It is commonly attached to doors of places like offices and dorm rooms to signal that the person inside is sensitive to issues faced by gays, lesbians, and bisexuals and considers himself or herself an ally.

Whatever your own sexual orientation may be, write in your film notebook about how you have felt in the past (or might feel in the future) seeing this triangle on a door you are about to enter. Can you imagine why the sign might be needed, useful, or appreciated by homosexuals and bisexuals?

Wide-Angle Lens: Historical Perspectives

History of Homosexuality

In 1993 when *The Wedding Banquet* takes place, the gay couple, Wai-Tung and Simon, lead "normal" lives publicly, but fear of prejudice and rejection are ever present. A look at the history of homosexuality reveals that the situation depicted in the film, while complicated and difficult, nonetheless represents enormous progress in society's acceptance of gays.

The history of homosexuality is not easily described, for as one scholar succinctly states, "Sex has no history" (Halperin 1993, 416). Among the serious obstacles encountered in constructing such a history are the absence of documentation and records, problems related to defining homosexuality (see below), political barriers such as universities' reluctance to legitimize research on homosexuality, and people's natural reluctance to divulge information related to their personal, private behavior. Because gays have been persecuted and oppressed in so many societies, they have kept much of what might be critical to an understanding of gay history hidden from view, leading some scholars to speak of the "hidden history" of homosexuals.

Despite these difficulties, over the past three decades historians and biographers have produced a substantial body of material to reclaim and illuminate the homosexual past. The books by Adam, Cowan, Cruikshank, Duberman, Katz, and Marcus listed in the Sequel are but a few of the key works that have appeared. Though gay history may be faced with particularly stubborn obstacles, you should remember that in the United States all "minority" histories—those of African Americans, Asian Americans, women, and others—have been long neglected in favor of the dominant story, which is white, Christian, heterosexual, and male. As is stated in an African proverb, "Until the lion writes his own story, the tale of the hunt will always glorify the hunter." In our own time, much excitement is being generated by so-called revisionist history—that is, the new sets of stories and truths as well as the new interpretations of our collective past that are emerging.

Scholars generally agree that homosexuality—in a wide variety of forms—has been known across virtually all cultures and time periods. We must be careful, however, not to apply the word *homosexuality* in its modern sense to non-Western, traditional, or early societies, where "same-sex love" or "same-sex unions" were understood very differently from today's notions. The ancient Greeks, for example, did not have a word for homosexuality (nor did the Hebrews or Romans). What was legitimized was a certain form of love between an older, usually well-to-do man and a youth, resembling a tutelage or initiation into manhood. As a further example, in many Native American societies, the *berdache* (a gender-mixed person who was usually a man but could be a woman) dressed in clothing of the opposite gender, had sexual and marital relations with the same gender, and assumed ceremonial roles in sacred rituals. Berdaches confound modern notions of heterosexuality and homosexuality, since they were seen as neither sex, or both, or in-between, being described by many Indians as "half men, half women." While some tribes looked down on berdaches, others, such as the Navajo, revered them.

Ancient Greece and Native America offer only two of numerous examples of societies able to accept and even appreciate forms of same-sex love. Overwhelmingly, however, homosexual love in Western societies has been feared, banned, and punished, leading some to speak of gay history simply as a "history of persecution." The church, the law, and medical science have all shared in condemning homosexuality, defining it in religious terms as a sin, in legal terms as a crime, and in medical terms as a disease.

A modern consciousness of homosexuality began to emerge in the late nineteenth century as a homosexual identity took shape and social movements began to develop. The term *homosexual* itself was first used in a pamphlet written in 1869 by a Hungarian physician, Karoly Benkert. The first human rights organization for homosexuals, the Scientific Humanitarian Committee, was founded in Germany in 1896. In the United States the first gay men's organization, called the Mattachine Society, was founded in Los Angeles in 1950, followed in 1955 by the first lesbian organization, the Daughters of Bilitis, in San Francisco.

However, the gay and lesbian rights movement was not born until 1969, when the famous Stonewall riot took place in Greenwich Village, New York. The police raid on the Stonewall gay bar on June 27–28 was not noteworthy in itself, since raids in which police harassed or arrested homosexual patrons were a common occurrence. Nor was resistance by gays to discriminatory acts unusual—many examples can be cited. But somehow the week of protest and riots that followed the Stonewall raid became the symbol for the new movement. A consciousness of gay liberation, gay power, and gay civil rights emerged, clearly inspired by the burgeoning civil rights movements of other minority groups in the 1960s. In *The Wedding Banquet*, Simon, in particular, is influenced by gay liberation; he wears T-shirts that express his gay consciousness and pride.

The decade following Stonewall was a period of unprecedented activism and change. Gay rights groups and organizations were formed in cities, in towns, and on campuses across the United States (as well as in numerous other countries). Among these were major national organizations such as the National Gay and Lesbian Task Force and the Lambda Legal Defense and Education Fund. The gay liberation press was founded and began to flourish, with publications such as *The Advocate* (to which Simon and Wai-Tung subscribe) gaining nationwide readership. Pressure brought to bear on the American Psychiatric Association resulted in the removal of homosexuality from its list of mental disorders in 1973. Lesbian/Gay Pride Day festivals and other parades and demonstrations made gays more visible and brought gay issues before the general public. The election to public office of two openly gay candidates, Elaine Noble in New York in 1974 and Harvey Milk in San Francisco in 1977, were considered major victories in the realm of politics.

After having made considerable progress, the gay community suffered a tremendous setback in the 1980s with the outbreak and spread of the AIDS (acquired immune deficiency syndrome) epidemic. A disease of the immune system caused by the HIV virus, AIDS damages the body's ability to fight other diseases. Because the virus can be transmitted through blood or semen, gay men are especially susceptible to it. AIDS is not a disease restricted to homosexuals, however, and can be spread by intravenous drug use, by blood transfusions, and in other ways. Outside the United States AIDS is primarily a heterosexual disease, reaching alarming proportions. The United Nations estimates that at the beginning of the twenty-first century nearly thirty-five million people worldwide were living with HIV/AIDS.

While the epidemic increased fears of gays and resulted in a new wave of discrimination (gays were fired, denied housing, refused health insurance), there were some positive effects as well. The deaths of tens of thousands of gay men, though an unequaled tragedy for the gay community, also galvanized many gays and lesbians to come out of the closet and become socially and politically active. Gays have been in the forefront of efforts to combat the disease, promoting educational efforts, advocating the use of condoms and other safe-sex practices, and raising funds and lobbying for medical research. Their often publicized struggles to care for dying friends and partners have revealed them to the public as caring and compassionate people.

A unique symbol of this compassion is the Names Project AIDS Memorial Quilt. Begun in 1985, this work of art now contains more than 44,000 three-by-six-foot individual panels, each one commemorating the life of someone who died of AIDS-related complications. Sewn together by lovers, friends, and family members—and including panels from all the states and many countries—the quilt has been displayed at numerous National Marches on Washington for Gay, Lesbian, and Bisexual Rights. It also tours the world in smaller segments.

As the gay community struggled with the AIDS crisis, it also faced a determined backlash from right-wing individuals and groups determined to halt the gains of previous years. One of the first to gain nationwide attention for her opposition to gay rights was Anita Bryant, well known as a pop singer, publicist for Florida orange juice, and born-again Christian. Her organization, Save the Children, founded in 1977, paved the way for many subsequent groups that preached homophobia under the guise of "family values." The explosive growth of the so-called "religious right" (this term encompasses a variety of organizations such as the Christian Coalition and the Traditional Values Coalition), combined with the lack of political support for gays during the Reagan years, made the 1980s a time of formidable opposition.

Having made enormous strides since Stonewall, the gay community still has a long way to go. Arduous struggles continue for what many gays and lesbians view as basic rights: legally accepted marriages, antidiscrimination laws in the workplace, domestic partner benefits (such as health insurance), and full acceptance in the military. Gays are still the frequent target of street violence, verbal abuse, and other hate crimes. They have also had to mobilize against sophisticated antigay forces which have brought antigay ballot measures to voters in the states of Oregon, Maine, Colorado, and elsewhere.

While a personal rather than a political film, *The Wedding Banquet* can only be understood in light of the ongoing public efforts of gays to achieve full acceptance in American society.

Why Do We Speak of Gay "Culture"?

As we discuss *The Wedding Banquet*, you might be surprised by our frequent references to "gay culture." Perhaps you have not heard this before or have never thought of homosexuals as having a distinct culture. If you are encountering this concept for the first time, you should know that it is relatively new and is becoming more widely accepted. To help you understand what it means, you might think in terms of a gay "subculture" or "coculture," or, since you are probably accustomed to using the word *culture* solely to refer to ethnic or national groups, in terms of a gay "community."

Related Terms

bisexual or bi People whose romantic and sexual feelings are for members of both sexes.

come out or **come out of the closet** Terms referring to the process of disclosing one's homosexuality to others and of accepting it oneself.

faggot, fag, homo, pansy, fairy, fruit Commonly used derogatory terms for gay men; insulting words for lesbians include *dyke, butch,* and *lezzy.*

gender One's psychological and emotional identity as a male or female, in contrast with one's biological sex. One is born with a sex but raised with a gender.

heterosexism Prejudice against gays resulting from the often unquestioned assumption that everyone is heterosexual; analogous to other -isms such as racism, sexism, and ageism; also called *heterosexual bias.*

heterosexual or **straight** People whose romantic and sexual feelings are primarily for members of the opposite sex.

heterosexual privilege Unearned benefits that heterosexuals enjoy in society simply because of their sexual orientation. See the further explanation and examples below.

homophobia Deep-seated fear and accompanying hatred of homosexuality and homosexuals; the adjective is *homophobic.*

homosexual or **gay** Men or women whose romantic and sexual feelings are primarily for members of the same sex.

in the closet Hiding one's homosexuality from others and possibly from oneself.

lesbian Women who are homosexual. The word derives from the Greek island of Lesbos, home of the poet Sappho.

(continued on next page)

Related Terms (continued)

lover, significant other, (domestic) partner, (longtime) companion   Terms used to refer to individuals in a same-sex relationship. None of these terms is completely adequate, since *lover* has sexual connotations some gays dislike, *significant other* is also used by heterosexuals to refer to their unmarried partners, *domestic partner* refers more to the legalities of those living together than to the emotional realm, *partner* seems like a business or professional relationship, and *longtime companion* seems too much like merely a friend.

outing   Practice of revealing a person's homosexuality against his/her will; often done for political reasons (to show that gays are more prevalent and in more prominent and prestigious positions than is commonly known) and to provide role models to other gays.

queer   Originally a derogatory term, but some gays and lesbians now prefer it to *gay* or *homosexual*. They feel that by reclaiming the term, they can transform it from a hateful word into a proud self-description.

sexual orientation   One's sexual inclinations; usually preferred by homosexuals to *sexual preference*, since the latter indicates there is choice, whereas many gays and lesbians believe they were born homosexual.

special rights   Term often used by critics of gays to suggest that in working toward equal rights (in the workplace, the military, etc.), gays are really asking for extra benefits, in other words, "special rights."

straight but not narrow   Slogan often seen on buttons and T-shirts to indicate that the wearer is heterosexual but an ally of homosexuals and bisexuals.

transsexual   Individuals who consider themselves to be of the opposite gender from their biological sex. These people feel "born into" or "trapped in" the wrong bodies. They may or may not seek surgery and other medical procedures to bring their bodies into conformity with their psychological and emotional selves. The term *transgendered* is often applied to those who have undergone such surgery.

transvestite   Person who dresses in clothing of the opposite gender; also referred to as *cross-dressing*. Male transvestites are sometimes referred to as *drag queens*. Males who cross-dress to perform in public are known as *female impersonators*. Transvestites may be heterosexual, homosexual, or bisexual.

Of course gay culture is not the same as the culture of an ethnic group or a nation. But many gays and lesbians believe that the concept is appropriate and that many characteristics of a culture apply. Homosexuals do, for example, have a sense of shared history. They also have a sense of geographical place, having carved out "gay neighborhoods" in many major cities such as Greenwich Village, New York (where Simon and Wai-Tung of *The Wedding Banquet* live), the Castro area of San Francisco, and South Beach in Miami. Gay neighborhoods have sprung up to serve many purposes: here gays can meet and socialize, feel comfortable and safe, and come together to achieve political goals.

In his article on "America's Emerging Gay Culture," Randall E. Majors (1994) explains that gays and lesbians have distinct patterns of communication by which they meet and recognize each other. These patterns consist primarily of nonverbal cues such as posture, voice, eye contact, dress, and touch. In exaggerated form, these nonverbals form the basis for stereotypes of gay behavior, particularly of men.

Randall also explains that gay culture abounds with symbols, such as the rainbow, the stud earring for men (now worn by many heterosexual men as well), and the color lavender. The pink inverted triangle, which gays were forced to wear in the concentration camps of Nazi Germany, has become a political symbol, and the red ribbon is a sign of support for AIDS victims and AIDS research.

A further rationale for using the term *culture* is that homosexuals, like many ethnic, religious, and other minority cultures, experience oppression and discrimination by virtue of being different from the mainstream. Living outside the locus of power, gays and members of many other subcultures derive a sense of unity and solidarity from joining together for moral support as well as for political and social action.

As you think about gay culture in this chapter, remember that culture is not easy to define. There is no accepted checklist of characteristics that must be present. Anthropologists offer us many different definitions and hundreds of books on the topic. Does a culture have to have its own foods, language, customs, dress? Are its common values and ideals what are most significant? In her book entitled *The Gay and Lesbian Liberation Movement*, Margaret Cruikshank says that the phrase "gay culture" designates "attitudes, values, tastes, artistic and literary works, groups and organizations, common experiences, festivals, special events, rituals, and their sense of a shared history" (1992, 119).

A final important aspect of a culture is that people identify with it. You might wear red shoes frequently, for example, without seeing yourself as part of a "red-shoe" culture. If, on the other hand, you see your personal identity as tied to being Japanese, or being Catholic, or being young or old—and if you feel a sense of shared identity with others like you—one can argue that you are then part of a particular culture or coculture. (This same idea applies to Deaf culture, discussed in the next chapter.)

In the United States, heterosexuals enjoy many benefits that are often denied to homosexuals. They range from big things, such as being welcomed into a wide variety of apartment buildings or neighborhoods, to smaller ones, such as being able to find appropriate greeting cards for a gay partner or spouse. Other examples include the following:

- being able to hold hands, show affection, or dance together in public without attracting unwanted attention
- being allowed to enter into marriage and to obtain the rights and recognition accorded that status
- being able to serve openly in the military

In your film notebooks, list at least five additional examples of heterosexual privilege in the United States or in your own country. Be prepared to discuss these examples.

Lights Out: Viewing the Film

For decades gays have either been ignored or portrayed in disparaging, superficial ways in Hollywood films. Often they have been depicted as evil, predatory, or perverted; sometimes they have been included simply for laughs. *The Wedding Banquet* (1993) distinguishes itself in film history as one of a small but rapidly growing number of films to present gay characters in nonstereotypical fashion and to reach large mainstream American and international audiences.

Director and cowriter Ang Lee, a native of Taiwan, attended the New York University Film School. His excellent cast includes noted Taiwanese actors Sihung Lung (Mr. Gao) and Ah-Leh Gua (Mrs. Gao) as well as Taiwanese singer and television star May Chin (Wei-Wei). Winston Chao (Wai-Tung) appears in his first film role with the openly gay actor Mitchell Lichtenstein (Simon), and Ang Lee appears in a cameo role at the banquet, com-

Major Characters in the Film

Wai-Tung Gao   gay Taiwanese American real estate entrepreneur
Simon   Wai-Tung's lover
Mr. and Mrs. Gao   Wai-Tung's parents
Wei-Wei   mainland Chinese woman artist who marries Wai-Tung
Little Sister Mao (Wu Ren Ren)   mainland Chinese woman chosen by computer to marry Wai-Tung
Bob Law   friend of Wai-Tung
Old Chen   restaurateur who knew Mr. Gao in China

menting that the raucous goings-on reflect "five thousand years of sexual oppression" in China.

The film became the biggest box-office success ever in Taiwan and made history there as the first film in which two men kissed. *The Wedding Banquet* was also the surprise winner of the Berlin Film Festival's Golden Bear. Filmed in English and in Chinese (with English subtitles), it is dedicated to the real-life couple whose story inspired the film.

Spotlight on Culture and Communication

This spotlight will focus on the process of "coming out of the closet." Review this and other terms in Related Terms (pages 166–67). The decision to conceal or reveal one's homosexuality plays a major role in many gay people's lives and greatly affects gay culture and patterns of communication. Gays who hide their sexual orientation do so for many reasons. They may fear discrimination or dismissal at work, rejection by friends or family, or harassment and violence from antigay individuals or groups.

Actually, the image of the closet is not the best one, since it suggests an either/or choice in which one either stays in or walks out forever. The real situation is much more complicated. To understand "coming out," remember that it is not a single act, but rather a lifetime process. It involves coming out to oneself as well as to others. For some gays it may take a long time to realize, or to admit to themselves, that they are gay. For most gays coming out to others is a selective, often painful process. It is not uncommon for gays to be "out" to some people—trusted friends or family—and in the closet at work or with casual acquaintances. Not only must gays decide with whom to be open about their sexuality, but also, in every case, they must find an appropriate way to inform the person at hand. Thus they must come out over and over again throughout their lives to people who do not know they are gay.

In small groups, select a clip from the movie that illustrates one or more aspects of coming out. Focus on the way in which the scene evolves, the details of the setting, and the words and actions of the characters, paying attention to both verbal and nonverbal behavior.

You may wish to consider the following:

- *Trust* deciding whom to confide in and why; whom not to confide in and why
- *Deception* handling the lies, complications, and awkward problems created by staying in the closet
- *Timing* deciding where and how to come out to a certain person
- *Long-term effects* dealing with and responding to reactions of family and friends after coming out

Two or more groups with different scene selections and themes may present their findings to the class.

True or False?

There is a great deal of misinformation surrounding homosexuality and bisexuality. To test your knowledge, read the statements below and circle true or false. You are not expected to know all the correct responses.

true false 1. Sexual orientation is a choice.
true false 2. Gays can have children.
true false 3. AIDS is a gay disease.
true false 4. You can be fired from your employment for being gay.
true false 5. Gays are estimated to comprise 2 percent of the adult population in the United States.
true false 6. Lesbians and gays are more of a danger to children than are heterosexuals.
true false 7. Homosexuality is a mental illness that can be cured.
true false 8. Some companies are gay-friendly and offer benefits to the partners of gay employees.
true false 9. Bisexuals are confused about their sexuality.

This quiz is based primarily on Eric Marcus' book *Is It a Choice? Answers to 300 of the Most Frequently Asked Questions about Gays and Lesbians.* Time permitting, read through this book and write one question and answer in your film notebook that you found particularly interesting. Be prepared to share this information with others in class discussion.

Answers are located on page 178.

Poetry: Reflections of a Gay Student

Read the following poem, written by an anonymous high school student and published in *Growing Up Gay/Growing Up Lesbian: A Literary Anthology*.

Does It Matter?

My father asked if I am gay
I asked Does it matter?
He said No not really
I said Yes.
He said get out of my life
I guess it mattered.

My boss asked if I am gay
I asked Does it matter?
He said No not really
I told him Yes.
He said You're fired, faggot
I guess it mattered.

My friend asked if I am gay
I said Does it matter?
He said Not really
I told him Yes.
He said don't call me your friend
I guess it mattered.

My lover asked Do you love me?
I asked Does it matter?
He said Yes.
I told him I love you
He said Let me hold you in my arms
For the first time in my life something matters.

My God asked me Do you love yourself?
I said Does it matter?
He said Yes.
I said How can I love myself? I am Gay
He said That is what I made you
Nothing again will ever matter.

- How did you feel as you progressed through the poem? What was the effect of the question and answer format? How does the voice of the poem change at the end?
- Does this poem make you think of any times in your own life when you have felt unfairly rejected by someone?

Zoom Lens: Choosing Your Own Topic of Interest

Hands-on Activities

1. If your campus has a gay and bisexual student organization, invite members to speak to your class. There may be students in the class who are gay or bisexual (and perhaps already "out" on campus) and who would like to help answer questions.

   If there is no gay student organization at your school or on your campus, you might invite a representative to speak to your class from Parents and Friends of Lesbians and Gays (PFLAG), the National Gay and Lesbian Task Force (NGLTF), or the Lambda Legal Defense and Education Fund (see the Sequel). The national headquarters of each group can put you in touch with people at the nearest local chapters.
2. Watch another film that focuses on the lives and concerns of gays and lesbians (see list of recommended films in the Sequel) and compare it in writing or discussion with *The Wedding Banquet*.
3. Contact one or more of the organizations mentioned above—or other gay rights organizations—to obtain information and materials. What do you learn from the activities of the organizations?

Research Papers or Oral Reports

1. Research the origins and history of the AIDS Memorial Quilt. You may wish to contact the Names Project Foundation (see the Sequel).
2. Gays of color often face double discrimination as members of two minority groups. Look into the issues that they consider relevant and pressing in today's society.

3. A number of books have now been written for children growing up with gay and lesbian parents. Contact Alyson Publications (see the Sequel) for a complete catalogue of books. Read several (one is listed in the Sequel under authors Newman and Souza, and another one is under Willhoite) and write about this growing segment of children's literature. In your paper, describe this body of literature with regard to content, style, and illustrations. Also give your views on what the books accomplish.
4. Research one of the following issues concerning gay rights:
   a. same-sex marriages
   b. status of gays in the military
   c. antidiscrimination laws in the workplace
   d. hate crimes against gays and efforts to enact protective legislation
5. Research the debate about homosexuals that is occurring within the Christian church. Include the controversy over specific Bible passages and the differing positions taken by different denominations. Alternatively, research attitudes and practices toward gays in another religion.
6. Find out more about the legal situation regarding homosexuality in your own country or, if you live in the United States, in your own state.
7. Obtain several issues of magazines such as *The Advocate, Out, Poz, Girlfriends,* and *Curve.* What insights do you gain from these magazines? How do they differ from the mainstream press?

Using Your Imagination

1. Design a poster, button, or other artwork to advocate for gay rights or AIDS awareness. (You might wish to look at Keith Haring's work—see the biography by Gruen in the Sequel. Note that in his first appearance Simon wears a Keith Haring T-shirt.)
2. Imagine you lived in a totally nonhomophobic society. Describe what life might be like and how it would be different from your own society.
3. Imagine you were to wear a Keith Haring or other T-shirt advocating homosexuality for a day. How might you feel? What reactions might you get from others?
4. Imagine that Wai-Tung and his mother write to each other (or send cassettes) three years after the parents' visit. Write one or both of the written or recorded letters.

5. Imagine a sequel to *The Wedding Banquet* (or a television situation comedy spin-off) in which the baby is featured as a teenager living with Wai-Tung, Wei-Wei, and Simon. Describe the major plot elements.
6. You are a heterosexual who is unsure about your feelings toward gays. Imagine you receive a letter in which a sibling or close friend comes out to you. Write your reply. Or imagine that you are a parent and your daughter or son comes out to you in a letter. Write your response.

Sequel: Further Suggested Resources

Readings

Adam, Barry D. 1987. *The Rise of a Gay and Lesbian Movement.* Boston: Twayne.

Bawer, Bruce. 1993. *A Place at the Table: The Gay Individual in American Society.* New York: Simon and Schuster.

Coote, Stephen, ed. 1983. *The Penguin Book of Homosexual Verse.* New York: Viking Penguin.

Cowan, Thomas Dale. 1988. *Gay Men and Women Who Enriched the World.* New Canaan, CT: Mulvey Books.

Cruikshank, Margaret. 1992. *The Gay and Lesbian Liberation Movement.* London: Routledge.

Duberman, Martin, Martha Vicinus, and George Chauncey Jr., eds. 1989. *Hidden from History: Reclaiming the Gay and Lesbian Past.* New York: New American Library.

Fahy, Una. 1995. *How to Make the World a Better Place for Gays and Lesbians.* New York: Warner Books.

Gruen, John. 1991. *Keith Haring: The Authorized Biography.* New York: Prentice Hall.

Halperin, David M. 1993. "Is There a History of Sexuality?" In *The Lesbian and Gay Studies Reader,* edited by Henry Abelove, Michele Aina Barale, and David M. Halperin, 416–31. New York: Routledge.

Helminiak, Daniel A. 1995. *What the Bible Really Says about Homosexuality.* San Francisco: Almo Square Press.

Hendricks, Aart, Rob Tielman, and Evert van der Veen, eds. 1993. *The Third Pink Book: A Global View of Lesbian and Gay Liberation and Oppression.* Buffalo, NY: Prometheus Books.

Herbst, Philip H. 2001. *Wimmin, Wimps & Wallflowers: An Encyclopædic Dictionary of Gender and Sexual Orientation Bias in the United States.* Yarmouth, ME: Intercultural Press.

Katz, Jonathan. 1976. *Gay American History.* New York: Thomas Y. Crowell.

Majors, Randall E. 1994. "America's Emerging Gay Culture." In *Intercultural Communication: A Reader.* 7th ed., edited by Larry A. Samovar and Richard E. Porter, 165–71. Belmont, CA: Wadsworth.

Marcus, Eric. 1993. *Is It a Choice? Answers to 300 of the Most Frequently Asked Questions about Gays and Lesbians.* New York: HarperCollins.

———. 1992. *Making History.* New York: Harper Perennial.

Miller, Neil. 1995. *Out of the Past: Gay and Lesbian History from 1869 to the Present.* New York: Random House.

Newman, Lesléa, and Diana Souza. 1989. *Heather Has Two Mommies.* Boston: Alyson Wonderland.

Singer, Bennett L., ed. 1994. *Growing Up Gay/Growing Up Lesbian: A Literary Anthology.* New York: New Press.

Stewart, William. 1995. *Cassell's Queer Companion.* London: Cassell.

Sullivan, Andrew. 1995. *Virtually Normal: An Argument about Homosexuality.* New York: Random House.

Willhoite, Michael. 1990. *Daddy's Roommate.* Boston: Alyson Wonderland.

Witt, Lynn, Sherry Thomas, and Eric Marcus, eds. 1995. *Out in All Directions: A Treasury of Gay and Lesbian America.* New York: Warner Books.

Zuckerman, Amy J., and George F. Simons. 1994. *Sexual Orientation in the Workplace.* Santa Cruz, CA: International Partners Press.

- -

Films

The Birdcage (1996)   Gay nightclub owner must ask his drag queen lover to be absent when his son's conservative prospective in-laws come to visit. This entertaining remake of the French *La Cage aux Folles* (1978) does not live up to the splendid original but is worth seeing for the performances of Robin Williams, Nathan Lane, and other fine actors. Directed by Mike Nichols.

Common Threads: Stories from the Quilt (1989)   The stories of five people who are memorialized in the AIDS quilt, as told by family and friends. Academy Award-winning documentary directed by Robert Epstein and Jeffrey Friedman (Facets).

Desert Hearts (1985)   A straitlaced English professor, recovering from her recent divorce on a dude ranch in Nevada, becomes romantically involved with a spirited young woman artist. Directed by Donna Deitch.

In and Out (1997)   A comedy about a high school English teacher (Kevin Kline) who is "outed" shortly before he and his fiancée are to marry. Directed by Frank Oz.

The Incredibly True Story of Two Girls in Love (1995)   An engaging lesbian romantic comedy about two teenage girls from different backgrounds who fall in love. Directed by Maria Maggenti.

Longtime Companion (1990)   A beautifully told story of a gay couple, one of whom is dying of AIDS; provides a glimpse into the devastating impact of the disease on the gay community in the 1980s. Directed by Norman Rene.

Personal Best (1982)   A sensitive portrait of track stars who enter into a lesbian relationship while training for the 1980 Olympics; starring Mariel Hemingway. Directed by Robert Towne.

Philadelphia (1993)   Successful corporate attorney (Tom Hanks) battling AIDS is fired from his firm and decides to sue for discrimination; important mainstream film about biases against people with AIDS. Directed by Jonathan Demme.

The Times of Harvey Milk (1984)   Academy Award-winning portrait of the slain gay political activist Harvey Milk. Directed by Robert Epstein (Facets).

Websites and Mailing Addresses

Alyson Publications, PO Box 4371, Los Angeles, CA 90078; phone: 800-525-9766; fax: 213-467-6805 (www.alyson.com)

Gay and Lesbian Alliance Against Defamation (GLAAD) 150 W. 26th Street, Suite 503, New York, NY 10001; GLAAD@glaad.org (www.glaad.org)

Lambda Legal Defense and Education Fund, 666 Broadway, 12th Floor, New York, NY 10012 (www.qrd.org/qrd/orgs/LLDEF)

Names Project Foundation, 310 Townsend Street, Suite 310, San Francisco, CA 94107; phone: 415-882-5500 (www.AIDSQuilt.org)

National Gay and Lesbian Task Force (NGLTF), 2320 17th Street NW, Washington, DC 20009; phone: 202-332-6483; (www.ngltf.org)

Parents and Friends of Lesbians and Gays (PFLAG), 1101 14th Street NW, Suite 1030, Washington, DC 20005; phone: 202-638-4200; (www.pflag.org)

Answers to true-false quiz on page 171

1. False. This matter, however, is controversial. Scientific experiments are being conducted to determine if sexual orientation is biologically determined, and some research on genetic and hormonal factors indicates that it may be. There is still no conclusive evidence; nonetheless most gays and lesbians testify that they have no more chosen their sexual orientation than heterosexuals have chosen theirs.

2. True. Some gays become parents when involved in heterosexual marriages or relationships (this is one plot element of the film *The Wedding Banquet*). Many gays are also choosing a variety of options for having children, including artificial insemination, adoption, coparenting, and surrogacy.

    Studies comparing children raised by gays and those raised by heterosexuals show no significant differences in the children's psychological growth, social adjustment, or development of sexual identity. It is a myth that gay parents raise gay children, just as it is not true that the children of heterosexual parents are necessarily heterosexual.

3. False. This is explained on page 164.

4. True. In most parts of the United States it is still legal to fire gays from their jobs. Laws that forbid discrimination against gays in employment, housing, and public accommodation (such as providing service in hotels) are in effect in only a handful of states. Many cities and corporations, however, have enacted their own antidiscrimination policies.

5. False. The most widely accepted statistic is 10 percent, based on landmark studies on human sexuality done by Albert Kinsey in the 1940s and 1950s. The accurate numbers are difficult to know, since many gays are in the closet and no definitive studies have been conducted in recent years.

6. False. Statistics from many reputable sources show that most child molesters are heterosexual men.

7. False. In 1973 the American Psychiatric Association removed the term *homosexuality* from its list of mental and emotional disorders. Today most psychologists, psychiatrists, and other mental health professionals agree that homosexuality is not a mental illness; thus, there is no need for a cure.

8. True. An increasing number of corporations include the phrase "sexual orientation" in their nondiscrimination policies. Some offer benefits to same-sex partners and encourage the formation of gay employee groups within the company.

    If you are interested in further information on gay-friendly corporations, contact the Gay and Lesbian Alliance Against Defamation (GLAAD) (see the Sequel).

9. False. Bisexuals are clear about being attracted to both men and women. Most people, whether they are aware of it or not, are bisexual to some degree. In his studies, Alfred Kinsey rejects a strict either/or approach to sexual orientation. According to the seven-point Kinsey Scale, those who are exclusively hetero-

sexual receive a 0, those who are exclusively homosexual receive a 6, and most people fall somewhere in between, thus having the capacity, in varying degrees, for relationships with both sexes.

9

Deaf Culture:
Children of a Lesser God

Setting the Scene: Freewriting and Discussion

The sculpture depicted in this photograph is located at the entrance to the Oregon School for the Deaf in Salem.

Imagine you are visiting the school and see this sculpture as you enter the campus. Freewrite what you imagine your feelings and impressions might be, and give your interpretation of the sculpture.

After you have completed this exercise, read the inscription from the plaque at the base of the sculpture.

Inscription reads: "The initial sculpture design was for the hand shape of FRIENDSHIP, but it was structurally impossible to create in cement. Retaining the concept of interlocking digits, the design was changed to the hand shape of BUTTERFLY...a creature of obvious symbolic significance. The last adaptation in the design resulted in the sculpture being rotated 180 degrees to face away from the campus suggesting the direction of flight and emphasizing the relationship between the school and the larger community."

Wide-Angle Lens: Historical Perspectives

Some Turning Points in Deaf History

The film *Children of a Lesser God* brings to light a question that might seem simple but has resisted a solution for centuries: do deaf people have the right to use their own language or must they be forced to learn to speak? The main character in the film, Sarah Norman, is determined to use sign language rather than speech, despite the well-meaning efforts of her speech teacher, James Leeds, who believes that speech will allow her to "get along" in life.

Sarah's situation is experienced in various forms by an estimated one to two million *prelingually deaf* people living in the United States today. The prelingually deaf include those who are born deaf (congenitally deaf) and those who become deaf at an early age before acquiring spoken language. Try to imagine for a moment how excruciatingly difficult it must be for prelingually deaf people to speak if they have never heard sound and thus have no auditory memory of sound upon which to base their learning and understanding of a spoken language. Remember as well that they cannot hear what they are saying and thus cannot know if they are speaking correctly. Also imagine what it must be like to try to read lips if you do not know what sounds the lip movements are shaping. A further difficulty is that many sounds are not visible on the lips, but are made in the sound cavity.

Having grown up without sound or spoken language, many prelingually deaf individuals see deafness as central to their identity and culture (see discussion of Deaf culture, pages 186–87), as do those *postlingually deaf* who lose their hearing at a young age or as adolescents. The situation is generally quite different for those postlingually deaf people who lose their hearing later in life. They have already assumed a place in the hearing world as adults and thus usually do not consider deafness as a part of their self-image. Similarly, the approximately fourteen million Americans who are hard-of-hearing generally do not see themselves as belonging to Deaf culture.

The history of deafness in the United States is marked not only by ignorance and misconceptions on the part of the hearing world but also by persistent attempts to control the deaf and force them to accept spoken language. For much of our early history, deaf persons experienced abuse, neglect, and discrimination. Because speech is so closely tied to notions of intellect, deaf persons were generally considered inferior and stupid (as evidenced by the long-used phrase "deaf and dumb," which meant "deaf and mute"). As described by Oliver Sacks in his book *Seeing Voices: A Journey into the World of the Deaf*, the situation of the prelingually deaf prior to 1750 was a calamity, not only in the U.S., but in many countries around the world as well:

> ...unable to acquire speech, hence "dumb" or "mute"; unable to enjoy free communication with even their parents and families; ...cut off, except in large cities, even from the community of their own kind; deprived of literacy and education...forced to do the most menial work; living alone, often close to destitution; treated by the law and society as little better than imbeciles—the lot of the deaf was manifestly dreadful. (1989, 13–14)

Forms of legal discrimination in some societies included prohibitions from inheriting or owning property and from marrying. In tragic cases throughout history, deafness in children went undetected, and deaf children were treated as mentally disabled.

A fascinating exception to this widespread intolerance was found on Martha's Vineyard, an island off the Massachusetts coast, where families who came from the same English town and carried a recessive gene for deafness began to settle in the seventeenth century. Due to intermarriage among the islanders, deafness eventually affected a significant proportion of the community, resulting in the widespread adoption of sign language, used freely and naturally for more than 250 years by deaf and hearing people alike. Rather than being stigmatized, the deaf were fully integrated and even enjoyed a privileged position in this society.

In the 1820s conditions for the deaf began to improve in the United States due to the efforts of Thomas Hopkins Gallaudet, a minister in Hartford, Connecticut. The story, a beloved part of Deaf history, begins when Gallaudet was observing some children playing in his garden and noticed that one little girl, Alice Cogswell, was left out. Upon learning that the girl was deaf, he talked with her father, the surgeon Mason Cogswell, about setting up what would become the first American school for the deaf. Sponsored by Alice's father, Gallaudet sailed in 1816 for Europe, where pedagogical methods were known to be more progressive than in the U.S., in the hope of finding a teacher for the school.

Gallaudet visited the Institute of Deaf Mutes in Paris, founded in 1755 by the Abbé de L'Epée, who had observed and learned the sign language of orphaned deaf children, given them shelter, and helped them develop a system of French Sign Language that could be used within the wider society. At this institute Gallaudet met the young teacher Laurent Clerc, himself deaf, who was to play a critical role in Deaf history in the United States. Though he had never traveled outside France or ventured much beyond the institute, Clerc agreed to accompany Gallaudet back to the U.S.

By the following year the two men had raised sufficient funds to found, with Mason Cogswell, the American Asylum for the Deaf and Dumb in Hartford. Clerc's French Sign Language was blended with indigenous sign languages already used by deaf Americans—such as the language of Martha's Vineyard—to create a unique language, known as American Sign Language (ASL). The success of the Hartford asylum led to the opening of other such schools around the country where deaf pupils received instruction from teachers fluent in ASL, many of whom were deaf and almost all of whom had trained in Hartford. In 1864 Congress created in Washington, D.C., the first college for the deaf in the world, known today as Gallaudet University.

Unfortunately, this "golden age" enjoyed by the American deaf was short-lived. A new movement called *oralism*, which requires the deaf to read lips and vocalize (a physical near-impossibility for many), was gaining support. Well-known inventor and speech expert Alexander Graham Bell lent his considerable prestige to the effort to force the deaf to speak. In 1880 at the International Congress of Educators for the Deaf held in Milan, Italy (and attended by delegates who were all hearing except for one), oralism was prescribed as the universal teaching method for the deaf, and an edict was passed to ban the use of sign language.

As a result of the Milan Congress, ASL was banned from American schools, effectively stripping deaf students of their native language. Disobedient students had their hands strapped or tied down in school. The number of deaf teachers of the deaf decreased rapidly, giving control of deaf education to the hearing. Rather than improving standards, oralism led to the deterioration of the level of literacy and the education of deaf students in general.

Not until eighty years later, in 1960, did ASL receive further consideration as the language of the deaf. In that year linguist William Stokoe of Gallaudet University published research demonstrating that ASL is a genuine language in its own right, with a sophisticated vocabulary and grammar, rather than (as was believed at the time) a primitive and random assortment of gestures. So revolutionary were Stokoe's findings that even many deaf people did not at first understand or believe his claims that ASL was equal to spoken language. (More information about ASL is included later in this chapter.)

Stokoe's work helped promote a growing consciousness of Deaf pride and advocacy in the wake of the civil rights movement of the 1960s. But the landmark event for Deaf rights came two decades later during a change in presidents at Gallaudet University. Although Gallaudet had never had a deaf president in its entire 124-year history, in 1988 the possibility was at hand. At a rally held prior to the final decision, thousands of students, faculty, staff, and alumni, wearing buttons that read "DEAF PRESIDENT NOW," gathered to express their views. One of the speakers at the rally, Professor Allen Sussman, said, "This is a historical event. You could call this the first Deaf civil rights activity" (Shapiro 1993, 77). Many in the audience were thus made aware for the first time of the link between the treatment of the deaf and civil rights.

When the lone hearing candidate was chosen by the board of directors a few days later, the campus erupted in protest. Students boycotted classes, gained the support of Deaf organizations across the country, received wide coverage in the national media, and organized marches on the White House and the Capitol. After a highly emotional week of resistance, the newly hired hearing president was forced to resign in favor of I. King Jordan, the popular dean of arts and sciences and one of the two Deaf finalists. This so-called Gallaudet Revolution was considered pivotal not only in instilling a new sense of pride in the Deaf community but also in giving powerful impetus to the disability rights movement across the country. Soon after the Gallaudet protest, the Americans with Disabilities Act was passed.

Despite the progress of the past few decades, the majority hearing population often continues to try to determine what is best for the minority deaf population. The debate over oralism and signing is far from resolved, and new sources of conflict, such as that of the cochlear implant (discussed later in this chapter), have emerged.

What Is Deaf Culture?

As the deaf have gained a new sense of identity and pride in recent decades, the idea of a Deaf culture (spelled with a capital *D* to indicate the culture rather than the audiological condition) has gained credence. This idea may seem an unusual concept because we so often link the idea of culture with ethnic identity, food, clothing, religion, and shared geographical space. Yet the Deaf indeed have a culture with their own language and nonverbal behavior, values, socializing patterns and etiquette, humor, arts and entertainment, social and political organizations, history, and traditions. Moreover, part of Deaf culture and consciousness is, like that of many other subcultures, a sense of what authors Harlan Lane and Robert Hoffmeister call "shared oppression" (1996, 159).

Certainly the key to Deaf culture is sign language. Through signing, with its specific hand and body movements and facial expressions, Deaf people create common bonds and form a community. They share and pass on their history, values, and traditions, and they express themselves artistically. Because sign language is spatial rather than written, Deaf arts are often very different from hearing arts. Mime, visual poetry, theater, and storytelling are highly valued among the Deaf. Other flourishing Deaf art forms that do not depend on the written word are dance, sculpture, and crafts.

Also intrinsic to Deaf culture and identity are residential schools for the deaf, such as the one depicted in the film. Because 90 percent of deaf children are born to hearing parents, they would have little or no access to their own language and culture were it not for their attendance at schools for the deaf. Many deaf children thus learn language not from their parents but at school, where they bond and develop unique social patterns, including specific styles of greetings, farewells, and touching. For example, deaf people cannot use their voices or sounds to get each other's attention, so they either wave their arms in the other person's visual field or touch the other person

---

Related Terms

deaf Audiological condition of deafness.

Deaf Deaf culture and those individuals who identify themselves with the culture.

deaf and dumb Term no longer acceptable but widely used historically to refer to deaf people who did not possess spoken language and therefore were considered stupid.

deaf and mute Term that has fallen out of favor because it tends to define deaf people from the point of view of the hearing.

person with disability Term preferred to *handicapped person* or *disabled person* because the emphasis is placed on the person rather than the disability. Many deaf people do not consider themselves as having a disability.

in a prescribed, appropriate way. So important are the residential schools to the Deaf that they usually include the name of their school when introducing themselves.

A final aspect of Deaf culture is Deaf humor, which tends to be visually based, making use of mime and gesture. Also much humor focuses on deafness itself, as does the following old joke.

> *Question: What is the greatest problem facing deaf people today?*
> *Answer: Hearing people.*

Viewing Deafness as a culture produces a profound shift in thinking from old models that define it as a handicap, disability, or illness to be cured. As Edward Dolnick explains in his article "Deafness as Culture," many deaf people "now proclaim they are a subculture like any other. They are simply a linguistic minority (speaking American Sign Language) and are no more in need of a cure for their condition than are Haitians or Hispanics" (1993, 37). And John Limnidis, a former Gallaudet football player who had a role in *Children*, explains, "Deafness is not a handicap. It's a culture, a language, and I'm proud to be deaf. If there was a medication that could be given to deaf people to make them hear, I wouldn't take it. Never. Never till I die!" (Shapiro 1993, 85).

In his article "Deaf Is Beautiful," Andrew Solomon describes his perception of the Deaf community as "close, closed, and affectionate" (1994, 44). Attending a reception for one thousand Deaf people, he observed "inviolable bonds of love of a kind that are rare in hearing culture." He says that "it is impossible," when you are among them, "not to wish that you were Deaf" (45), an astonishing statement that illustrates the transformation taking place in how the Deaf are viewed by the hearing and in how they view themselves.

Lights Out: Viewing the Film

 Children of a Lesser God, a play written by hearing playwright Mark Medoff, made its debut at the Mark Taper Theater in Washington, D.C., in 1979. Widely acclaimed and the winner of Tony Awards, it was adapted as a motion picture by Medoff and screenwriter Hesper Anderson in 1986.

Set at a fictitious school for the deaf in Maine (but filmed in New Brunswick, Canada), the story focuses on the changes in the lives of

Major Characters in the Film

Sarah Norman   deaf custodian and former pupil

James Leeds   new speech teacher

Curtis Franklin   superintendent

Mrs. Norman   Sarah's mother

Lydia   deaf student

Glen   deaf student

Johnny   deaf student who refuses to speak

Orin   deaf teacher

the two main characters, one deaf and one hearing. The hearing character, James Leeds (played by William Hurt), is a newly appointed, ambitious speech teacher. Using innovative techniques, he attempts to force oralism not only on his students but also on Sarah (played by Deaf actress Marlee Matlin), the school's deaf janitor and a former pupil. Despite considerable pressure, Sarah refuses to cooperate with James, insisting on her right to sign rather than to speak and lip-read.

Children of a Lesser God has been instrumental in bringing the situation of deaf people to the attention of a wide audience. Marlee Matlin's role in her film debut as a confident, strong, and articulate (in sign language) character has served to break down film stereotypes of the deaf as victims and sufferers. In a noteworthy success, Matlin won the Academy Award for Best Actress in 1986. Film director Randa Haines and producers Burt Sugarman and Patrick Palmer can be praised not only for hiring a deaf actress to play the lead but for hiring deaf or hearing-impaired actors to play other parts as well.

Spotlight on Culture and Communication

This spotlight will focus on the theme of *ethnocentrism*.

First review this term in Essential Vocabulary on Cultures (page 10). Then working in small groups, select a clip from the film in which you perceive the occurrence of ethnocentric attitudes or behavior. How do the characters express their insensitivity and feelings of superiority—through words, actions, or nonverbal behavior? How do others react? Can you explain the beliefs and values that might lead the character(s) to behave in ethnocentric ways?

Two or more groups who have chosen different scenes may present their clips and perspectives to the whole class for discussion. Remember to include examples of film techniques that accentuate ethnocentric behavior.

Sign Languages

Sign language has universally been misunderstood by hearing people. Undoubtedly, part of the confusion comes from the fact that it is extremely difficult for a hearing person to imagine how language can be created manually, other than by stringing word pictures together. Sign language, however, is not a sequence of word pictures. While some signs look like the objects they represent (e.g., a house is made with two hands formed into the shape of a roof and then moved down to shape walls), most signs do not. If they did, after all, a hearing person would be able to understand signing (such as Sarah's in the film) quite easily. Much to the contrary, the task of learning sign is long, complicated, and arduous.

What makes ASL so difficult for the hearing to learn and understand is that it is spatial rather than linear. Whereas in spoken language meaning is created by the combination of specific sounds combined into words arranged in a certain order, in ASL meaning is created in three dimensions. That is, the shape and orientation of the hands, their movement, and their location in relation to the body combine in a three-dimensional mode to create meaning. Additionally, other movements such as eye and eyebrow movements, facial expressions, and the tilt of the head play a role. For example, whereas negatives in English are expressed by words like no and by tone of voice, in ASL the face is a grammatical marker, expressing negatives and questions.

The grammar and syntax (arrangement of words or signs into sentences) of ASL are radically different from English as well. If you know only how English or other spoken languages are structured, you undoubtedly imagine that sign must be structured similarly. As Matthew Moore and Linda Levitan, authors of *For Hearing People Only*, explain, "With ASL you have to abandon 'English thinking' and think *visually*. It's not easy" (1992, 53).

Thus ASL is not a way to communicate in English through signs. In fact one of the most startling realizations for hearing people is that children who grow up in a signing environment from birth have no knowledge of English. They are not thinking in English (or any other spoken language) or translating from English—rather, they are thinking in sign. If they wish to understand English, they must learn it, as hearing people might learn a foreign language. And in order to read, they must first learn English or another written language, since sign languages cannot be written.

Another surprising realization for hearing people is that there is not a universal sign language. Just as there is no universal spoken language, deaf people in different parts of the world sign differently.

They use French Sign, British Sign, Israeli Sign, and so on. In fact, there is even such a thing as a regional accent in sign.

As we have learned in this chapter, much of Deaf history has been marked by the dispute over whether the Deaf can use their own sign languages. And the controversy extends to the question of whether the Deaf should use ASL or other types of sign that more closely resemble English (the so-called Manually Coded English Systems), such as Signed English or Signing Exact English.

Let's look at the differing viewpoints. Imagine for a moment that you are the hearing parent of a deaf child. You do not wish to enforce oralism on your child, but you have tried unsuccessfully to learn ASL. It is much easier for you to learn signed English or Signing Exact English instead. If you and your child learn such a system, you will be able to communicate with each other, and you believe as well that your child will be able to function more successfully in the larger world.

Now imagine that you are the Deaf parent of a Deaf child (approximately 10 percent of deaf children are born to deaf parents). You are fluent in ASL, the primary language of perhaps as many as two million people, and you consider this language to be the true and natural language of the deaf. In your view the various manual English systems are much inferior to ASL and will leave your child with an incomplete, inadequate means of communication with hearing and deaf people alike. You believe that your child's intellectual and emotional growth will be hampered by not having a full, rich, and expressive language. You are outraged that others want to revise your native language to bring it more closely in line with the hearing world.

In attempts to find compromises and solutions, specialists have developed various new signing methods and philosophies in the past several decades. The approach called Total Communication, for example, encourages the use of all means available to communicate, including ASL, English, fingerspelling, and pantomime. The more recent Bi-Bi (*bi*lingual/*bi*cultural) movement advocates that deaf children first learn ASL as their native language and then, using ASL as their base, learn English as their second language.

For now, Signed English and ASL are both employed. The signing system you will see used on closed-captioned television or by sign interpreters at public events is likely to be Signed English. In the film both Signed English (between Sarah and James) and ASL (at the Deaf party) are used. Interestingly, Signed English is the official language at Gallaudet University, although ASL is also taught and may be preferred by some students in informal settings.

In future years the two fundamental struggles—oralism versus sign and ASL versus manual English systems—will no doubt continue, and the outcomes will have an enormous effect in determining the quality of life for deaf people.

Arrange to learn some sign language, either from a person in your class or from an invited guest who has a basic familiarity with the language. In the absence of a knowledgeable person you can use a videotape or appropriate site on the Web (see Sequel).

•Begin by working in pairs or small groups and learn to sign your first names using the manual alphabet that appears on the following page. This alphabet is used by signers of ASL and English-based systems primarily to communicate proper names and words that have no easy translation from English. If you have a nickname, learn to sign it as well. Deaf people often choose as their nickname a particular sign that indicates some aspect of their character.
•Now learn a few simple phrases (greetings, apologies, thanks) in ASL with the appropriate facial expressions.

After the sign language lesson, write your reactions in your film notebook.

•How did it feel to be using signs rather than words?
•What insights into Deaf culture did you obtain from this brief introduction?
•Would you like to learn more sign language? Explain your reasons.

Sign Language Alphabet

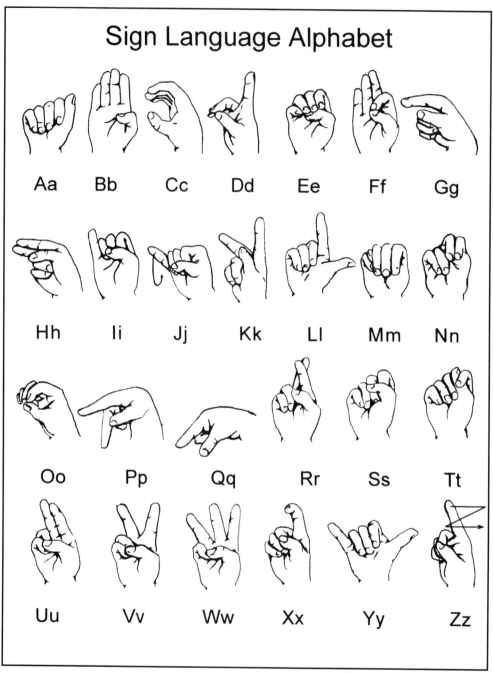

drawings by Steven Shoffner

Poetry: The Deaf Perspective

Read Robert Panara's* poems "Lip Service" and "The Deaf Experience" from the anthology *No Walls of Stone,* edited by Jill Jepson, and respond to the following questions in your film notebook.

- How does "Lip Service" illustrate some of the ideas about sign language presented in this chapter and in *Children of a Lesser God*?
- In "The Deaf Experience," explain which images had the greatest impact on you and why.
- How do you react to the tone of the poems?

Lip Service

You want to rap
you said
and let it all hang out
this thing about
the communication gap
that keeps us separate
your kind
from mine.

You want to rap
you said
you want to integrate
but you decline
to change your line
of crap
from speech
to sign.

---

* Robert Panara, who became deaf at age ten, learned sign language at the American School for the Deaf in Hartford, Connecticut, and attended Gallaudet University. His subsequent teaching career at Gallaudet and other schools for the deaf spans more than forty years. Panara is one of the best-known Deaf writers in the United States and has received numerous awards for his teaching and poetry.

The Deaf Experience

Looking at the speaker
thru uncomprehending
eyes
trying to decipher *make out the meaning of*
the word
unheard
the sleight of tongue
and talking mouth
which opens
and shuts
instamatically
enigmatically
traumatically...

Reaction
in action
a flutter of fingers
a show of hands
the mimic movement
of silent symphony
suddenly
shattered
with cymbalic force
endorsed
of course
by smug recourse
to verbal intercourse.

Controversy over Cochlear Implants

One of the most heated controversies affecting deaf people today surrounds what is called a *cochlear implant,* an electronic aid that provides profoundly deaf people with a sense of hearing. Requiring a surgical procedure, the implant is regarded by many Deaf people as experimental, invasive, and ethically questionable. But many others, both deaf and hearing, disagree, asking why a profoundly deaf child or adult should not be given the chance to hear if that possibility exists.

A cochlear implant has three main components. The first is the implant itself, a tiny chip less than a quarter of a millimeter in size that is surgically implanted in the coils of the cochlea—the part of the inner ear that contains nerve endings necessary for hearing. The second component is a microphone that receives sounds and is worn behind the ear, similar to a hearing aid. And the last part is a box (about the size of a pocket calculator) containing a speech processor that can be attached to clothing or carried in the wearer's pocket. Sometimes referred to as a "bionic ear," the microphone transmits sounds to the microprocessor and then via the implanted chip to the auditory nerve and brain. In short, the cochlear implant tries to replicate the job the cochlea would normally do.

In its first years of use from the mid to late 1980s, only adults who had lost their hearing later in life, and therefore had speech, could be candidates for implants. But in 1990 the Federal Drug Administration approved the cochlear implant for use in children, and soon thousands of operations had been performed worldwide. Presently a cochlear implant, including the necessary rehabilitation and training, generally costs $30,000–$40,000 in the United States, and some insurance companies are willing to share in the costs.

The sounds heard by means of the implant, however, seem to be different from those heard by a hearing person. Thus deaf children need intensive speech therapy to learn to understand the sounds they hear and to produce them as recognizable speech. Indeed, much of the success with cochlear implants in young children has been accredited to intensive training of the child and parents with speech pathologists in weekly sessions over a period of one to five years. Where this postoperative therapy has been negligible, results have been unimpressive. Some families and implantees have actually given up and reverted to sign language.

Among the deaf, those who favor the implant point to ongoing improvements in technology and cite "success stories" with young children over the past ten years. Though there are still no studies of long-term results, some children do seem to have adapted well to the technology and are leading happy, fulfilled lives as teenagers. One such case received widespread coverage on the CBS news magazine *60 Minutes*. Young Caitlin Parton, who lost her hearing to meningitis before the age of two and underwent the implant surgery, appears as a well-adjusted thirteen-year-old who attends a mainstream school and is on the honor roll. She requires no more therapy, just adjustments to her cochlear processor several times per year. Caitlin talks with her friends on the phone, listens to CDs, and plays piano.

Deaf proponents of cochlear implants think it wrong to deny a child the chance to experience these and other great pleasures of life made possible by the devices. They do not minimize the risks of surgery or the difficulties of therapy, but they are willing to weigh them against the benefits they see for children who can join the hearing world. Deaf author Bonnie Poitras Tucker approves of the implant and other means of enabling the deaf to become part of the hearing community. She says that many Deaf leaders who argue convincingly for a separate Deaf culture are themselves the product of oral training and thus can function in the hearing world. It is precisely their oral education, she claims, that has enabled them to become the Deaf cultural leaders they are today.

But many Deaf remain unconvinced and deeply opposed to the technology. They are angered by the hearing world's eagerness to "fix" their deafness for them, when in fact they do not view deafness as a disability at all, but as their identity. As explained in earlier sections of this chapter, the emergence and growth of Deaf culture are rooted in its history as an oppressed culture in which ASL has been repeatedly threatened by oralism. The promotion of cochlear implants, therefore, is easily seen as yet a further invasion by the hearing world to normalize or "cure" the Deaf and to destroy Deaf culture. These vehement feelings are illustrated by the sign for a cochlear implant in ASL: a two-fingered stab to the back of the neck, indicating a vampire in the cochlea.

Cultural reasons aside, the National Association of the Deaf has traditionally opposed implants in children due to risk factors from the surgery itself, postoperative complications, and the lack of any long-term studies on young children. Recently, however, the association has assumed a more moderate stance. In its "Position Paper on Cochlear Implants" (October 2000), the group recognizes the right of parents to make informed choices for their children and voices respect for the decision to proceed with cochlear implantation. At the same time parents are encouraged to research options other than implantation.

The third major party in this discussion (in addition to Deaf proponents and Deaf opponents) is the hearing community, including parents of deaf children and medical specialists. For the former the cochlear implant may seem to be the ideal solution, the one that will open the door to the hearing world and a better future for deaf children. The hearing parents' hopes are often echoed in the medical field; doctors, audiologists, and therapists can point to positive results with children who are leading full and satisfying lives with the implant.

This optimism, however, is not shared by professionals such as James Tucker, Superintendent of the Maryland School for the Deaf, who has had experience with implant "failures." Tucker explains how he has invited surgeons to come see for themselves what it is like when a teenager yanks off the processor and refuses to put it back on. But according to Tucker the doctors never visit. "We are the dumping ground," he says (Arana-Ward 1997).

What has become clear in the debates is that new technology brings with it problems as well as solutions. There are no clear-cut answers, only challenges for deaf and hearing people alike.

The above reading describes the complexity of the medical, social, and ethical questions surrounding cochlear implant surgery. Once you have thought carefully about the issue, make a list of points in your film notebook in response to the following questions:

- What more would you want to know about cochlear implants before making any decisions about possible surgery if you were the hearing parent of a deaf child?
- Where and from whom would you seek advice?

Zoom Lens: Choosing Your Own Topic of Interest

Hands-on Activities

1. Obtain information on the deaf from one or more of the following (see Sequel):
   a. The Deaf World Web
   b. Gallaudet University's home page
   c. DeafWeb
   d. The National Association of the Deaf
   e. Alexander Graham Bell Association for the Deaf and Hard of Hearing
   f. American Society for Deaf Children
2. Find out about the teaching of American Sign Language (ASL) in schools in your city, state, or country. Is ASL listed as a language in school catalogues? Do students receive credit for it as they would for other languages? If you are interested, sign up for classes in ASL.
3. Watch the People in Motion video series hosted by Marlee Matlin (see Sequel). Of particular interest is the video of Evelyn Glennie, a deaf woman who is the world's leading solo classical percussionist. There is also a viewer's guide to this series which contains an extensive list of resources.

4. Visit the nearest residential school for the deaf. Prepare questions for your visit and learn some basic greetings in sign language beforehand.

5. Watch the documentary *In the Land of the Deaf* (see Sequel). This film, produced in French with English subtitles, permits a glimpse into the lives of deaf children and their parents, teachers of the deaf, a woman placed in an asylum because of her deafness, and a newlywed deaf couple. What perspectives does the video present that are new to you?

6. Watch the scenes from the video *Mr. Holland's Opus* in which (a) Mr. Holland and his wife learn that their son is deaf and discuss "what is best" for him with a doctor (0:56–0:58), and (b) Mrs. Holland argues with her husband about sign language (1:03–1:04). How do these scenes illustrate the oralism/sign conflict?

7. Watch a television news anchor for several minutes with the sound off and try to lip-read. How successful were you? How did it feel to try to lip-read?

Research Papers or Oral Reports

1. Study and report on an important figure in Deaf history, such as Thomas Hopkins Gallaudet, Alice Cogswell, Abbé de L'Epée, or Laurent Clerc.

2. Locate information on Deaf theater, paying special attention to the role and activities of the National Theater of the Deaf (see Sequel). Alternatively, focus on another art form important to the deaf for your report.

3. Read *The Mask of Benevolence* (see Sequel) by Harlan Lane and describe Lane's clear-cut position as a hearing and signing ally of the Deaf community.

4. Investigate further the controversy over cochlear implants. Begin with Harlan Lane's *The Mask of Benevolence*, but search further for the latest developments to gain a clear understanding of both sides of the issue.

5. Research the history of the Deaf community on Martha's Vineyard, using Nora Ellen Groce's *Everyone Here Spoke Sign Language: Hereditary Deafness on Martha's Vineyard* (see Sequel).

6. Learn about deaf actors such as Marlee Matlin and Louis Merkin (Orin), and describe their careers and their role in the Deaf community in your paper.

7. If you are not from the United States, locate John Van Cleave's *Gallaudet Encyclopedia of Deaf People and Deafness* (see Sequel) to learn about deafness in your country of origin.

8. Study the Americans with Disabilities Act and its implications for deaf people.

9. Locate several publications popular among the Deaf, such as *Deaf Life*, *Silent News*, and *Deaf American*. What do these publications provide that the mainstream press does not?

10. Find out about TDD (telecommunications device for the deaf, sometimes referred to as TTY, or teletypewriter).

Using Your Imagination

1. Try to experience silence as James does at the end of the movie. Place yourself in as quiet a place as possible and try to imagine how it would be to always be surrounded by this silence. Try to view the silence not as a void but simply as a different world. Write a poem about the experience.

2. At the end of the film James asks Sarah, "Do you think that we could find a place where we can meet, not in silence and not in sound?" In your opinion is such a meeting place possible? If not, why not? If so, imagine what it might be like. Write a poem or short narrative to explain your opinion.

3. You are James. Write a film notebook entry for those days at the end of the movie when you try to imagine and understand Sarah's world.

4. Imagine you are Mrs. Norman and write one of the following:
   a. a letter of complaint to Curtis Franklin after James' first visit, explaining your feelings about James' "interference"
   b. a letter to James after James and Sarah reconcile, apologizing for and explaining your earlier attitudes

5. You are Johnny. What are you thinking as you watch your classmates interact with Mr. Leeds? Alternatively, imagine you are Sarah watching from the back of the room as the students perform for their parents, teachers, and peers. What is going through your mind? Freewrite your thoughts.

6. Write a poem or draw an illustration to show Sarah's thoughts and feelings as she swims in the pool.

Sequel: Further Suggested Resources

Readings

Arana-Ward, Marie. 1997. "As Technology Advances, a Bitter Debate Divides the Deaf." *Washington Post*, 11 May, Sec. A.

Butterworth, Rod R., and Mickey Flodin. 1989. *Signing Made Easy*. New York: Perigree Books.

Cohen, Hager Leah. 1984. *Train Go Sorry: Inside a Deaf World*. New York: Vintage Books.

Dolnick, Edward. 1993. "Deafness as Culture." *Atlantic Monthly*, September, 37–53.

Gannon, Jack R. 1981. *Deaf Heritage: A Narrative History of Deaf America*. Silver Spring, MD: National Association of the Deaf.

Greene, Laura, and Eva Barach Dicker. 1981. *Discovering Sign Language*. Washington, DC: Gallaudet University Press,

Groce, Nora Ellen. 1985. *Everyone Here Spoke Sign Language: Hereditary Deafness on Martha's Vineyard*. Cambridge: Harvard University Press.

Humphries, Tom, and Carol Padden. 1992. *Learning American Sign Language*. Englewood Cliffs, NJ: Prentice Hall.

Jepson, Jill, ed. 1992. *No Walls of Stone: An Anthology of Literature by Deaf and Hard of Hearing Writers*. Washington, DC: Gallaudet University Press.

Kisor, Henry. 1991. *What's That Pig Outdoors?: A Memoir of Deafness*. New York: Penguin Books.

Klima, Edward S., and Ursula Bellugi. 1979. *The Signs of Language*. Cambridge: Harvard University Press.

Lane, Harlan. 1992. *The Mask of Benevolence: Disabling the Deaf Community*. New York: Vintage Books.

Lane, Harlan, and Robert Hoffmeister. 1996. *A Journey into the Deaf-World*. San Diego: Dawn Sign Press.

Mindess, Anna. 1999. *Reading Between the Signs: Intercultural Communication for Sign Language Interpreters*. Yarmouth, ME: Intercultural Press.

Moore, Matthew S., and Linda Levitan. 1992. *For Hearing People Only: Answers to Some of the Most Commonly Asked Questions about the Deaf Community, Its Culture, and the "Deaf Reality."* Rochester, NY: Deaf Life Press.

Padden, Carol, and Tom Humphries. 1988. *Deaf in America: Voices from a Culture*. Cambridge: Harvard University Press.

Sacks, Oliver. 1989. *Seeing Voices: A Journey into the World of the Deaf*. Berkeley: University of California Press.

Shapiro, Joseph P. 1993. *No Pity: People with Disabilities Forging a New Civil Rights Movement*. New York: Random House.

Solomon, Andrew. 1994. "Deaf Is Beautiful." *New York Times Magazine*, 28 August.

Tucker, Bonnie Poitras. 1998. "Deaf Culture, Cochlear Implants, and Elective Disability." The Hastings Center Report 28, no. 4 (July–August): 6–14.

Van Cleave, John V., ed. 1987. *Gallaudet Encyclopedia of Deaf People and Deafness*. 3 vols. New York: McGraw-Hill.

Films

Beyond Silence (1997) Story of a young gifted musician whose struggle for independence is difficult for her deaf parents to grasp (German with English subtitles). Directed by Caroline Link.

The Heart Is a Lonely Hunter (1968) Heartwarming drama of the relationship between a troubled adolescent girl and a lonely deaf man. Directed by Robert Ellis Miller.

How to Talk to a Person Who Can't Hear (1996) Lighthearted, accessible video that teaches more than 300 words in ASL. Stars charming deaf actor Anthony Natale. Directed by Brady Connell. (CJ Sign Language; phone: 888-532-7674; TDD: 818-788-5977)

In the Land of the Deaf (1994) Unique and moving look inside the world of the deaf. In French and French Sign Language with English subtitles. Directed by Nicolas Philibert (Facets; phone: 800-532-2387; or Sign Enhancers, Inc.; phone and TTY: 800-767-4461).

The Miracle Worker (1962) Classic film about the bond between Helen Keller (Patty Duke), who was both deaf and blind, and her teacher and lifelong companion Anne Sullivan (Anne Bancroft). Directed by Arthur Penn.

Mr. Holland's Opus (1995) A deaf boy is long neglected by his father, who lives in the world of music. Directed by Stephen Herek.

People in Motion (1996) Documentary series tells the stories of people who confront their disabilities with courage and creativity. Directed by Vicki Sufian, Gail Freedman, Jan Legnitto, and Lyn Goldfarb. (Films for the Humanities and Sciences; phone: 800-257-5126).

CD-ROM

Sternberg, Martin L. A. 1994. *The American Sign Language Dictionary on CD-ROM for Windows*. New York: HarperCollins.

Websites and Mailing Addresses

Alexander Graham Bell Association for the Deaf and Hard of Hearing, 3417 Volta Place NW, Washington, DC 20007-2778; phone: 202-337-5220; TTY: 202-337-5221 (www.agbell.org)

American Sign Language Dictionary (www.bconnex.net/~randys)

American Society for Deaf Children, 2848 Arden Way, Suite 210, Sacramento, CA 95825-1373; phone: 800-942-ASDC (www.deafchildren.org)

Central Institute for the Deaf (www.cid.wustl.edu)

CyberSchool (on-line ASL course): (www.cyberschool.k12.or.us)

Deaf Life (www.deaf.com)

DeafWeb (www.deaflibrary.org)

The Deaf World Web (www.deafworldweb.org)

Gallaudet University (www.gallaudet.edu)

National Association of the Deaf, 814 Thayer Avenue, Silver Spring, MD 20910; phone: 301-587-1788; TDD: 301-587-1789 (publishes *Deaf American*) (www.nad.org)

National Information Center on Deafness, 800 Florida Avenue NE, Washington, DC 20002; voice: 202-651-5052; TTY: 202-651-5052; e-mail: nicd@gallux.gallaudet.edu

The National Theater of the Deaf, Hazel E. Stark Center, P.O. Box 659, Chester, CT 06412 (www.ntd.org)

SERI Hearing Impairment Resources (www.seriweb.com/hearing.htm)

Sign Enhancers, Inc.; phone and TTY: 800-767-4461 (extensive catalogue of videotapes, CD-ROMs, and other sign language products)

Silent News, 133 Gaither Drive, Suite E, Mt. Laurel, NJ 08054-1710; e-mail: silentnews@aol.com

Flashback/Flashforward

We have now come to the end of our journey through some of America's diverse cultures. We hope you have learned more about yourself and have gained a better sense of your own cultural identity. We hope that you will be more open to new cultural experiences in the future and able to enjoy cultural differences. And we hope that you have become more aware of how much still needs to be done to create a more equitable society for all of us who live, study, and work in the United States.

In this final activity, we would like you to flash back to three times in this course when you felt you learned something important. In your film notebook, describe the flashbacks.

Now flash forward to one time in the future when your thinking or behavior might be affected by what you have learned in this course. Describe the flashforward.

11

To the Instructor

Behind the Scenes: Why, How, What, Who

Why Film?

Film has proven itself to be a splendid tool for cross-cultural learning. By using film you will be able to expose your students to American cultures and cocultures they might seldom encounter. You will be provided entry into topics that might otherwise seem too controversial or too sensitive. You will be able to increase your students' understanding of the profound ways in which cultures differ, including values, histories, and verbal and nonverbal modes of communication. And you will help your students view these differences with interest and respect.

Because most of your students have grown up with films and videos—and love watching them—a course focusing on film captures their attention. Although they are already sophisticated viewers in some ways, we place emphasis on helping them develop the tools to evaluate what they see more critically.

How Did We Choose the Films?

Early on, we decided to select feature films rather than documentaries, partly because they tend to become less dated. Also, the fictional story lines and characters provided us with rich material upon which to base exercises for cultural observation and analysis. In addition, we needed to keep in mind sheer practicality. Feature films are generally more readily available and less expensive than documentaries. The films we chose are fairly recent and can be rented from local video stores or purchased quite reasonably.

We established a set of criteria to help us select feature films appropriate for a course of this nature. Above all, we searched for films that depicted cultures with insight, care, and authenticity. Though films that stereotype, bash, or misrepresent cultures can sometimes be used as negative examples, we strictly avoided them here. We tried to choose films of high artistic quality in the belief that these tend to hold greater appeal and provide more interesting material for analysis. We wanted films that would heighten our students' cultural curiosity and pose thought-provoking questions.

While we recognized the importance of including chapters on the major cultural groups within American society, we would also have liked to focus on less frequently discussed cultures such as Arab Americans and Asian Indians. We were, however, unable to find suitable films on many cultures. We spent a great deal of time previewing and screening, and we sought opinions from friends, students, and teachers who belong to the respective cultures. We also tested the materials in different kinds of classes and workshops over several years and used our students' feedback to make the final selections and to create, rethink, and revise the exercises.

What Are Our Goals?

Our primary goal is to broaden students' awareness, understanding, and appreciation of the many cultures and cocultures in the United States today. As we have used and experimented with different parts of the text, we have seen both American and international students benefit enormously from an exposure to the breadth of multicultural America. Despite an increasing emphasis on multicultural education in our schools, most of our students seemed to know only a smattering about the various cultures we discussed, and they appreciated the opportunity to learn more.

In learning about others, students will, of course, reflect on their own culture, language, and lifestyle and use them as benchmarks for comparison. Students have noted with surprise how much more they now want to learn about their own cultural background.

As mentioned above, we also try to help students learn to analyze and evaluate more critically what they see on film—and by extension, in the media generally. Whereas at the beginning of the course students might be tempted to "believe" what a film tells them about a culture they do not know, by the end they will know how to ask probing questions. Bombarded daily by media images as we are, this skill seems to us indispensable.

In addition to emphasizing critical thinking and viewing, we also aim to help both native and nonnative speakers of English develop and refine their language abilities. The course is designed to provide them with tools to become more attentive listeners and readers, more thoughtful and articulate discussants, and better writers. Because students are often working with topics in which they are vitally interested, they are motivated to understand the materials thoroughly and to express themselves with precision and vitality.

Who Is Our Audience?

Seeing the Big Picture can be used in a wide range of educational settings with students of different ages, cultures, and language backgrounds. We believe the text is suitable for introductory college classes in areas such as American studies, English composition, film, communications, history, anthropology, and ethnic studies. We have designed the materials to meet the needs of both native and nonnative speakers within the same classroom. For example, we have used it successfully for a number of years in a Linfield College course (for all first-year students) called the "Inquiry Seminar" in which there are generally quite a few international students.

We also encourage adoption of the text by instructors of English as a second language (ESL). It has been enthusiastically received over a period of years in our own ESL courses for advanced speakers—those with Test of English as a Foreign Language (TOEFL) scores of 500 and above on the paper-based test, and 173 and above on the computer-based test. Some of our most advanced nonnative speakers (with scores above 550 or 213 on the respective tests), who would not otherwise have taken an ESL class, have been intrigued by the topic and have found the course a worthwhile introduction to the diverse cultures of America.

Though we have written the text with students in America in mind, we hope that instructors of English or other subjects in countries abroad might find it useful and interesting. We can also envisage its use as a training tool for diversity workshops in the workplace.

Rolling the Camera: Technical Considerations

How to Get Started

Before showing any of the films, you will want to prepare your students for the cultural journey on which they are about to embark. We advise you to invest at least three fifty-minute class sessions (or the equivalent) on the following introductory sections:

Sneak Preview

Why American Cultures?—This reading and the accompanying exercises encourage students to analyze and define their own perceptions of American culture(s) as they begin the course.

Viewing Films in New Ways—This section enlists students to become active observers of film. We ask students to develop their "film eyes" by looking at film in new ways and questioning what they see. Their careful observation of cultural clues and details as well as verbal and nonverbal communication patterns will be the starting point for many class discussions.

Script

Essential Vocabulary on Cultures—We have provided students with a selection of cultural terms and their definitions. We encourage you to review these lists as you prepare for each chapter and incorporate them in class discussions. Note that in the Spotlight exercises the students are often asked to review and work with one or more of the terms. As the course progresses, your students should become more adept at using the terms and applying them to the films.

Essential Film Vocabulary—Similarly, we have provided a list of film techniques and definitions that we believe students will find interesting and useful, particularly as they work through the Spotlight exercises. For example, in *Dances with Wolves* your students may want to discuss the panoramic shots or Dunbar's voice-over narration of his journal. The film vocabulary helps students analyze and describe what they see on film, and thus become less susceptible to manipulation.

Stage Directions: Guidelines for Discussion

Your students will spend a great deal of time discussing the films and readings with the entire class, in small groups, and in pairs. They will need to step out of their comfort zones and take risks as they express their opinions. To help students do this, we have found it essential to set up certain guidelines at the outset of the course (see pages 14–16). The principle underlying these guidelines is a willingness to listen respectfully to each other's views, regardless of differences of opinion. We advise you to introduce the guidelines to your students at an early point, asking them to add others if they feel inclined and to review them from time to time during the course.

To ensure that each student has a chance to speak in class discussions, we suggest the use of discussion roles (see pages 15–16)—at least in the early weeks of the course. Read through these roles with your students. They show students

that they do not have to make a brilliant remark or be an expert on the subject at hand in order to join a discussion. Rather, they can simply ask a question or request clarification. Timekeeper and questioner are good roles for those who may at first lack confidence.

Of course you must decide whether these roles should actually be assigned or simply used informally. In any case we caution you not to overuse them, since discussions could easily become stilted. Perhaps you can incorporate them in the early discussions and gradually withdraw them as students gain more confidence. You will likely use them more formally in an ESL class than in a class of mostly native speakers. Students can keep track of the roles they have played on their self-evaluation sheets (see page 219).

Forming Groups

If we are working with classes of twenty to thirty students, we create four or five groups on the first or second day of class. We ask students to select their own groups with as diverse a composition as possible. It is then up to us and our students (and you and yours) to decide how often and when to change groups. In our experience, we have found it necessary to change groups at least after every film (even if students want to remain together), as this keeps discussion fresh and allows students to get to know all of their classmates and to hear as many different views as possible.

Ask students to give you occasional feedback about how well they think their group is working. This can be done on the self-evaluation sheet (see page 219), via e-mail, or in film notebooks. One important lesson we have learned is to allow students to select their own work partners (though they should change partners regularly).

We also recommend making a master list of the instructor's and students' phone numbers and/or e-mail addresses at the beginning of a course and distributing a copy to each student. In this way students are able to contact you and each other outside class and to arrange group meetings.

Sequencing the Films

In the courses we have taught, we have usually chosen to follow the sequencing of films as they appear in the text. While you may wish to change this order, we suggest leaving Mainstream White Culture until students have had experience with Spotlight exercises in other chapters. Also, we advise handling more sensitive material, such as the chapter on homosexuality, later in the course, after students have become better acquainted and built trust with you and one another.

How Much Time to Spend on Each Film

We have designed *Seeing the Big Picture* primarily for use as the core text either in a quarter or semester of ten to fifteen weeks, meeting at least three hours per week.

In this format we suggest that you spend one week discussing the Sneak Preview, Script, and Stage Directions. These introductory chapters are essential preparation for the films and exercises that follow. You will then probably want to spend about two weeks on each feature film (this also applies to the chapter on mainstream white culture) and one class session on Flashback/Flashforward. Assuming that you follow this schedule, you will be able to select four to five feature films that best meet your students' interests and needs.

In the first chapter you will find two Native American feature films. If you are teaching an ESL class, we advise using *Dances with Wolves* rather than *Thunderheart*. The former introduces early Native American history, with which some international students may not be familiar. Also, Dunbar's voice-over as he reads his journal facilitates comprehension of the plot. *Thunderheart*, on the other hand, is more complex in terms of both language and plot. Our classes of native speakers with whom we used both films preferred *Thunderheart*, explaining that they were already familiar with much of the material in *Dances* but had very little knowledge of the situation of more contemporary Indians. They did not think we should cut *Dances* entirely, but recommended that we study only a few sections (Setting the Scene, Wide-Angle Lens, and Spotlight) in order to spend most of our time on *Thunderheart*.

If you are teaching in a course shorter than a quarter or semester, you may need to limit your film selection to only a few, but we do stress the importance of using the Sneak Preview, Script, and Stage Directions to introduce your course and Flashback/Flashforward to conclude effectively.

On the next page is an example of how a two-week unit of work on *Dances with Wolves,* including a field trip, might be organized for a class that meets four days per week.

Sample Two-Week Unit on *Dances with Wolves*

	Class Activity	Assignments
■ Week 1		
Day 1	Setting the Scene: Freewrite and share responses.	Wide-Angle Lens: Read, reread, and respond in film notebook.
Day 2	(1) Map Exercise: Work in pairs. (2) Lights Out: Viewing the film. Read and discuss.	Watch the film. Write down questions in film notebook.
Day 3	(1) Whole class discussion of questions/ reactions to the film. (2) Spotlight: Define nonverbal communication and begin Spotlight preparation in small groups.	Spotlight: Groups meet to select clips illustrating nonverbal communication. Prepare ideas/clips for class discussion.
Day 4	Spotlight presentations and discussion with whole class.	Point of View: Read all four reviews and respond in film notebook.
■ Week 2		
Day 1	Point of View: Share reactions to reviews in small groups.	Indian Languages: Write a poem, essay, or letter in your film notebook.
Day 2	Share Lakota poem, essay, or letter in small groups.	Prepare field trip questions.
Day 3	Zoom Lens: Field trip.	Write up field trip reactions in film notebook.
Day 4	Debriefing on field trip. Group writing: field trip thank-you letter/article for student newsletter.	Using Your Imagination: Final writing assignment.

How to Use a Film Notebook

In our courses students collect all their writing, from the roughest notes to more formal, polished entries, in a three-ring binder. As the course progresses, the film notebook becomes a valuable resource, providing ideas for future essays, research papers, and oral reports. Students should be encouraged to use their film notebooks not only for the exercises in the text but also as a place to jot down thoughts while watching the films or listening to class discussions. They should remember to take their notebooks (or pages to be inserted later) with them when working on hands-on activities or participating in fieldwork/field trips.

We have found it important to collect the film notebooks at regular intervals. We do not promise to read every word; rather, we skim through, commenting in the margins and annotating with a check mark (✓), plus (+), or minus (–) to indicate that adequate thought and energy are being applied to the task at hand. Of course, you may wish to assign more formal grades to the polished pieces of writing. More than the grades, however, students seem to appreciate receiving our notes and comments.

For us as instructors the film notebooks are an important source of information. We are able to track the students' academic progress and also gain insights into their struggles with the emotional content of the material. Again and again we read in the notebooks of problems and questions that simply do not surface in class discussion. Depending on the student and the issue, we can then decide how best to respond.

When we see particularly creative, interesting, well-written work, we ask students to read aloud from their writings. Or we might ask a student's permission to read something aloud ourselves. Students are often amazed at their peers' capabilities and are inspired to do better themselves.

- -

How to Use the Readings and Exercises to Teach Culture and Language Skills

- -

Certain key readings and exercises recur in most chapters and are essential to an understanding of the culture being studied and the related film. Here are some of the ways in which you can use them:

Setting the Scene: Freewriting and Discussion

This exercise introduces students to the chapter in a way intended to capture their attention. It is a nonthreatening, relatively quick activity that asks students to freewrite in their film notebooks in response to a picture, cartoon, quote, or similar prompt. We explain the concept of freewriting to students on page 7.

Wide-Angle Lens: Historical (and Geographical) Perspectives

This section provides vital background information that should be read and discussed before viewing the film. At first we were unsure whether to include so much history, but we were soon reassured by students' enthusiastic reactions. We worried that the sections were too long, but students actually requested more. Most of our students have felt that the histories and maps were not only indispensable to their understanding of the films, but extremely interesting as well. Even students who already knew a great deal about aspects of American history—one group of Dutch students, for example, had prepared for extensive examinations on Native Americans and were quite knowledgeable—were glad to refresh their memories.

For us as authors, this section makes the statement that cultures simply cannot be understood without history. If we are to undertake the hard and important work of understanding each other, we must be willing to study the past. How, for example, could a white, black, or Asian person claim to understand American Indians without a familiarity with Wounded Knee, Red Cloud, Pine Ridge, the Ghost Dance, Leonard Peltier, and AIM? Any attempt to do so can only result in superficial interpretations of present-day attitudes, values, and behavior of people from cultures different from one's own.

The Wide-Angle Lens sections also provide excellent opportunities for both native and nonnative speakers of English to develop their reading skills. We have developed a number of reading tasks (see below), one or two of which could be used for each Wide-Angle Lens, depending on the specific needs and interests of your students. You may decide to assign tasks other than the ones we have recommended, or even have students devise some. In any case students should understand that marking the text and performing some type of exercise in their film notebooks will help them become active, critical readers.

Reading Task Suggestions for Students

1. Read Wide-Angle Lens twice. The first time, read for an overview of the historical background. In the second reading you should concentrate on attending to details and raising questions.

2. Annotate the margins as you read. Your annotations should help you relocate important information at a later date and recall your questions or comments in readiness for class discussions or quizzes.

3. Based on the reading, create a quiz of five to ten factual or opinion-related questions for your peers to answer verbally in pairs or small groups.

4. Your instructor will provide each group with a different set of three or four short answers based on information in Wide-Angle Lens. In your groups formulate questions to fit the answers and then pair up with other groups to test each other with your set of questions.

5. Create a chronological table of historical events mentioned in Wide-Angle Lens. (This is especially helpful in those chapters including map exercises—Dances with Wolves, Come See the Paradise, and Lone Star.)

6. Respond in a focused freewrite in your film notebook to these cues:

   Before reading this text, I had assumed that...
   After reading this text, I learned that...
   The authors provoked my curiosity about...*

7. Imagine that you are the instructor for this course. Develop two research topics or two oral presentation topics and justify your choices.

8. Select a key historical event or figure mentioned in the text. Research your selected topic or person briefly and be ready to provide your group with further information in the next class meeting. Choose the topic or person in your groups and make sure none of the choices overlap.

---

*This exercise is adapted from a similar one described in John C. Bean's *Engaging Ideas*, San Francisco: Jossey Bass, 1996, 142.

Map Exercises—Maps are included in several chapters to complement the historical readings. In the chapter on Japanese Americans, for example, we have inserted a map to show the location of World War II internment camps. The maps will mean more if students study and discuss them. Thus we ask them to do accompanying exercises. Our experience shows that pair or small-group work is the most effective way to tackle these map exercises.

Lights Out: Viewing the Film

In each Lights Out we first give students noteworthy information on the films. For example, does the film break new ground in its depiction of a culture? Are the actors credible representatives of the culture? What are the director's credentials for making a particular film? Are the setting and props authentic? How successful was the film? The information provided helps students to focus their "film eyes" and "ears" and begin asking new questions about a film's credibility and importance.

In most cases viewing is best done by the students outside of class to save class time. If your school or university has a media center or viewing facilities, you may wish to buy or rent the film and put it on reserve for students to borrow. Usually our students have chosen to share the rental cost of a film and have watched it with their groups at home or on campus. When the schedule permits, we try to make film watching a weekend assignment so that students have a little more time to schedule it and to relax. Watching the film with peers gives students the opportunity to point out details to each other and to share their initial reactions immediately after the viewing. This kind of group activity outside the classroom also helps to reinforce trust and foster positive small-group dynamics.

Spotlight on Culture and Communication

In this section we provide a selection of readings and exercises that relate to the specific culture and film under discussion. The first of these is always a pivotal group task in which students select and analyze brief film clips that clarify and illustrate a specific cultural term or concept. This is followed by a smorgasbord of activities from which teachers and students may choose.

We have found that the variety in each Spotlight section appeals to a wide range of students' interests and keeps them engaged. For example, in Dances with Wolves the focus for the exercise is non-verbal communication, so the students might choose one of the Lakota council meetings. By playing their clips repeatedly in preparation for Spotlight, students begin to pick up small details that otherwise might go unnoticed. They are thus able to sharpen their ability to identify cultural clues.

Furthermore, this exercise integrates skills important to the course—critical thinking, listening, and speaking (also reading and writing if the exercise is varied as described below). Success of the activity depends on the students' ability to arrive at a consensus on the choice of film clip(s), to present their views and ideas to one another, and to decide how to structure the presentation. We estimate that group presentations should take no longer than ten to fifteen minutes, including one short film clip. (All groups should designate a timekeeper.) Each student in the group takes responsibility for and gives part of the presentation. So that presentations are well organized, students need to take responsibility for setting up a time and place to meet outside of class.

The introductory Spotlight exercise can be varied if you feel that students need a change of pace or if time is limited. For example:

1. The group discusses, organizes, and agrees on the content of the presentation, then selects a spokesperson to give the presentation. (This option works well in small classes where each person eventually has a chance to be spokesperson.)
2. Groups can pair up and compare their findings. They can simply explain which clips they used rather than actually showing them.
3. Working individually, students can write a one- to two-page response to the exercise, including a brief description of the clip they have chosen. You may wish to ask students to read sections of their written responses aloud in class.

For native and nonnative speakers alike, this component of Spotlight has proved to be a popular exercise. Our students have greatly enjoyed the challenge of choosing their own clips. Additionally, the activity has helped students develop self-confidence in oral presentation and discussion skills; even the shyest students are able to participate with the support of their peers.

Zoom Lens: Choosing Your Own Topic of Interest

This section is divided into three parts, from which you can choose activities that suit your needs and objectives.

Hands-on Activities—As the title suggests, these are practical activities, ranging from field trips and interviews to surveys to searching the World Wide Web. The value of this section is that students can become involved in *doing* something, in taking some type of action, in conducting fieldwork. The activities are a great way to bring alive much of what otherwise might remain abstract and to link the classroom with the outside world.

In our classes the students have especially liked and benefited from field trips we have organized. Field trips do require considerable time and energy to set up, but we encourage you to organize at least one or two; the payoff is enormous. Obviously, your geographic location will very much determine the type of field trip you can organize. Some examples from our area in Oregon include a visit to the local Grand Ronde Tribal Council, a meeting with Hispanic workers at Monrovia Nursery, and a visit to the Oregon School for the Deaf. We have been able to establish good relationships with people at these sites and have returned several times with different classes. We have also tried to offer something in return; students at the school for the deaf, for example, visit our college as part of what has now become a reciprocal visitation. Great interest in ASL and Deaf culture has even led to classes in American Sign Language being set up at Linfield College.

Please note that we intend every hands-on activity to lead to some kind of reflective "product," be it written or spoken. For example, if students conduct a survey, watch a film, or search the Internet, we expect them to present the results in class or incorporate them into a formal report or paper. Similarly, if students participate in a field trip, they can record their reactions in their film notebooks and share them with the class in the next meeting. Since we can well imagine that most instructors prefer to adapt the hands-on activities to fit their own course, we have refrained from prescribing specific final assignments in the Hands-on Activity sections. We do recommend that students always take their film notebooks (or loose-leaf paper to be inserted later) with them when involved in hands-on activities, so that they can jot down ideas and observations as a basis for the specific assignments you decide are most appropriate.

Research Papers or Oral Reports—We assume some of you will wish to require a formal report or paper. With this in mind, we have provided lists of suggested topics. These lists are intended as starting points only, since students should be encouraged to follow their own areas of interest. For example, a music major might enjoy exploring Native American music and musical instruments. A history major might be interested in learning more about the "No-No Boys."

Using Your Imagination—This section breaks away from traditional writing exercises, allowing students to be more imaginative, informal, and personal than in research papers. Our rationale for this exercise is to provide an open-ended format that will appeal to different learning styles. Below are some examples of a poem and illustration written and drawn by our students in response to the questions posed in these two sections.

While the above exercises form the key elements of each chapter, there is a range of other supplementary readings and exercises. For example, we have chosen several poems that help students relate to how people from various cultures feel and what prejudices they face. You will also find sections on controversial issues, such as cochlear implants, and sections on languages used in the films, such as Black English and American Sign Language.

Ideally, you would be able to work through all the exercises. But in any given chapter, you will probably decide to pick and choose those that best suit your course goals and your students' needs. If you have time to try at least one of the supplementary sections in each chapter, we think they will make for lively and interesting sessions.

Examples of Student Responses

On Children of a Lesser God   *by Lia Sur*

Imagine watching the world as it passes you by
Unable to converse or hear yourself cry
When you try to speak, others just seem to stare
It is as if you are living in a silent nightmare
You "listen" to music through the vibrations in the floor
And watch sporting events, unable to hear the crowd's roar
ASL is your language, the deaf's "unspoken speech"
It is also what the hearing world refuses to teach
Why is it that society accepts Braille for the blind,
But refuses to acknowledge the deaf's desire to sign.

For The Wedding Banquet   *by Trisha Wilder*

How to Use Flashback/ Flashforward

This section is intended to bring closure to the course. Students are asked to make some concluding entries in their film notebooks as a way of reflecting on what they have learned and of thinking about the future.

Before the Premiere: Easing Anxieties

Some Commonly Asked Questions

I am neither a historian nor a film expert. How can I teach this course?

Neither are we! But one of the most enjoyable aspects of teaching these materials is that we continue to learn more with each new class of students. Certainly, extra background reading and viewing always help, and for that reason we have included suggestions for both teachers and students in the Sequels given at the end of the chapters.

A lack of historical or film expertise should definitely not deter you from using this text. We explain to our students at the beginning of each course that this is a cooperative learning experience about cultures—a learning experience for all of us.

Which books and films will provide me with useful background information?

The Sequel contains books and films you may wish to order in advance of the course, as personal or library copies. We have found them to be indispensable, both as reading for ourselves and as references. You will want to acquaint your students with them and to place as many as possible on reserve in the library.

How do I find films or film reviews?

The feature films we have used or listed in the Sequels are fairly easy to locate in your local video stores. The documentaries (and the feature films as well) are available from various distributors, some of which require a membership fee. A few of the most important distributors for our purposes are

Facets Multimedia Center:
    800-331-6197 (www.facets.org)
Home Film Festival: 800-258-3456
    (www.homefilmfestival.com)
California Newsreel: 414-621-6196
    (www.newsreel.org)
Filmakers Library: 212-808-4980
    (www.filmakers.com)
NAATA/Crosscurrent Media:
    415-552-9550 (www.naatanet.org)
PBS Video: 800-328-7271
    (www.pbs.org)

In the Sequels we have provided the names of these and other distributors from which the documentaries can be rented or purchased. Because we assume that you will locate feature films in video stores, we did not provide distributors for them.

The most important reference work for reviews of feature films released in major markets in the United States is Jeremy Ozer's *Film Review Annual* (Englewood, NJ: Jerome S. Ozer). The volumes appear yearly, and each volume contains several important reviews of films released that year. You can find these annuals in the reference section of most public or university libraries. The *Film Review Annual* is a marvelous resource, is very user-friendly, and saves tedious hours of searching for reviews. In addition the following three film resources on the World Wide Web have proved to be very reliable:

1. The Movies, Race and Ethnicity, Media Resources Center, Moffit Library, U.C. Berkeley at www.lib.berkeley. edu/MRC/EthnicImagesVid.html. This resource provides information on African Americans, Asians and Asian Americans, Latinos and Chicanos, Jews, and Native Americans in film. It gives film titles with a brief synopsis, along with a list of related film reviews and their sources.
2. Internet Movie Database Search at www. us.imdb.com/search. This resource gives information not only on reviews, but on all aspects of filmmaking as well, including biographical information on directors and actors.
3. Asian Educational Media Service at www. aems.uiuc.edu. This site provides a wealth of information, including reviews, for Asian and Asian American films and documentaries.

Will the language of the films be too difficult for my ESL students?

Yes and no. Certainly the culturally rich words, phrases, and expressions will be challenging but no more so than the language our students encounter every day outside the classroom—on the street, on the radio, or on television. So far both our ESL students and our native speakers have enjoyed the linguistic challenges of these films. We believe that if students follow the carefully constructed exercises, they will not become frustrated but rather will feel a sense of achievement at completing the various film-related tasks.

If, however, ESL teachers wish to focus more closely on the actual language of the films, then the Spotlight sections present an ideal vehicle. Actually, you may find that while students are preparing their Spotlight presentations, some are motivated to practice the language on their own. We have witnessed, for example, nonnative-speaking students repeatedly replaying and transcribing their film clips, sometimes with the assistance of native-speaking culture partners (described below) in order to hear and come to grips with unfamiliar phrases and idioms. Although it is not our intention in this text to provide traditional language exercises, you could select specific film clips to focus on those grammatical structures, vocabulary words, or idioms that you wish to highlight for your students.

What are culture partners?

Culture partners are primarily used in ESL classrooms to facilitate small-group discussions and to contribute to cross-cultural exchanges. They should be native speakers or excellent speakers of English. They may be students or volunteers from your community. Some of our student culture partners have been able to receive regular or internship credit for the course. The culture partners themselves have commented on how much they have learned about other cultures, and about their own, as a result of participating in this course.

What are cultural informants?

Our students have especially enjoyed class sessions in which we have invited guests or speakers as informants of the cultures under discussion. For example, we have invited a Japanese American from the Oregon Nikkei Legacy Center to tell students of his firsthand experiences during internment at Tule Lake during World War II. Our students have been greatly moved by student visitors from the Oregon School for the Deaf, and some have gone on to take classes in American Sign Language as a result.

Cultural informants do not need to be experts or specialists. Clearly, the students in your class will be able to serve as informants about their own cultures, but they should not automatically be expected to do so. Some students may not feel that they know enough about a specific topic, and some may have personal reasons for declining this role (such as a gay student not wanting to come out to peers). Students from minority cultures are often placed in the role of representative (or ambassador) and may resent this extra responsibility and expectation.

On the other hand, many students will be pleased to talk about their own cultures. We have been happy to see a number of reticent or diffident students blossom in the role of cultural informant. After all, this course is based on the idea that every student will have something to share about his or her culture, so no one minority student is being singled out as having to "represent" an entire culture. We recommend that you state on your syllabus the expectation that students will help others understand their specific cultural backgrounds.

What if my students have already seen the films?

Many of our students have already seen some of the films, but they do not seem reluctant to watch them a second time. We explain that our viewing goals in this class are very different from watching films for entertainment. In fact most of our students comment on how the reading exercises and ensuing discussions help them to look at the films from a new standpoint. They learn to develop their "film eyes" and focus on aspects of culture and communication they might otherwise have overlooked.

How is "Mainstream Culture: Film of Your Choice" different from the other chapters?

Mainstream Culture provides a change of pace for both you and your students. By this point in the course, students have become familiar with the chapter format and are quite experienced in selecting film clips for Spotlight. In Mainstream Culture, each group becomes responsible for choosing a full-length feature film that illustrates some values or beliefs of white culture. In our experience, students have thoroughly enjoyed this challenge. Even though we provide a list of suggested films, many groups have come up with excellent alternative suggestions.

You will need to emphasize to students that they will only be able to show a short clip, just as in Spotlight, and that the clip need only illustrate one significant white cultural value or belief. Discourage your students from trying to present too many ideas.

It is important for peer observers to watch and listen carefully to the presentations. We provide a post-viewing exercise immediately after the presentations so that the presenters can obtain prompt feedback from the class.

Please note that we have not included a Zoom Lens section in this chapter so that students have more time to become familiar with cultures other than mainstream white culture. However, in our courses some white students (particularly Irish Americans) have become interested in exploring their roots and have asked to do relevant individual projects. We have been glad to encourage such initiatives.

How can I evaluate my students in this course?

We find this course difficult to grade because we want students to write and speak freely, without reluctance to admit doubts or lack of knowledge, and without fear of making mistakes. We emphasize to students that they will not be judged on whether their views are "right" or "wrong." What is important is that they participate in an honest and open inquiry, and that ultimately they be able to express their views in an articulate fashion and with adequate substantiation.

In particular, we have found self-evaluations to be a valuable tool, as they give students the chance to demonstrate responsibility for their own learning. We ask students to complete evaluation sheets (a sample follows) at three intervals during the semester. They grade themselves on criteria designed to meet course goals and write a prose evaluation of their performance in the course.

If we believe that a student is either overestimating or underestimating a grade in the self-evaluation, we set up a conference to discuss the discrepancy. We advise students to bring their film notebooks to these conferences so that they can refer to specific assignments.

Self-Evaluation

Name_____ Date _____ Numerical Grade_____

Directions: Use the criteria below to help you arrive at a numerical grade from one to five—five being the highest. Circle the appropriate number and then write a prose evaluation (several sentences) of your performance in this course.

1 2 3 4 5   I attend class regularly.

1 2 3 4 5   I am up-to-date on readings, exercises, and preparation for class discussions.

1 2 3 4 5   I experiment with different discussion roles in whole-class and small-group discussions.

1 2 3 4 5   I encourage others to speak by asking thoughtful questions.

1 2 3 4 5   I take a fair share in the preparation of Spotlight exercises.

1 2 3 4 5   I make regular meaningful entries in my film notebook.

Self-Evaluation:

Final Word

In writing this book and teaching our classes, we have discussed content and pedagogy with colleagues from different disciplines—communications, history, anthropology, and modern languages. We hope that as you use this text, you too will find opportunities to interact with others across the curriculum. In our own experience this exchange has helped us discover more creative teaching methods and has given us confidence to venture into content areas that were new for us. For example, we developed ideas for writing exercises in Setting the Scene and Using Your Imagination from talking with professors in our English department. We spoke with Chinese colleagues before teaching the chapter on *The Joy Luck Club*. We have sought the advice of our ASL instructor in our presentation of Deaf culture. And our Linfield College group Fusion, a gay/straight alliance, has visited our classes many times and provided invaluable assistance with the chapter on gay culture.

In all our discussions with colleagues, we have tried to keep in mind the impact the materials will have on our students. The films in this text deal with sensitive topics, and your students may be profoundly affected by at least some of them and by the questions they raise. If students become upset, be sure to offer them the chance to talk as soon as possible after class. Maybe they will take you up on the offer; maybe they won't. Perhaps they just need time to reflect on the class discussions and opinions presented by their peers. At the end of the course, we hope your students will leave the class with many of their questions addressed—in part by their peers—and also with a more critical awareness of their own culture and a greater responsiveness to the cultures around them.

Resources for Instructors

Readings

Auerbach, Susan, ed. 1994. *Encyclopedia of Multiculturalism*, 6 vols. New York: Marshall Cavendish.

Ballantine, Betty, and Ian Ballantine, eds. 1993. *The Native Americans: An Illustrated History.* Atlanta: Turner Publishing.

Banks, James A. 1997. *Teaching Strategies for Ethnic Studies.* 6th ed. Boston: Allyn and Bacon.

Bennett, Lerone Jr. 1988. *Before the Mayflower: A History of Black America.* 6th ed. New York: Penguin Books.

Giannetti, Louis. 1982. *Understanding Movies.* Englewood Cliffs, NJ: Prentice Hall.

Herbst, Philip H. 2001. *Wimmin, Wimps & Wallflowers: An Encyclopædic Dictionary of Gender and Sexual Orientation Bias in the United States.* Yarmouth, ME: Intercultural Press.

———. 1997. *The Color of Words: An Encyclopædic Dictionary of Ethnic Bias in the United States.* Yarmouth, ME: Intercultural Press.

Hirschfelder, Arlene, and Martha Kreipe de Montaño. 1993. *The Native American Almanac: A Portrait of Native America Today.* New York: Prentice Hall.

Houston, Jeanne Wakatsuki, and James D. Houston. 1973. *Farewell to Manzanar.* New York: Bantam.

Marcus, Eric. 1993. *Is It a Choice? Answers to 300 of the Most Frequently Asked Questions about Gays and Lesbians.* New York: HarperCollins.

Moore, Matthew S., and Linda Levitan. 1992. *For Hearing People Only: Answers to Some of the Most Commonly Asked Questions about the Deaf Community, Its Culture, and the "Deaf Reality."* Rochester, NY: Deaf Life Press.

Rosales, Arturo F. 1997. *Chicano! The History of the Mexican American Civil Rights Movement.* Houston: Arte Publico Press.

Shapiro, Joseph P. 1993. *No Pity: People with Disabilities Forging a New Civil Rights Movement.* New York: Random House.

Sowell, Thomas. 1981. *Ethnic America: A History.* New York: Basic Books.

Summerfield, Ellen. 1997. *Survival Kit for Multicultural Living.* Yarmouth, ME: Intercultural Press.

———. 1993. *Crossing Cultures through Film.* Yarmouth, ME: Intercultural Press.

Takaki, Ronald. 1993. *A Different Mirror: A History of Multicultural America.* Boston: Little, Brown.

———. 1989. *Strangers from a Different Shore: A History of Asian Americans.* Boston: Little Brown.

Zinn, Howard. 1980. *A People's History of the United States.* New York: HarperCollins.

Films

The Color of Honor (1988) Vivid documentary looks at the exceptional contributions of Japanese American men who served in the military during World War II, in both combat and intelligence. Also tells the story of those who chose to resist military service. Directed by Loni Ding (NAATA).

Eyes on the Prize: America's Civil Rights Years (1986) Six-part series. The story of the civil rights struggle between 1954 and 1965 comes alive through news footage, photographs, and personal recollections. Winner of dozens of national awards. Directed by Henry Hampton (PBS Video).

Incident at Oglala (1992) Documentary traces the dramatic events that occurred on the Pine Ridge Indian Reservation in the 1970s, focusing on the trial and imprisonment of

Leonard Peltier. Provides fascinating insights into this period in history. Directed by Michael Apted (Facets).

Paha Sapa: The Struggle for the Black Hills (1993) Memorable interviews with Lakota and Cheyenne shed light on their ongoing struggle to regain the Black Hills. Directed by Mel Lawrence (Mystic Fire Video; phone: 800-292-9001).

Unfinished Business (1986) Award-winning film tells the stories of three Japanese Americans—Fred Korematsu, Gordon Hirabayashi, and Minoru Yasui—who challenged the constitutionality of Executive Order 9066. Directed by Steven Okazaki (NAATA).

Compact Discs

African American Spirituals: The Concert Tradition (Wade in the Water Volume I). Smithsonian/Folkways Recordings and National Public Radio. 1994; phone: 301-443-2314.

Negro Spirituals (Osceola Davis, Jorma Hynninen, and Ilmo Ranta). Ondine Oy, 1988.